THE SHILOAH CENTER FOR MIDDLE EASTERN AND AFRICAN STUDIES
THE MONOGRAPH SERIES

THE AFRO-ASIAN MOVEMENT
IDEOLOGY AND FOREIGN POLICY OF THE THIRD WORLD

The Shiloah Center for Middle Eastern and African Studies
Tel Aviv University

The Shiloah Center is, with the Department of Middle Eastern and African History, a part of the School of History at Tel Aviv University. Its main purpose is to contribute, by research and documentation, to the dissemination of knowledge and understanding of the modern history and current affairs of the Middle East and Africa. Emphasis is laid on fields where Israeli scholarship is in a position to make a special contribution and on subjects relevant to the needs of society and the teaching requirements of the University.

The Monograph Series

The studies published in this series are the work of the Research Associates and Visiting Research Associates at the Shiloah Center. The views expressed in these publications are entirely those of the authors.

URIEL DANN/IRAQ UNDER QASSEM

DAVID KIMCHE/THE AFRO-ASIAN MOVEMENT

ITAMAR RABINOVICH/SYRIA UNDER THE BA'TH 1963–66

ARYEH YODFAT/ARAB POLITICS IN THE SOVIET MIRROR

THE AFRO-ASIAN MOVEMENT
IDEOLOGY AND FOREIGN POLICY
OF THE THIRD WORLD

David Kimche

ISRAEL UNIVERSITIES PRESS, Jerusalem

HALSTED PRESS
A Division of JOHN WILEY & SONS, INC., New York

ISRAEL UNIVERSITIES PRESS
is a publishing division of the
ISRAEL PROGRAM FOR SCIENTIFIC TRANSLATIONS, LTD.
P. O. Box 7145, Jerusalem, Israel

IUP Cat. No. 360610
ISBN 0 7065 1265 0

Manufactured by Keter Press, Jerusalem, Israel

PREFACE

Afro-Asia provides a vast canvas to paint, so vast, indeed, that individual details tend to blur and become indistinct. I wish to stress this fact, for I have by no means attempted to fill the canvas with all the component parts which together make up the 'Third World.' Rather I have sought to trace the history of the Afro-Asian Movement *per se,* analyzing the causes for its rise and decline, and endeavouring to place it within its proper context in contemporary history. At the same time, by means of a number of case studies—of India, Indonesia and Tanzania—I have tried to give added depth to the picture as a whole.

The most important sources for this work have been the speeches and writings of those leaders of Asia and Africa who not only led their countries to independence but who also forged the links of Afro-Asian solidarity in those first fateful years of their countries' independence. The large number of conferences held under the aegis of Afro-Asianism provides a mass of source material; so do the press and radio of the countries concerned. Moreover, I have had the good fortune of travelling widely in many of the countries which comprise the 'Third World,' and of meeting personally some of the figures who played a leading role on the Afro-Asian stage. Unfortunately, not all of them have allowed me to acknowledge the aid they gave me, nor even to quote them. I prefer, therefore, to forego the pleasure of name-dropping, and to thank all those who gave me assistance without divulging their identities.

There are, however, a number of exceptions: Oscar Kambona, who spent many hours with me describing the attitudes he took towards the Afro-Asian Movement as foreign minister of his country, Ambassador Jha of India, Professor Poplai of the Indian Council of World Affairs, and, in particular, my two mentors at the

v

Hebrew University in Jerusalem who supervised my Ph.D. thesis on which this present book has been based, Professor Harold Zvi Shiffrin and Dr. Nehemia Lev-Zion. My debt to them is great, as it is to Professor Shimon Shamir, head of the Department of the History of the Middle East and Africa, Tel Aviv University and present director of the Reuven Shiloah Research Center, who made this book possible. And last, but by no means least, my wife Ruth, for the encouragement she gave me throughout the writing of this book.

August 1972   David Kimche

CONTENTS

Preface   v

1. The Historical Setting   1
2. The Political Setting: Search for a Foreign Policy   17
3. The First Steps   29
4. Bandung   59
5. Post-Bandung: The Official Follow-Up   80
6. Cairo and Algiers: The Demise of Afro-Asianism   114
7. The Militants Take Over   126
8. The Solidarity Movement Takes Root   144
9. The Sino-Soviet Split and the Solidarity Movement   174
10. Havana—Broadening the Solidarity Movement   198
11. The Case of India   214
12. The Case of Indonesia   229
13. Africa (South of the Sahara) and the Afro-Asian Movement—with Special Reference to Tanzania   238
14. The Decline of the Afro-Asian Movement   250

Conclusions   263
Appendix 1   273
Appendix 2   275
Bibliography and Sources   279
Index   287

1 THE HISTORICAL SETTING

The first indications that the Afro-Asian Movement had achieved
conscious political form became apparent only in the late 1940s.
The movement reached its high point with the first Asian-African
conference, held at Bandung in Indonesia in 1955, and remained
a political force until the failure of the "Second Bandung" meeting
at Algiers in 1965 marked its demise. The antecedents of the movement, however, go back far beyond the first official expressions
of an Afro-Asian solidarity in the late 1940s. They are found in
the first stirrings of national sentiment among Asians and Africans
at the turn of the century, and in the ideals of Pan-Asianism, Pan-
Africanism and Pan-Arabism which these sentiments produced.
The establishment of the Indian National Congress in 1885, and
of its counterpart, the All-India Muslim League in 1906, the convoca-
tion of the first Pan-African Congress in 1900 and of the Arab Congress in 1913, the uprising of Asians against Occidentals, such as
the "Boxer" rebellion in China in 1900, and, even more so, the
Japanese victory over Russia in 1905—all evidenced a new awakening
among the coloured peoples, the gathering of momentum of ideas
and emotions which were to develop into national movements and
finally into sovereign nation-states.

Full analysis of the causes and process of the emergence of an
Asian, and, at a later stage, of an African nationalism, falls outside
the scope of this work.[1] At its earliest stage, this nationalism was the
product of a heightened intellectual activity on the part of Westernized
elites in Asian countries and among Negro[2] communities. The new
intellectual activity centred on a re-examination of indigenous values
and cultures, using terms of reference supplied by Western political
thought. This tendency was exacerbated by World War I which
brought about the weakening of the colonial powers and the emer-

gence of liberal and radical thought as an international political factor—on the one side expressed in US President Woodrow Wilson's principle of national self-determination and at the Bolshevik extremity, by Lenin's denunciations of imperialism.[3]

The intellectual ferment among the Asian and Negro elites led to attempts to organize political movements. Though isolated from one another, they developed virtually identical objectives, namely, the search for a new Asian, or African, personality, and, closely linked with it, freedom from colonial domination.

This dichotomy of aims runs like a thread through virtually all the nationalist movements of Asia and Africa. However, while the yearning for a new image, a reincarnation of Asia or of Africa in modern terms but based on intrinsic Asian or African values and culture, was vaguely defined and universalistic in character, the particularistic aims of achieving independence and of hastening on the process of decolonization were more sharply defined. These two objectives formed the foundation stone on which Asian and African nationalism rested. Their presence in all the particularistic national movements of Asia and Africa provided the ideological basis for sentiments of Afro-Asian solidarity and for what is called in this study the Afro-Asian Movement.

These national movements, however, remained largely isolated from one another until the aftermath of World War II. The colonial powers maintained a policy of keeping their colonies in watertight compartments, with links only to the "mother-country" in Europe. A glance at a pre-1960 map of Africa, for example, reveals that the road networks of, say, the Ivory Coast and the Gold Coast stop considerably short of the common frontier between them. Communication between the two colonies was extremely difficult, and even in 1972 there still existed no road between Abidjan and Accra, while telephone communication between these two capitals, so close to each other, was still conducted via Paris and London.

There was thus, in these early years of Asian and Negro nationalism, very little horizontal cooperation among the various nationalist movements. Each of them arose and developed according to the conditions prevailing in the particular area in which it formed. This naturally led to a broad diversification in the character of these movements, despite the uniformity of their basic objectives. The attitude taken by the colonial powers to the nationalist movements added to this diversification and substantially affected the degree to which the new tenets of Communism succeeded in influencing the nationalist movements. Jawaharlal Nehru of India pointed out, "the tendency of Asian nationalist movements to follow the leadership of the Communist Party is dependent on the degree to which their deep-rooted anti-colonial impulse is ignored by the Western powers."[4]

Despite this isolation and diversification the intellectual elites of Asia and Africa found opportunities of meeting, of getting to know each other, and of benefiting by one another's experiences. It remains a common dictum in Africa that "all roads lead to Paris and London." In these two capitals the Asian and African elites found common ground and at the same time formed an intellectual symbiosis with radical political thought in Europe. The teachings of Karl Marx, and of Harold Laski at the London School of Economics, both had enormous influence in moulding the political orientations of the Asian and African nationalists. In Paris the Communist influence was prevalent, affecting young Asian, African and West Indian students there, who were later to become national leaders, among them Ho Chi Minh, Félix Houphouët-Boigny and Aimé Césaire. In London, the London School of Economics under Laski held sway, casting its influence over such diverse personalities as Jomo Kenyatta, Kwame Nkrumah and Krishna Menon.

The rise to power of the Bolsheviks by the end of World War I early had an electrifying effect on the young nationalists, particularly of Asia. Lenin's dicta, such as his declaration that "colonialism is the worst and the most extreme form of capitalism, but also its last" could not fail to impress the anti-imperialists from Asia and Africa. The Congress of Eastern Peoples at Baku, in 1922, to which Asian delegations were invited, expanded the theme of a united struggle against imperialism, while the writings and activities of such men as the Bolshevik leader Karl Radek and Sultan Galiev, who sought to set up an "International" of the peoples under colonial rule, "the real vanguard of the social revolution," made a strong impact.[5] The denunciation of Galiev in 1923 by the Soviet Communist Party marked the first disenchantment of Asian nationalists with the Soviet Union; it sounded a discordant note in what had been, till then, perfect harmony in a common anti-imperialism. Yet, despite this setback, the attraction of the Soviet Union remained powerful; Nehru, invited to Moscow to attend the October Revolution celebrations in 1925, was much impressed by what he was shown and became a warm admirer of Soviet Communism. His approval, however, was tinged with dislike of the totalitarian system of government of the Soviet Union.

Both the Communists and the far-left radicals of Western Europe served as important catalysts in bringing together the Asian and African nationalists on European soil. One such occasion was the International Conference for World Peace, held at Bierville, France, in 1926, at which the European delegates were presented with a common memorandum submitted by the Asian delegates.[6] The second, and by far the more important, was the Congress of Oppressed Nationalities, held in Brussels in February 1927. The congress had been organized by the Association of Oppressed Peoples which had been founded under the name of "Anti-Imperialist League" in 1924 and held its first conference in Moscow that year.[7]

The Association of Oppressed Peoples had strong Communist leanings, but a number of non-Communist nationalists and radicals, centred mainly in Berlin, cooperated with it from the start, and both the Mexican government and the Kuomintang provided it with funds.[8] The Brussels conference provided the first real opportunity for direct contact among Afro-Asian leaders; 175 delegates from thirty-seven countries and territories attended, including Asian and African leaders such Jawaharlal Nehru, Ho Chi Minh, Muhammad Hatta, Madame Sun Yat-sen and Léopold Senghor.[9] There were, in the words of Nehru, "representatives from the national organizations of Java, Indochina, Palestine, Syria, Egypt, Arabs from North Africa and African Negroes."[10] This was, in fact, the first real Afro-Asian conference, though under a European aegis, and one of the themes most heard was the need for solidarity of the Asian and African peoples. "The Communist element was . . . strong there," wrote Nehru of the conference. "Ideas of some common action between oppressed nations *inter se,* as well as between them and the labour left wing, were very much in the air. It was felt more and more that the struggle for freedom was a common one against the thing that was imperialism; and joint deliberation, and where possible, joint action were desirable."[11] Nehru himself played a major role in propagating such ideas at the conference. After noting in his speech there on February 9, 1927, that there was "much in common" in the struggles of the various oppressed peoples, Nehru declared: "Contact between the various peoples will lead to a better understanding of each others' problems and difficulties, and is bound to result in closer cooperation which is bound to bring success nearer to all."[12] In a second speech the following day he hammered home the point that the freeing of India would affect the position of all other countries under imperialist domination. India, he implied, was the kingpin of one giant freedom movement.[13] One of the decisions taken by the Asian participants at the conference was to meet regularly thereafter, but nothing came of this resolution. As Nehru himself remarked, they "found it was not possible for us to meet anywhere except in some country of Western Europe."[14]

Hardly less important, however, was that the Brussels conference made the Asian and African participants aware that they were not alone and that cooperation among them could strengthen them in their struggle for independence. In this sense, the Brussels meeting was the father of Afro-Asian solidarity, the forerunner of the conference at Bandung. Indonesian President Ahmad Sukarno mentioned Brussels in his opening address at the Bandung conference[15] and Nehru, when asked by Professor M. Brecher about Bandung, replied: "I will tell you an old story. Perhaps you have come across the fact that I attended a conference in Brussels in 1927 . . ."[16] Coupled with his earlier trip to Moscow, the Brussels conference had a profound effect on the political thinking of Nehru. Nationalist ideas began to combine with socialism. The need for solidarity among the peoples of Asia and Africa was reinforced by the need for close cooperation with the peoples of the Soviet Union, who, according to Nehru's view after the conference, were fighting the same battle against imperialism as the oppressed peoples of Afro-Asia. Above all, however, the realization was driven home that the struggle waged by the Indian National Congress was part and parcel of a much wider movement encompassing Asia and Africa, and that each victory and setback in that struggle would have repercussions throughout the movement. "The Brussels conference, as well as the subsequent meetings of the League . . . helped me to understand some of the problems of colonial and dependent countries," wrote Nehru in his autobiography.[17] It heightened his conception of internationalism. Freedom means freedom for the human race, and not only for Indians, Nehru was often quoted as saying.[18]

This principle was no new orientation on the part of Nehru and the Indian National Congress; it was only the strengthening of an attitude which had existed since the end of World War I. As early as 1920 Mahatma Gandhi had written that "common lot no less than territorial homogeneity and cultural affinity is bringing the Asiatic races wonderfully together, and they now seem determined to take their fullest share in the world politics."[19] Subsequently the Indian National Congress paid increasing attention to the struggles of other nationalist movements. In 1922 it demanded the restoration of the Turkish nation to a free and independent status; a year later it demanded the removal of all foreign control from Arab lands,[20] and in 1924 it expressed its sympathy for the Egyptian people. The situation in China evoked its special interest. In 1925 the Indian National Congress passed a resolution expressing sympathy to the Chinese people in their struggle for national unity,[21] and a number of other resolutions it passed denounced the use of Indian troops as part of the British colonial army in China and elsewhere.[22]

It was against this background that Nehru brought back his report on the 1927 Brussels conference to the Indian National Congress. It had been an event of great importance, he wrote, "likely to have far-reaching results."[23] He urged Congress to maintain links with the newly established League against Imperialism which was a useful channel for propaganda, and offered facilities for closer contact with other Asian nationalists. Largely as a result of Nehru's report the Indian National Congress decided, in 1928, to establish a Foreign Department to develop contacts with other anti-imperialist forces; one of the more important resolutions it passed that year declared that the Indian struggle was part of the general world struggle against imperialism. The contacts of the Congress Foreign Department were channelled mainly through the League against Imperialism.

Nehru was elected as one of the five honorary presidents of the League's Council, together with Madame Sun Yat-sen, Albert Einstein, British Labourite George Lansbury, and the French author Romain Rolland. Nehru's relations with the League continued until

1930. He was then expelled for having supported Gandhi's acceptance of the declaration on Dominion status for India by the governor-general Lord Irwin. Acceptance was considered a betrayal of the anti-imperialist struggle by the League, which, in Nehru's own words, "veered more towards Communism in later years."[24]

At the same time, and independently from these activities, Pan-Asian and Pan-African sentiments were being increasingly expressed elsewhere. In China, under the influence of Sun Yat-sen, the Pan-Asian Front had been established shortly after World War I. The Front was a creation of the powerful Black Dragon secret society which played a key role in the political life of China at that time. Its Pan-Asianism was directed principally against the European presence in China and in Asia as a whole. Its militancy infected Japanese nationalists who enthusiastically espoused the pan-Asian cause, creating an Association for Greater Asia in 1924. This Sino-Japanese interest in Asianism gave rise to a conference of Asian peoples, held in Nagasaki in 1926, at which delegates from several Asian countries attended. The Indians sent a strong delegation, headed by the leftist Subhas Chandra Bose. Later the Indian National Congress expressed its "fascination" with the idea of an Asian federation.[25]

Meanwhile Pan-Africanism was already feeling its way in the American hemisphere. A series of Pan-African congresses was organized by Dr. William du Bois, an American Negro intellectual of mixed blood who, with his rival Marcus Garvey, dominated the Pan-African Movement in its formative years.[26] Four congresses were held between 1919 and 1927. The majority of participants still came from the United States and the West Indies, but an increasing number of African students in Europe took an interest in du Bois' activities, including Jomo Kenyatta and other future leaders in Africa like Wallace Johnson, and Dr. Nnamdi Azikiwe.

The momentum of both Pan-African and Pan-Asian activity which had marked the 1920s, however, appeared to peter out in the 1930s. After the Pan-African Congress held in New York in 1927 no further congresses took place until eighteen years later when the decisive Pan-African Congress met in Manchester in 1945. Similarly the Pan-Asian conference at Nagasaki in 1926 was not repeated in the interwar years and there was no attempt to translate the dreams of

an Asian federation, to which the Indian National Congress subscribed, into a reality. There were a number of reasons for this
interlude up to the end of World War II. Crucial was the change in
world conditions as a result of the 1929 depression and the rise to
power of fascist regimes. The hopes for a better world, so rosy in the
immediate post-war years, gradually subsided in the realization that
the millennium had not yet arrived. By 1933 Nehru could write of
Asian nationalism: "The great revolutionary nationalist urge in the
Asia of the after-war years gradually exhausted itself for the time
being . . ."[27] In Asia, Japan's attack on the Chinese in Manchuria
in 1931 and the gradually developing Japanese conflict with China
made a mockery of the Pan-Asian ideals which had generated mainly
from both China and Japan. In India, Nehru spent long periods in
prison, while the Indian National Congress was occupied increasingly
in its own struggle against the British. In Indonesia, the three leading
nationalists, Ahmad Sukarno, Muhammad Hatta and Soetan Sjahrir,
spent most of the 1930s in a detention camp, first in New Guinea,
and later in the Moluccas. They were only released by the Japanese
in 1942.

The advent of World War II made a revolutionary impact
on colonialism. In the words of the Swedish sociologist Gunnar
Myrdal, "it was during and immediately after the Second World
War that all the forces and pressures that had been gradually weakening the European colonial power system came together to effect
its final collapse."[28] A debacle immediately visible to the peoples
of Asia and Africa was the occupation by the German armies of
three major colonial powers—France, Belgium and Holland—
and the progressive weakening of Great Britain, the fourth and major
colonial power, in a protracted and costly war. The United States,
once it had been drawn out of its isolationism into the war, took up
an anti-colonialist stand. The Atlantic Charter signed in 1941 between
F. D. Roosevelt and Winston Churchill on the guiding lines of the
post-war settlement underwrote the Wilsonian rights of national
self-determination. The embroilment of African and Asian troops
in the "white man's war" and the lessons they learned from it,[29]
the rousing declaration to the peoples of Africa made by General
de Gaulle at Brazzaville in January 1944, and, last, but by no means
least, the shattering effect which the Japanese victories had on Asian

nationalists additionally contributed to a far-reaching metamorphosis in the attitudes of colonizers and those under colonial rule alike which led to the downfall of the colonial empires in the aftermath of the war. Above all, the results of the war finally exploded the myth of white superiority and unleashed among non-Europeans the ideas of freedom and equality. Such ideas were no longer terms confined to nationalist elites; they became household words of the masses. The Zimbabwe nationalist leader, Rev. Ndabaningi Sithole, describes the process in the following words:

World War II . . . has had a great deal to do with the awakening of the peoples of Africa. During the war the African came in contact with practically all the peoples of the earth. He met them on a life-and-death-struggle basis. He saw the so-called civilized and peaceful and orderly white people mercilessly butchering one another just as his so-called savage ancestors had done in tribal wars. He saw no difference between the primitive and the civilized man. In short, he saw through European pretensions that only Africans were savages. This had a revolutionizing psychological impact on the African. But more than this, World War II taught the African most powerful ideas. During the war the Allied Powers taught the subject peoples (and millions of them!) that it was not right for Germany to dominate other nations. They taught the subjugated peoples to fight and die for freedom rather than live and be subjugated by Hitler. Here then is the paradox of history, that the Allied Powers, by effectively liquidating the threat of Nazi domination, set in motion those powerful forces which are now liquidating, with equal effectiveness, European domination in Africa.[30]

The consequences were immediate. In the African colonies themselves, the immediate post-war years were marked by a period of heightened political, social and economic instability. The hundreds of thousands of African ex-servicemen, who had served both in the British army and with the Free French, returned home with ideas which were often diametrically opposed to the traditionalist values and mores that had governed their lives in the pre-war era. Tribal barriers, and in many cases even family ties, had broken down. Many of the ex-servicemen abandoned their villages and flocked to the towns, stepping up the process of urbanization which had already become a feature of most of Africa, with its concomitant rampant unemployment. The general situation in the post-war years was one of acute and worsening poverty. An urgent need for raw materials in Europe had led to an emphasis on cash crops in Africa which diverted attention from subsistence farming, with a resultant lack of local foodstuffs. Shortages of imports also led to a spiralling of prices. It was in these circumstances that the Afro-Asian nationalist leaders increased their pressure on the colonial powers: in French Africa with demands for full equality with Metropolitan France and in British Africa with demands for self-government.

These political demands—made at least by the Africans from British colonies—found full expression in the Pan-African Congress held immediately after the end of the war, in October 1945, in Manchester. The Congress had been organized by a group of Africans and West Indians who, in 1937, had formed the International African Service Bureau. Grouped under its leadership in 1944 were thirteen African political student and welfare organizations centred in Great Britain.[31] The Manchester Congress was notable for a number reasons. For the first time the African element, and not that of the US Negro and West Indian, dominated the proceedings, represented by Jomo Kenyatta, Wallace Johnson, Kwame Nkrumah, Joe Appiah, Chief Akintola and Peter Abrahams, to mention only a few.[32] For the first time a Pan-African Congress demanded outright independence for Africa and threatened the use of force if independence was denied them,[33] and, again for the first time, an African political movement voiced its solidarity with independence movements in Asia. The Congress expressed the hope, went one of its resolutions, that before long the peoples of Asia and Africa would have broken their centuries-old chains of colonialism. Then, as free nations, they would stand united to consolidate and safeguard their liberties and independence from the restoration of Western imperialism, as well as the dangers of Communism.

The Manchester Congress was thus a turning-point in the history of the African nationalist political movement. In Asia also the war years marked the end of the old era and the beginning of the new. The speed of the Japanese advance through South-East Asia brought home to the Asian nationalists the vulnerability of the European colonial powers. Just as they had done in 1905, the Japanese once more underscored the fact that the white race was by no means necessarily superior to the yellow. The swift surrender of the Dutch, the French, and, above all the British, to the Japanese armies destroyed the last vestiges of Western prestige. The Japanese, for their part, fostered nationalist ideals in the territory they occupied. They freed nationalist leaders imprisoned by the colonial powers, installed nationalist governments, and encouraged the creation of volunteer armies. Above all, they revived the slogan of "Asia for the Asians" previously heard in 1926 at the Nagasaki conference, and launched a scheme by name of the "Greater East Asiatic Coprosperity Sphere" which culminated in the holding of a Pan-Asian congress in Tokyo in November 1943, attended by a number of leading nationalists from the occupied countries.

The Japanese presence was not welcomed by all the Asian nationalists in the countries under Japanese occupation. Those on the left wing, and in particular the Communists, looked at Japanese militarism and expansionism as a new imperialism which had to be fought no less than the old. Underground movements were formed, and resistance to authority grew. When the Japanese withdrew at the war's end these organizations were in being, side by side with the governments and armies the Japanese had created, and adding to the anti-colonial momentum already in operation. In Burma, for instance, the British had to recognize the largest of the underground movements, the Anti-Fascists People's Freedom League, as the most genuinely representative of popular opinion. In Indochina the Vietminh (League for the Independence of Vietnam) had formed the only effective resistance to the Japanese occupation, emerging after the war as the only genuine nationalist movement in the country. In Malaya, the Chinese Communists continued armed insurrections which they had formerly waged against the Japanese, switching them against the British authorities after the war ended. Even in Indonesia, where the Japanese had done more than anywhere else to encourage local nationalism, a leftist resistance movement had come into being, led by, among others, the nationalist leader Soetan Sjahrir.

Thus the Japanese, both positively and negatively, served as a catalyst fermenting nationalist aspirations in Asia. The independence of Burma, Indonesia and the Democratic Republic of Vietnam came as a direct result of Japanese occupation of these territories. The independence of Malaya—another Japanese-occupied territory —was delayed until 1957 because of the communal structure within the peninsula and the fear of the Malays that political power would pass into local Chinese hands. In the case of the Philippines, the United States government had already promised to grant independence by 1946, without any tangible pressure on the part of the Filipinos having been employed.

It was, however, the developments in the Indian sub-continent and in China that were decisive in setting the pattern for the new Asia of the post-war era, with effects that spread outside it. Gunnar Myrdal has pointed out, "the achievement of political independence on the Indian sub-continent was the decisive impulse that set in motion a wave-like movement of emancipation from colonial rule all over South Asia—and beyond it into West Asia and Africa."[34] The Indian struggle for independence had for long been in the vanguard of other such movements, especially those within the British Empire. The success of this struggle served, therefore, as a beacon for other efforts in this direction and heralded a process of decolonization which gathered momentum—in Burma, Ceylon, Malaya and South-East Asia, and finally in Africa. Many factors led up to Britain's abdication of power in India in 1947, not the least being the rise to power in London of a Labour government committed to decolonization.[35] The basic determinant, however, was that the national demand for immediate independence had reached such dimensions in India that Britain would have been faced with a major revolt if this demand had not been met. If a revolt had broken out, Britain, both psychologically and physically, would hardly have been in a position to quell it.

The communal rioting in the Indian sub-continent followed by the establishment of the sovereign states of India and Pakistan, together with the civil war in China culminating in victory for the armies of Mao Tse-tung, were the crowning events of that historical period which came to an end in the aftermath of World War II.

In the years that followed the events in India and China an increasing number of countries gained independence, at first in eastern and southern Asia and in the Middle East, and later in Africa. This process of decolonization was, in itself, a development of global consequences, but it went forward at a time when the world was partitioned into two hostile camps. The breakdown of the Moscow Conference of Foreign Ministers in the spring of 1947 marked the collapse of the wartime entente between the Western powers and the Soviet Union. Thus, during the period which witnessed the beginnings of the end of the great colonial empires, the two super-powers were consolidating their positions and jockeying for influence in the areas of the world which had not yet been drawn under the aegis of one power or the other. Nowhere was this more conspicuous than in China during the last phases of the civil war or in Asia after the establishment of the Communist regime in Peking in September 1949. The latter engendered increased intervention by the United States in Asian affairs and led to the embroilment of Asian countries in the cold war through their inclusion in the system of military pacts and treaties which the US promoted in the early 1950s.

This was the setting against which the first concrete steps towards Afro-Asian solidarity were taken in the late 1940s. It was marked by chronic weakness and instability of the newly independent states and by the aggressive foreign policies of the two super-powers as each sought to broaden its zone of influence and prevent the other from making gains. With the unleashing of the cold war in all its fury, the new regimes had, perforce, to adjust their foreign policies accordingly. The fact that the majority of these regimes were confronted with a similar situation—weakness and instability in the face of the uncertainties and dangers of the cold war—led to a desire for association and for brotherhood. Hence the reasoning behind the foreign policy orientations of the new regimes led, almost naturally, to the ideas on which Afro-Asian solidarity was founded. These foreign policy orientations will therefore be examined more fully.

NOTES

[1] There have been numerous books on this subject, some of which have been mentioned in the Bibliography at the end of this volume. Books to be found in the Bibliography are mentioned in these notes in brief.

[2] The term "Negro" is used here instead of "African" because the beginnings of Pan-Africanism occurred among the Negro communities of the United States and the West Indies, and not in Africa itself.

[3] The Indian historian and diplomat K. M. Panikkar writes that in Asia Wilson's "fourteen points" were acclaimed as "a doctrine of liberation" (*Asian and Western Dominance,* p. 263).

[4] F. Moraes, *Jawaharlal Nehru, A Biography,* New York, 1956, p. 45; see also Myrdal, *Asian Drama,* p. 141: the impact of Communism "was most marked in those regions where the regenerative and constructive role of colonialism, in the sense of educating the intellectual elite in the powers and responsibilities of governments, had been least developed."

[5] For an excellent summary of Sultan Galiev's views, see Benningsen, in *Journal á Plusieurs Voix,* 20.12.1956

[6] For the text of the memorandum, see K. M. Panikkar, "Asia and Peace," *India Quaterly,* Vol. II, No. 2, pp. 193–5. See also Poplai, *Asia and Africa,* pp. 1–2, 10.

[7] See Queuille, *Histoire de l'Afro-Asiatisme,* p. 52.

[8] See Brecher, *Nehru,* p. 54.

[9] Among the prominent Europeans and Americans attending the conference were Albert Einstein, Upton Sinclair, George Lansbury, and Romain Rolland.

[10] J. Nehru, *Towards Freedom,* London, 1936, p. 125.

[11] *Ibid.,* p. 123.

[12] *Indian Quarterly Register,* Vol. I (1927), p. 204, quoted in Norman, *Nehru, the First Sixty Years,* p. 121.

[13] The full speech is given in J. S. Bright, *Before and After Independence,* pp. 365–8.

[14] Brecher, *Nehru,* p. 54.

14

[15] The texts of Sukarno's and other opening speeches are given in *Asia-Africa Speaks from Bandung,* Jakarta, 1955.

[16] Brecher, *Nehru,* p. 54.

[17] J. Nehru, *An Autobiography*, London, 1936, p. 163.

[18] See Char, *Profile of Nehru,* p. 49.

[19] *Young India,* 14.4.1920.

[20] The resolution is quoted in Brimla Prased, *The Origins of Indian Foreign Policy: the Indian National Congress and World Affairs, 1885–1947.* Calcutta, 1962, p. 76.

[21] *The Indian National Congress, 1924,* New Delhi, 1926, p. 4.

[22] Notably the resolution passed by the Indian National Congress at its 1927 conference at Madras. The resolution is printed in full in Karuna-karan, *India in World Affairs, August 1947–January 1950,* p. 10.

[23] Brecher, *Nehru,* p. 112.

[24] Nehru, *Towards Freedom,* p. 125.

[25] Prasad, *op. cit.,* p. 85.

[26] A history of the Pan-African Movement falls outside the scope of this book. There exists a great deal of literature on this subject. Legum's *Pan-Africanism* gives an excellent brief summary of the movement.

[27] In "Whither India," one of Nehru's best-known essays, published in 1933, and reproduced in full in his *India and the World,* p. 39 ff. For quotation, see p. 51. Nehru's change in emphasis in his speeches of the 1920s and those of the 1930s is worth noting. Whereas in his presidential address in 1929 to the National Congress of Lahore (the first essay in *India and the World*) the stress is still on the role that Asia had to play in the world, this is completely lacking in later speeches. Thus, in his address in April 1936 to the National Congress at Lucknow (*India and the World,* p. 64 ff.) he pays more attention to the division of the world between the forces of fascism and imperialism on the one side and those of nationalism and socialism on the other than to any geographical division. In this ideological division India belonged fairly and squarely to the second grouping, Nehru stresses.

[28] Myrdal, *Asian Drama,* p. 143.

[29] The African and Asian demobilized soldiers became in many instances the vanguard of national unrest in the post-war years. An example of this is the role played by the war veterans in the Ghanaian nationalist movement.

[30] Sithole, *African Nationalism,* p. 23.

[31] See Legum, *op. cit.,* p. 30.

[32] Dr. Nnamdi Azikiwe of Nigeria was one of the active organizers of the Congress but could not be present at the proceedings.

[33] "We affirm the right of all colonial peoples to control their own destiny. All colonies must be free from foreign imperialist control, whether political or economic. . . . We demand for Black Africa autonomy and independence. . . . If the Western world is still determined to rule mankind by force, then Africans, as a last resort, may have to appeal to force in the effort to achieve freedom, even if force destroys them and the world"—extracts from the "Declaration to the Colonial Powers" of the Manchester Pan-African Congress.

[34] Myrdal, *op. cit.,* p. 153.

[35] For the situation in Great Britain at the time the decision was taken to withdraw from India, see Chapter 3, p. 31.

2 THE POLITICAL SETTING: SEARCH FOR A FOREIGN POLICY

A Soviet political commentator, Lev Stepanov, in attempting to define the concept of Afro-Asianism, wrote, "Afro-Asia is not just a sum of two geographical units, it is a concept whose substance is the community of the Afro-Asian peoples' fundamental national interests." He summed up these interests in the following terms: "Anti-colonialism, the need for a world at peace, the vital interest in preserving independence and territorial integrity—these are the major factors in Afro-Asian unity."[1]

This chapter will examine whether there exists a community of fundamental national interests of the people of Asia and Africa, what these are, and how they have determined foreign policy orientations. Countries which form obvious exceptions are Japan, Thailand, Turkey, and Israel.

Basically the common denominators which could lead to such a community of interests rest on social and economic factors, and on a psychological element. In the first category are the common bonds created by underdevelopment. The stage of development in the countries of Asia and Africa is at such a different level from that in either the Western or the European Communist bloc, that there exists a wide gulf between them which has nothing to do with political ideologies, and has inevitably created a feeling of solidarity among Asian and African peoples. Mamadou Dia of Senegal has described it in the following words:

> Much less than Marxism-Leninism, it is . . . the consciousness of solidarity in poverty, the weakness of the standard of living, the inadequacy of the public services, the presence of all the elements characteristic of the underdevelopment that provide the most solid foundation for the new proletariat, officially

17

constituted as the 'Third World' since the Bandung conference
... it is the consciousness of economic inequality that gives
birth to a proletarian national sentiment, aligning the nations
of Africa and Asia on the same battlefront against the West.
With the consciousness of underdevelopment, a new idea
appears, that of proletarian nations grouped 'on the life-line of
imperialism' confronting rich nations with a geographical unity
that widens the gap between them.[2]

The consciousness of being socially and economically the world's
underdog, the proletariat of the world, played an important role
within the Afro-Asian Peoples' Solidarity Organization (AAPSO),
as will be seen later. It was largely this common sentiment which the
Chinese Communist ideologists have sought to exploit in their
ideological dispute with the Soviet Union.

Less tangible, but having no less an effect, is the psychological
element in the feeling that a racial bond unites the non-white peoples.
This is closely interconnected with the sentiment of proletarian
solidarity, since the coloured people of the underdeveloped countries
see themselves confronted with the exclusive and privileged society
of the "whites," which includes the European Communist bloc.
The colour factor, again, has been exploited by the Chinese, but it
forms a powerful and overriding bond, quite apart from the polemical
overtones added by Chinese propaganda. As long ago as 1900,
at the first Pan-African Congress in London, William du Bois declared
that "the problem of the twentieth century is the problem of the
colour line—the relation of the darker to the lighter races of men
in Asia and Africa, in America and the islands of the sea."

Superimposed on these two basic common denominators which
might lead to a community of fundamental interests are the historical-
political factors, foremost among which is the common heritage of
colonial subjugation and the concomitant struggle for national
independence. Their common past has provided the countries under
colonial rule with a uniform social and cultural veneer which shows
itself in many ways. The different colonial empires, in particular
those of the British and French, provided various forms of public
service—in the educational and other spheres—having similar
characteristics in all the colonies under their rule. Thus there exists

today a common understanding between say, an educated Indian and a Ghanaian, which goes far deeper than the common language bequeathed to both of them by the British colonial power. In the former French colonies this uniformity is even more marked: there is, for instance, even a certain physical similarity in lay-out and architectural style between the capital of a former French colony in Asia, such as Pnompenh, and most capital cities in former French Africa, while both the Asian and the African elites of former French colonies have imbibed deeply of French culture and been profoundly influenced by it. However, the solidarity formed by a common colonial past goes much deeper. There exists the bond of the oppressed peoples, so passionately described by Franz Fanon in his *Wretched of the Earth*. More tangibly, as shown in the previous chapter, the struggle for independence against the colonial regimes brought Asian and African leaders together. C. S. Jha, one of the foremost Indian diplomats who played a leading role in most Afro-Asian conclaves, goes so far as to say that "the objective of freeing the people of Asia and Africa from foreign domination became a cementing factor and created a common bond; *and from that arose the beginnings of the concept of Afro-Asian Solidarity.*"[3]

The corollary to a common colonial past is a common anti-colonial policy in the post-independence period, and this constitutes another important common denominator embracing most of the countries of Asia and Africa. There exist a number of motivations, apart from the purely ideological ones, for the strong anti-colonialism which has become such a marked feature in the policies of most of the countries within this group. The struggle for independence against the colonialist powers engendered a certain built-in dynamism in the colonies themselves, and provided the cohesive force which gave the nationalist movement strength and kept it together. After independence was achieved it provided the legitimatization for the nationalist leaders who had led the struggle for independence to take over power and to rule in place of the colonialist regimes. It thus became a cardinal objective of the post-independence rulers to maintain this legitimatization by prolonging the anti-colonial struggle; hence emphasis on anti-colonialism has been a fundamental element in the foreign policy of many countries of Asia and Africa.

There are, however, additional reasons why so many Afro-Asian leaders had recourse to a policy of anti-colonialism. These are bound up with the problem of achieving a national consciousness within many of the newly independent states themselves. In many of the new countries, especially those of Africa, a number of the elements which usually help to form nationalist sentiments are lacking, such as a common history, customs, language, religion, habits and mores. Even the demarcation of national boundaries has frequently been the result of arbitrary decisions of the colonial powers. Thus the only experience that many of the Afro-Asian peoples previously had in common has been the former colonial rule. For example, the only common feature uniting the Hausa and the Fulani of northern Nigeria with the Yoruba of western Nigeria has been British rule. Similarly the only reason for the division of the Hausa of Nigeria from the Hausa of Niger was the arbitrary boundary drawn between the British and the French colonial empires. Afro-Asian nationalism is therefore closely bound up with experience under colonial rule, and the myth of the threat of imperialism, whether in the form of neo-colonialism[4] or in the guise of an international danger of a colonialist conspiracy, must thus be maintained as long as possible by those in power in order to consolidate national consciousness.

Given this additional unifying element in Afro-Asia, conferences of Afro-Asian countries provide a convenient platform for voicing anti-colonialist sentiments. The unifying factor thus works both ways: it provides a motivation for holding the conferences, and the theme of anti-colonialism enables the maintenance of unity at gatherings of Afro-Asian countries on an international level. The anti-colonialism of Afro-Asian leaders thus satisfies the internal political needs of their countries—their internal dynamism, the legitimacy on which the power of the nationalist leaders can be based, the fostering of national consciousness—while at the same time it is the expression of protest and revolt created by both the economic and psychological common denominators described above. It is the class cry of the proletariat of the colonized, to use Mamadou Dia's expression. Protest at the inequality between ex-colonized and ex-colonizer, revolt against the privileges of "white" society—these are the overtones which make anti-colonialism such an appealing battle-cry for the Afro-Asian peoples, and provide it with the passion which colonial rule has engendered.

Once independence has been achieved new political problems arise which create additional common factors for most of the Afro-Asian countries. Independence can all too often be a very fragile plant. It must be watched over, nursed to strength, above all, be given aid to make it flower and bloom. In all too many cases, there exists very little relationship between political independence and economic viability. The less its viability the more the newly independent country must depend on outside aid. However, the national leaders are aware that the more a country needs to lean on outside factors in order to reach economic viability, the greater will its political independence be jeopardized. The evils of political strings attached to economic aid, of neo-colonialism, of a continuing dependence on the donor country, which is generally the former colonizing power, give a bitter taste to the pill of economic aid which most newly independent countries need to swallow in order to gain economic health. For common to the leaders of most newly independent countries, and especially those who had to struggle against colonial powers in order to attain that independence, is a powerful desire to assert that independence, and to express it in as many ways as possible. In the oft-quoted words of Nehru, "far too long have we in Asia been petitioners in Western courts and chancelleries. . . . That story must now belong to the past. We propose to stand on our own legs . . . we do not intend to be the playthings of others."[5] Colin Legum goes so far as to declare that this assertion of independence is the principal factor creating the concept of Afro-Asianism. Thus, in his words, the new countries "are too freshly free from foreign control to be willing to accept its re-establishment in any shape or form. This characteristic is the *principal factor* linking together the widely diverse Muslim, Christian and Hindu states of Africa, Asia and the Middle East."[6]

Faced with staggering economic and social problems at home, the leaders of the newly independent countries generally find it easier to seek a means of expressing their independence externally. One such means, obviously, is the United Nations. The world assembly offers opportunities to all its members, large and small, powerful and weak, to express themselves on all subjects. The UN General Assembly has thus become a projection of political independence, a means to uphold the self-respect and the dignity even of those newly independent countries most dependent on outside aid and whose actual power is negligible. Another means is by association with other states on an *equal* footing. There exists a strong desire for solidarity, even of brotherhood, to act as a buttress to one's limited strength. This serves as a powerful stimulant to Afro-Asianism. The mere act of belonging to such an association becomes a symbol of one's independence and adds prestige and respect to its members. Afro-Asianism is regarded by many in Asia and Africa as a status symbol elevating its members to a new international grading and rank, which, by the sheer weight of the number of its adherents, is far higher than the rank that the single state could ever hope to attain. [9]

Such an association of equals, however, satisfying though it may be in itself, does nothing to minimize the quandary of how to equate economic dependence with political independence. The problem is connected with the entire gamut of relationships between the newly independent states and the donor countries, and, indeed, between them and the two world blocs. This is one of the fundamental issues in the foreign policy orientations of the countries of Asia and Africa, and although the problem is common to them all, their method of solving it has by no means been the same. Basically, however, the problem can be reduced to what the attitude of the newly independent country should be towards the cold war.

There exist two diametrically opposed attitudes to the cold war among Afro-Asian countries, both of which have played a dominant role in the foreign policy orientations of the countries of the two continents. The one, expounded supremely by India and Burma, views the rivalry between the two power blocs as a constant threat to world peace, a sword of Damocles hanging over the heads of humanity. According to this view the cold war must be neutralized. An "area of peace" must separate the two rivals, and the leaders of Afro-Asia must labour on the world scene in order to bring about a détente in the cold war. The second attitude is rarely expounded publicly, but is ever-present in the foreign policy calculations of certain Afro-Asian countries, notably of Egypt. This attitude views the cold war as a triple blessing: as long as the cold war exists the countries of Africa and Asia are assured of outside support, as both world blocs seek to buy political gains in Afro-Asia by means of economic aid; as long as the rivalry between the two blocs continues, the countries of Afro-Asia can ask for help from one of the blocs if they feel that the other is seeking to encroach on their independence— the existence of the cold war thus becomes a guarantee for their independence and solves the problem of a possible limitation on it through taking foreign aid; and, thirdly, any détente in the cold war could lead to a dividing up of the world into spheres of influence between the two blocs, which is one of the possibilities most to be feared. There are thus a number of tangible advantages in the con- tinuation of the cold war, and, indeed, one of the reasons why the Egyptians publicly voiced their approval of the Russian invasion of Czechoslovakia in August 1968 was because of the setback to the growing détente between the Soviet Union and the United States which this move caused.[7] Thus, according to this viewpoint, it is not a détente in cold war relations which should be the aim of Afro-Asian leaders, but a continuing balance in rivalry, for a preponderance of one power over the other would erase the advantages which the cold war affords.

It is significant that in neither of these two approaches to the cold war does the ideological factor play a preponderant role. It is not the choice between the Communist and the Capitalist systems which determines the attitude of the majority of countries of Africa and Asia to the cold war, but much more pragmatic factors. The ideological struggle, on which spokesmen of both the Communist and the Western blocs have placed such stress, is rejected. "The ideological conflict is not, I repeat, not the main problem of our time. It is not a problem which affects the majority of mankind, such as poverty, disease, illiteracy and colonial bondage," declared President Ahmad Sukarno, at the 1961 Belgrade conference of non-aligned nations.[8] "As exponents of a national form of socialism, we can only be indifferent to foreign ideologies," was Cambodia's Prince Sihanouk's way of putting it,[9] while Patrice Lumumba of the Congo declared simply that "les questions idéologiques ne nous interessent pas."[10] These statements are typical of a host of others, all of which point to an indifference to, and even distate of, the ideological manifestations of the cold war. This was particularly true of the Arab countries. The ideological struggle of the cold war was far from the Arab mind, wrote Fayez A. Sayegh; both Communism and Western- style democracy were found to be ill suited and alien. There was no respect for democracy in the Western countries, nor for the caricature of democracy which had existed in Arab countries, concludes Sayegh.[11]

Nehru, indeed, insisted that there was "room for a third ideology,"[12] and that "there is a third way which takes the best from all existing systems . . . and seeks to create something suited to one's own history and philosophy." India's planning under a democratic pattern of socialism had, in Nehru's opinion, "set a new pattern for African and Asian development."[13]

These two approaches to the cold war, and the general rejection of the two dominant world ideologies, form the backdrop to the political behaviour of the countries of Africa and Asia with regard to the two world blocs. The overriding need for world peace and the advantages to be gained in perpetuating the balance between the Communist and the Capitalist world systems are the two major determinants of Afro-Asian attitudes to the cold war. To these are added subordinate factors, as will be seen below. Neither of these determinants are concomitant with membership of one of the two world blocs, and both objectives can be attained only if the new countries remain outside the sphere of influence of either of the two world systems. There thus exist powerful motives for the formal non-adherence to either the Western or the Communist bloc which has characterized the foreign policy orientations of the majority of Afro-Asian countries. Exceptions are countries directly evolving from the cold war (the two Vietnams and the two Koreas), countries whose geographical position puts them under quasi-exclusive dependence on one of the powers (Mongolia, and to a lesser extent the Philippines), countries menaced by more powerful neighbours (Israel, Pakistan, Iran, Turkey, Taiwan), countries never before colonized and thus not sharing anti-colonial sentiments (Turkey, Thailand, Liberia), and countries whose regimes are dependent economically and politically almost entirely on their former colonizers (the Philippines, Dahomey, Upper Volta, Niger, Chad, etc.).[14] In addition, there is the special case of China, at first adhering closely to the Soviet bloc but later forming a power centre itself.

Apart from these major exceptions, the general trend in Asia and Africa has been one of non-adherence to power blocs, or, to use the more fashionable term, of non-alignment. There have been a great many interpretations of non-alignment, but for the purpose of this chapter we use simply the literal meaning, namely, non-alignment with either of the world blocs—no regular, permanent, and automatic taking of sides in the cold war, whether for reasons of ideology, benefit or pressure.

We have examined two basic underlying reasons for non-alignment. To these must be added a number of more concrete motives. One is the emphasis placed by the newly independent countries on their full political independence and their need to assert it which has already been mentioned. The two blocs are, obviously, dominated by the large powers in their sphere, and relations within the blocs are inevitably very unequal; to enter into such a relationship would, therefore, be tantamount to limiting a lesser partner's independence. Moreover, a member of a bloc is obliged to judge issues according to the interests of the bloc and not according to its own national interests; worse still, the issues are often judged by the leader of the bloc and the bloc members must automatically accept the judgment. This, again, must be considered a severe limitation on the rights of independence. Non-adherence to blocs, or non-alignment, therefore, becomes a reaffirmation of that independence, a continuation of the struggle for political liberty and against colonialism. Resistance to pressure to become aligned—especially the pressure mounted by the United States in the early 1950s—becomes synonymous with the defence of newly won independence against the encroachment of a new form of colonialism. Non-alignment thus gradually became one of the elements of Afro-Asian solidarity, and, in the years after Bandung, a country openly aligning itself with one of the blocs risked isolation within the Afro-Asian context. It must be stressed, however, that alignment with a world bloc was generally considered in the narrowest term of formal adherence to a military pact dominated by one of the blocs. Singapore, with its vast British military base, was considered non-aligned, while Pakistan, although it had no foreign bases on its soil and despite its pro-Chinese leanings, was considered aligned because of its adherence to the Central Treaty Organization (CENTO) and the South-East Asia Treaty Organization (SEATO).

There existed another motive in the choice of non-alignment "La politique de la bascule," to use a phrase of Leo Hamon[15]—

of playing one bloc against the other and gaining aid from both—was found to be more advantageous than being allies of one bloc only. The Soviet Union, particularly in the post-Stalin era, placed great emphasis on economic aid to non-aligned countries of Asia and Africa. These countries were thus offered a choice, an alternative to the ties which had bound many of them economically to the former colonizing countries; moreover, there existed an opportunity to obtain aid from both blocs at the same time, as was, for example, ably demonstrated by Egypt and later by Tanzania. Additionally, as has been pointed out earlier, the presence of the two competing blocs, both willing to give aid, provided a safety valve enabling the newly independent country to escape from undue economic or political pressure when necessary.

The question of non-alignment will be gone into more fully later. In the context of examining whether a community of fundamental national interests of the peoples of Asia and Africa exists, and how this has determined foreign policy orientations, non-alignment and non-adherence to world blocs can be generally described as a typical foreign policy orientation of countries in the Afro-Asian group.

It can thus be seen that there do exist a number of real common denominators on which the solidarity of the peoples of Afro-Asia could rest. These include the economic and social factors of under-development, the consciousness of a racial bond among the non-white peoples, and a common colonial background with its concomitant struggle for independence. All this has made for a militant anti-colonialism, a need to assert political independence once it was obtained, a desire to associate with other states on an equal footing, and a common attitude of non-alignment to the cold war between the two competing world power systems.

This formed the political setting for the first steps towards an Afro-Asian solidarity which were taken in the immediate aftermath of World War II. The setting is a broad and generalized one, and, as we shall see, these common denominators have not been sufficiently binding to maintain that solidarity over the years. However, on this community of interests grew the concept of Afro-Asianism; the following chapter will examine the first steps which led to its development.

NOTES

[1] Lev Stepanov, "Future of Afro-Asia," *New Times,* No.51, 22.12.1965, p. 6.

[2] Dia, *African Nations and World Solidarity,* p. 13.

[3] Jha, "The Algiers Conference," in *India Quarterly,* Oct.–Dec. 1965, p. 376. (Present author's italics.)

[4] The term "neo-colonialism" has been used to villify many "evils." It was first widely used at the All-African Peoples' Conference, held at Cairo in 1960. The term was enlarged upon at the Council meeting of the Afro-Asian Peoples' Solidarity Organization at Bandung, in April 1961, where it was used broadly to mean all efforts on the part of the Western countries to interfere in the strivings for self-sufficiency and equality on the part of the newly independent countries. See Ardant, in *Revue Française de Science Politique,* Oct. 1965, p. 837 ff.

[5] Nehru, *India's Foreign Policy: Selected Speeches . . . 1946–61,* p. 242 ff. The passage here quoted was part of Nehru's inaugural speech at the First Asian Relations Conference, held at New Delhi in 1947. See Chapter 3.

[6] C. Legum, *Bandung, Cairo and Accra,* Africa Bureau, London, 1958, p. 3. (Present author's italics.)

[7] Cairo Domestic Radio, for example, claimed on Aug. 24, 1968, that "the Soviets had not wanted to send troops into Czechoslovakia, but had been compelled to do so by the part played by world Zionism." Baghdad Radio, on Aug. 21, 1968, described the invasion as "a national self-defence and a defence of the cause of international liberation"—quoted in *New Middle East,* London, No. 1, October 1968, p. 7.

[8] *Conference of Heads of State and Government of Non-Aligned Countries: Belgrade, Sept. 1–6, 1961,* Belgrade, 1961, p. 36; see Chapter 4.

[9] Prince Sihanouk, in *Foreign Affairs,* p. 582.

[10] At a press conference at the UN on July 26, 1960, quoted by Leo Hamon, "Non-Engagement et Neutralisme des nouveaux Etats," in J. B. Duroselle et J. Meyriat (ed.), *Les Nouveaux Etats dans les Relations Internationales,* Paris, 1962, p. 408.

[11] Sayegh, *Dynamics of Neutralism in the Arab World,* see pp. 167–74.

[12] Karanjia, *Mind of Mr. Nehru,* p. 93. Karanjia's book consists of a series of interviews of Nehru.

[13] Karanjia, *ibid.,* pp. 100–1.

[14] See Centre d'Etude des Relations Internationales, *"Les pays nouvellement indépendants dans les relations internationales," colloque de 26– 27 Nov. 1960.* Fondation Nationale des Sciences Politiques, Paris, 1960; Rapport Générale par J. B. Duroselle et J. Meyriat, p. 11.

[15] Hamon, *op. cit.,* p. 368.

3 THE FIRST STEPS

In the late afternoon of March 23, 1947, some 250 delegates coming from twenty-nine countries and territories of Asia[1] gathered together at the Perana Qila of the Red Fort of New Delhi for the inaugural session of the first Asian Relations Conference. The occasion was, in Nehru's words, unique in history. From the Asian point of view, this was the first conference on such a scale encompassing so many peoples of that far-flung continent: in the wider Afro-Asian context it completed the cycle of post-war regional groupings which had begun in 1945 with the Pan-African conference in Manchester and with the establishment in Cairo in the same year of the Arab League.

The idea of holding an Asian conference had been fermenting for some time in the minds of several Asian leaders. "It so happened that we in India convened this conference, but the idea of such a conference rose simultaneously in many countries in Asia," declared Nehru in his inaugural address to the gathering at the Red Fort.[2] Only a year earlier, on returning from a tour of South-East Asia in March 1946, Nehru had declared that the desire for holding an Asian conference had been expressed by General Aung San, the Burmese leader who was to become the first premier of independent Burma, and by others.[3] In India itself, the need for closer cooperation among the countries of Asia was being increasingly voiced. In September 1945 the All-Indian Congress Committee declared that free India would seek the formation of common policies for defence, trade and economic and cultural growth with China, Burma, Malaya, Indonesia, Ceylon and the countries of the Middle East.[4] On January 1, 1946, Nehru declared that some kind of close association between the countries of Asia was necessary for defence and trade[5]; in a broadcast nine months later he returned to this theme, stressing

29

that the future was bound to see a closer union between India and South-East Asia on the one hand, and Afghanistan, Iran and the Arab world on the other.[6]

The conference, though Nehru's brain-child, had been organized by the non-official Indian Council of World Affairs, a body which had been formed in 1943 by the Indian Congress for the study of international affairs. It was thus a non-official conference, and the delegates were not official representatives of states. Indeed, it could hardly be otherwise, as scarcely any of the Asian states had yet attained full independence, not even India, the host country, which was to become independent only five months later. The dates and the lack of official status were by no means accidental; for one thing the Indian hosts feared that many of the delegates would not have received the necessary exit permits from their colonial regimes in order to attend an official conference; for another, the Indians had no wish at that early stage to antagonize Britain by inviting unwelcome guests, such as the delegates from the Asian republics of the Soviet Union, to an official conference.

The lack of official standing in no way lessened the importance of this first meeting of Asian representatives of independence. Although the organizers had sought to prevent controversial and even political issues from being raised,[7] the conference was soon dominated by three themes: decolonization, the problems arising out of the sub-development of Asia, and the need for Asian solidarity. Nehru himself made a highly political inaugural address. Asia, he declared, was emerging from the isolation into which it had been cast by the colonial regimes. It had "suddenly become important again in world affairs." But this was no Pan-Asian movement directed against Europe and America. "We have no designs against anybody; ours is the great design of promoting peace and progress all over the world," Nehru stated. Yet Asia had to assert itself. "Far too long have we of Asia been petitioners in Western courts and chancelleries. That story must now belong to the past. We propose to stand on our own legs and to cooperate with all others who are prepared to cooperate with us. We do not intend to be the playthings of others." The need for peace remained for Nehru the one supreme objective, but there could be no peace "unless Asia plays her part. . . . Peace can only come when nations are free." Significantly, even at this early stage Nehru was already thinking in terms of African as well as Asian freedom. "We of Asia have a special responsibility to the people of Africa. We must help them to their rightful place in the human family," he stressed.[8] Six months previously, in September 1946, Nehru had written to Kwame Nkrumah, Jomo Kenyatta and other African leaders that he had always considered the struggle for the freedom of India "as a common heritage for all, and more especially for those who have been deprived of it." Nehru continued in his letter: "We are particularly interested in the people of Africa, who have suffered so much in the past . . . . You have referred to the Inter-Asian Relations Conference, which we propose to hold in March next in New Delhi. As its name implies, this conference is more or less limited to Asia, but I am sure that friendly observers from Africa will be welcome at this conference and we can then confer together as to what we should do for developing closer relations between Asia and Africa."[9] The seed of Afro-Asianism had already been implanted in Nehru's mind, though no African body was invited to send observers to the conference.

Nehru's call for Asia to assert itself in world affairs found a ready echo in the conference. For the international context in which it was held must be borne in mind. In the early months of 1947 Europe, and in particular Great Britain, appeared to be on the brink of total breakdown. As the Asian leaders met in the warmth of the New Delhi sun, Britain lay paralysed in the throes of a severe winter facing a shortage of wheat, potatoes and other food supplies, and, particularly of coal. Lack of fuel caused factories to close down with a resultant spiralling of unemployment figures, which, at the time of the New Delhi conference, had topped the two million mark. As Britain reeled from the economic crisis, her leaders hastened to curtail her commitments abroad. On January 28, 1947, the decision was taken to quit Burma. Less than a month later, on February 18, Ernest Bevin, the British foreign secretary, told the House of Commons that it had been decided to submit the Palestine question to the United Nations. Two days after this announcement the prime minister, Clement Attlee, informed Parliament that the government of India would be transferred "into responsible Indian hands" not later than June 1948. On February 25, the US government was infored that Britain would have to give up its military and financial commitments in Greece by March 30.This headlong abdication of power was not lost on the Asian leaders assembled at New Delhi. The spectre of the British imperialist, which had overshadowed the countries of Asia for so long, ceased to provoke sentiments of awe and fear. In this setting, the talk of the new importance of Asia, and the need for Asian solidarity, becomes more understandable.

Thus Solomon W.R.D. Bandaranaike, the delegate from Ceylon, and later its prime minister, expressed the hope that the conference would be the beginning of a federation of free and equal countries of Asia, and Aung San of Burma hoped that the conference would be guided by a new consciousness of the oneness of Asia and by the supreme necessity on the part of all Asian countries to stand together. At the suggestion of Wen Yuan-ning of China, the following resolution was adopted:

> The members of the delegations from the Asian countries assembled in the first Asian Relations Conference in New Delhi . . . are unanimously of the opinion that the contacts forged at this conference must be maintained and strengthened . . . they accordingly resolve to establish an organization to be called the Asian Relations Organization.[10]

This first post-war attempt to institutionalize Pan-Asian sentiments was not very successful. The aims of the new organization [11] were only vaguely defined, and the work of its Provisional General Council, with Nehru at its head, soon became bogged down in inter-Asian quarrels. Indeed, the lack of unity had already been evident at the conference itself; not only did the Arab delegates present strongly criticize the presence of delegates from the Jewish community in Palestine, but a number of delegates—notably those from Burma, Malaya and Ceylon—expressed their fear that their countries would be submerged by the inflow of Indian immigrants. Underlying these fears was a growing uneasiness that India was seeking the leadership of free Asia. This fear was openly expressed by the Indian Muslim Congress, which refused to take part in the conference, dubbing it as "a thinly disguised attempt on the part of the Hindu Congress to boost itself politically as the prospective leader of the Asian people."[12] The sanguinary inter-community strife which erupted in India in 1948, the worsening civil war in China, and the fighting between Indonesian and Dutch forces were sufficient to push, momentarily at least, thoughts of Asian solidarity into the background. Nehru himself, in those fateful years for Indian independence, was too preoccupied with immediate matters concerning India herself to pay much attention to the Asian Relations Organization.

Yet if the 1947 conference brought forth no tangible results, it did have an importance of its own; it marked the break with Asia's subservience to Europe and provided the opportunity for the leaders of Asia to assemble together and get to know each other. Thus the New Delhi conference hastened the process of inter-Asian cooperation which was to lead to Bandung and to the birth of Afro-Asianism.

The second inter-Asian conference had been tentatively scheduled to take place in China in 1949. But those two years had seen momentous changes over the face of Asia. The independent states of India and Pakistan had been hewn out of the shambles of Hindu-Muslim relations. In China the victory of Mao Tse-tung over Chiang Kai-shek had reverberated throughout Asia; its effects were already being felt in Indochina, Burma, Malaya and the Philippines, where Communist uprisings threatened the existing regimes. The confrontation between Indonesian and Dutch forces was reaching a critical stage, with the Dutch holding on tenaciously to their Far Eastern possessions. It was this rearguard action of one of the major colonial powers in the Far East which increasingly drew the attention of the new Asian heads of state. On December 18, 1948, the Dutch forces launched an offensive against the Indonesian nationalists, many of whose leaders they arrested and jailed. A Security Council ruling demanding the release of the leaders and a cessation of hostilities was ignored by the Dutch. Neither the US nor any of the European powers appeared willing to take any action to curb the Dutch activities. Against this background Burmese Premier U Nu proposed to Nehru that he urgently convene a conference of independent Asian countries to discuss the Indonesian problem. Nehru agreed, invitations were dispatched, and on January 20, 1949, the representatives of the governments of Afghanistan, Australia, Burma, Ceylon, Egypt, Ethiopia, India, Iran, Iraq, Lebanon, Pakistan, the Philippines, Saudi Arabia, Syria and Yemen convened in New

Delhi. The list of participants is interesting, both with regard to those omitted as well as those included. The Soviet Asian republics, present at the first inter-Asian conference, had not been invited to the second. China chose to attend the conference in the capacity of observer. On the other hand, Australia was to make her debut in an Asian conference; she was invited because of her strong stand in favour of Indonesia's independence. The inclusion of Egypt and Ethiopia (though for some reason Liberia was not invited) gave the conference an Afro-Asian tint. Above all, this was the first conference to be held on governmental level, and this gave the second New Delhi conference an importance of its own. For the first time 14 representatives of African and Asian governments, and in addition a delegate from Australia, met to discuss a specifically Asian question. Although the subject matter of the conference was a specific and limited one, a number of delegates took the opportunity to demand that this precedent should be continued, and that a permanent machinery allowing for inter-Asian consultation be established. Nehru, in his inaugural address, put the problem in his usual succint manner:

> The Americans have already recognized a certain community of interest and have created machinery for the protection and promotion of common interests. A similar movement is in progress in Europe. Is it not natural that the free countries of Asia should begin to think of some more permanent arrangement than this conference for effective mutual consultation and concerted effort in the pursuit of common aims. . . . [13]

The representatives of Afghanistan, Syria, the Philippines, and Yemen all echoed these sentiments. Yet nearly all the speakers were at pains to stress that such cooperation should not be construed as side-stepping the United Nations; on the contrary, it should be within the framework of that body. Thus, Dr. Nazim el-Qudsi declared that Syria "welcomes the strengthening of political and economic ties with the countries of Asia here present, for our mutual safety and prosperity. Syria believes that a regional and permanent understanding within the framework of the United Nations will be beneficial to all the nations taking part in it."[14] General Carlos Romulo, of the Philippines, who was one of the staunchest advocates of a regional organization, proposed the establishment of "a small permanent Secretariat in New Delhi, or maybe, at Manila." He added: "It is to be hoped that out of such methods of cooperation in nuclear form, we shall be able to evolve a potent permanent organization of Asian States, functioning as a regional body alongside other associations of its kind, as contemplated by Article 52 of the [UN] charter."[15]

If the final resolutions of the conference on the subject of Indonesia were clear and forceful, those dealing with future cooperation were couched much more tentatively, revealing the hesitations still felt by some of the delegations on this subject.

Resolution II stated:

In order to ensure close cooperation among themselves on matters dealt with in Resolution I, this Conference recommends to the participating Governments, whether Member States of the United Nations or not:
(a) That they should keep in touch with one another through normal diplomatic channels;
(b) That they should instruct their representatives at the Headquarters of the United Nations and their diplomatic representatives to consult among themselves.

Resolution III read:

The Conference expresses the opinion that participating Governments should consult among themselves in order to explore ways and means of establishing suitable machinery, having regard to the areas concerned, for promoting consultation and cooperation within the framework of the United Nations.[16]

This was still a far cry from the "potent permanent organization of Asian States" that General Romulo had envisaged. But these resolutions did supply the legitimization for the informal gatherings of Asian representatives which had already been taking place at the United Nations. A formal frame of reference was set for the establishment of the Asian and Arabo-Asian group as it came to be known at the UN, and, with the inclusion of

Egypt and Ethiopia, the nucleus was created for the burgeoning of this body into the Afro-Asian group.

There had existed a great deal of unofficial cooperation between Arab and Asian delegations at the UN from the very first meeting of the General Assembly.[17] It is, therefore, difficult to pinpoint the exact date of the initiation of the Afro-Asian group at the UN.[18] After the second New Delhi conference, however, the cooperation between the UN representatives of the countries which participated at the conference progressively increased, and by the end of 1950 they were formally known and recognized as a separate grouping. This group now assumed a new importance.

Two months after the second New Delhi conference, the Peoples' Republic of China was formally proclaimed, and the spotlight of history shifted inevitably from Europe eastwards. This trend was heightened in 1950 when, in July, Communist forces crossed the 38th parallel and the Korean War erupted, to be followed shortly by the first guerilla activities of the Vietminh in the Gulf of Tonkin area. Asia was now in the centre of the world stage, and such a situation offered an opportunity to India's volatile premier to demonstrate his capacities as a world statesman, which he exploited to the full. Nehru's treatment of the Korean question—which briefly elevated India to the front line of the world's diplomatic powers—falls outside the scope of this study. But this question, and the masterly way in which the Indians steered between alignment with either the Western or the Communist camp helped to cement the Afro-Asian grouping, which had been gradually coming together in the United Nations as a result of the second New Delhi conference, behind Indian leadership. The first formal meetings in 1950 were attended by twelve Arab and Asian members out of the twenty countries from the African and Asian continents which were, at that time, represented at the UN. Those attending were Afghanistan, Burma, Egypt, India, Indonesia, Iraq, Iran, Lebanon, Pakistan, Saudi Arabia, Syria and the Yemen, i.e., six Arab countries, four non-Arab Muslim countries and only two non-Muslim countries. Thailand and the Philippines joined at a later stage, and in 1953 Liberia and Ethiopia joined the group, transforming it from an Arab-Asian into an Afro-Asian group. The remaining four countries from Africa and Asia in the UN were Turkey, Israel, Nationalist China and South Africa.

Of these only Israel was eager to join the group, but was barred from doing so by the Arab members. The number of the group gradually increased as new members joined and additional countries of Asia and Africa were admitted to the UN. By 1956 the group had swelled to twenty-eight, and had become the largest single regional bloc, able to prevent any proposal from obtaining a two-thirds majority in the General Assembly without the support of at least some of its members.

Despite its size, the power of the Afro-Asian group in the UN remained largely fictional. From the outset the consensus of opinion in the group was limited largely to questions which had little reference to cold-war issues. Thus, on matters of human rights, socialism, the economic development of underdeveloped countries, and, to a lesser extent, on colonialism, the group was able to act in a coordinated fashion. In regard to the majority of problems brought before the UN, however, the group was faced with wide divergences, as its members voted in accordance with the specific interests of their particular foreign policy requirements, without reference to any Afro-Asian consensus. Some of the members, particularly those generally supporting the United States in cold-war issues, joined the group only half-heartedly, and, more often than not, absented themselves from council meetings. This happened with Ethiopia and Liberia in the first years of the group's existence.[19] Thailand joined with the principal aim of gaining support over the question of Vietminh infiltration into neighbouring Laos, while at least some of the Arab delegates regarded the group as a lever to increase Arab voting power to muster support over the issues of Palestine and North Africa.

The question of territories in North Africa, and in particular that of French rule in Tunisia, which provided one of the main subjects for attention of the Afro-Asian group in the pre-Bandung period, is well worth examining since it gives an insight into the methods employed by the group in those early days. The subject was brought before the UN General Assembly for the first time at its seventh session, in 1952, after exhaustive preparatory work had been carried out by the Arab delegations in the preceding session. Thirteen delegations representing Arab and Asian countries sought vainly to convoke a special session of the Assembly to debate the situation in Tunisia; they succeeded, however, in introducing a motion in the ordinary session which called, inter alia, for the establishment of a three-member commission to examine the entire question. This motion was heavily defeated; notable among those who refused to support it were the delegates of Ethiopia and Liberia. In its place the Latin-American delegates proposed such a mild formula that even the French saw no need to oppose it.

There now occurred an interesting and little-publicized sidelight to the Afro-Asian Movement. Disappointed by the results at the General Assembly, the Arab and Asian delegates assembled at the behest of the Arab League in Cairo in December 1952 to discuss further moves on North Africa.[20] The delegates decided to send a strong protest to France and to arrange a full-dress Arabo-Asian conference, to be attended by prime ministers and presidents, to discuss the North African situation. In the words of the final communiqué, published on December 4, "the member states agreed to view this conference, which is of historic importance, as a preparatory meeting to another conference, at which the heads of government of the bloc will participate and which will be called together to discuss the steps that should be taken (over North Africa) if French policy remain obdurate."[21] Nothing came of this attempt on the part of the Arab League to organize a repeat performance of the New Delhi conference on Indonesia. Asian delegates met again in Cairo with the Political Committee of the Arab League in August 1953, at the request of the Indonesian delegate, but decided to await the outcome of the eighth session of the UN General Assembly before taking further action. However, the efforts of the Arabo-Asian group fared no better than they had done the previous year; even the watered-down proposal they submitted this time did not obtain a majority of votes.[22]

In a sense, the 1953 discussions in Cairo marked the heyday of Arabo-Asian relations within the Afro-Asian group. Some of the more Western-oriented countries were reluctant to enter into an open fight with France over North Africa, and when the new government of Pierre Mendes-France embarked on a vigorous new policy in its relations with its overseas territories, this reluctance even spread to the more moderate of the Arab countries, and in particular to French-oriented Lebanon. An Arab effort to raise the question of Algeria in the UN Security Council received no support whatsoever from the non-Arab Afro-Asians. At this early stage, non-alignment, even when the subject dealt with was French colonization in North African territories, was still the exception rather than the rule. The change was to come much later.

The North African effort proved a dismal failure. The changes which were eventually wrought in the relations between France and her North African territories had nothing to do with the efforts of the Arabo-Asians at the UN. The Arabs drew further apart, disillusioned by the weakness of the Afro-Asians. In February 1954 the Washington correspondent of Cairo's *al-Ahrām* was already forecasting the disintegration of the group. The Arab delegates, he wrote, refused to support India's bid for leadership of the group, mainly because of Pakistan's violent opposition.[23] The winds of dissent were already blowing strongly. Several month later, *al-Ahram* again reported the group's impending disintegration. This time the cause for the crisis was that India, Pakistan and Iraq had voted for the postponement of the debate on the Cyprus issue, after the Political Committee of the Arab League had taken a stand to the contrary.[24] Persistent reports of differences between the Arab League and the Afro-Asian group at the UN brought an official denial from the League's secrctary-general 'Abd al-Khāliq Hassūna who rejected the assertion that the group was on the verge of falling apart.[25]

Although the denial was justified, for the Afro-Asian delegates continued to meet regularly, the group had, in effect, become moribund. It had its brief spell of glory during the Korean affair, due mainly to India's prestige and because the two world blocs had reached a political stalemate over Korea, but it had not since succeeded in making its mark in regard to any of the major problems it had tackled. It was only in the year of the Bandung conference, and with the influx of additional members into the UN, that new life was injected into the Afro-Asian group. This post-Bandung development belongs, however, to a later chapter.[26]

At the New Delhi conference on Indonesia in January 1949 a decision was taken to explore possibilities of greater cooperation among the Asian states. Two months later, in a speech in the Lok Sabha (Indian Parliament), Nehru informed the House that "perhaps in the course of a month or two and perhaps more we may have some more definite results to consider; possibly we might have another conference to consider the possible lines of cooperation." But Nehru made it plain in that speech that whatever the form of cooperation, "there will be no binding covenant in it, and this will largely be an organization for the consultation and cooperation that naturally flow from common interests."[27]

Nehru had, in fact, become considerably less enthusiastic over pan-Asianism, in any form, than he had been on the eve of the first New Delhi conference in 1947. There were a number of reasons for this change of attitude. One was the growing fractionalism within Asia itself, as the newly independent countries increasingly took sides in the developing cold war. There was the emergence of Communist China towards the latter half of 1949, and the uncertainties emanating from this momentous development. There were strained relations between India and Pakistan, which in 1949 and 1950 appeared to be steadily deteriorating. There were troubles within India herself, with the Communist Party in particular. Above all, there was Nehru's own reading of the international situation as the cold war unfolded in those bleak post-war years. As he himself said time and again, the main preoccupation of all nations should be to work for peace. The two ways in which India could contribute to this effort were, according to Nehru, by standing aloof from the two power blocs and by creating an "area of peace" between them. The situation in Asia at that time, especially after the Korean War erupted, made it appear to him that he could achieve his objectives more efficiently by working through the UN than by becoming bogged down in controversial issues raised in inter-Asian confabulations. The Korean War in particular had created a sharp cleavage in the stand taken on this issue by the various Asian countries. On the other hand, the success of Indian diplomacy at the United Nations over the Korean issue strengthened his belief that India had a world role to play, beyond the horizons of Asia. Nehru, who at heart was a true internationalist, cast himself in the role of world arbitrator. Yet this internationalism was not at the expense of India's interests; on the contrary, by pursuing what Nehru considered to be India's international obligations, he was at the same time defending her national interests. The pursuit of peace was not a mere act of humanism, but an essential factor for the fulfillment of India's ambitious economic programmes. India needed, just as the Soviet Union had needed in its infancy, twenty years of peace to develop her economy. A new world war could reduce her economy to a shambles and shatter the plans for a more prosperous India which were being laid in those first years of her independence. Basic national interests dictated India's international role. Her dire need for aid on a massive scale from every quarter able to supply it was the foundation on which India's policy of friendship to both power blocs rested. These sentiments created the desire to remain free from any involvement, even in an inter-Asian framework. They caused Nehru to emphasize that India would not be confined "by any binding convenant," and they, together with the other factors mentioned above, led Nehru to hold back from further initiative to establish any form of regional organization.

Such initiative was not slow in coming from another quarter. By the end of 1949 the Republic of Indonesia had reached virtual sovereign status and was accepted as a full member of the United Nations in September 1950. The Indonesian approach to international relations was very different from that of India. The anti-Western indoctrination by the Japanese during the years of World War II, the four-year struggle for independence against Western countries in the immediate post-war years, the support given to the Netherlands by the US all combined to produce militantly anti-Western sentiments in Indonesia. These feelings crystalized in an anti-Western foreign policy, which was only partly modified by the urgent need for economic aid from the West, and from the very first days of Indonesia's existence had strong overtones of anti-colonialism. There was a crusading quality in Indonesia's foreign policy reflected in the words of President Sukarno: "We do not belong to either of the two blocs but our policy is not one of neutrality. It can never be neutral as long as tyranny exists in any part of the world."[28] Thus from the start, whereas Nehru emphasized the need for world peace, Sukarno put all his weight behind a war against colonialism and imperialism. This difference coloured all the actions taken by Indonesia to bring about an Afro-Asian encounter. Indonesia's special interest in such an encounter stemmed from a number of reasons, not least this anti-colonialist zeal. But there were other, less altruistic ones: a desire for friendship with Communist China[29] and a wish to distract public attention from the grave economic, political and security situation existing within the more than two thousand islands which together make up the Republic of Indonesia, and, the necessity therefore to strengthen the government image.

The first initiative of the Indonesians on the Afro-Asian plane was taken in 1952. The Korean War was subsiding, the fractionalism in Asia which it had exacerbated was lessening; in Indonesia herself, a new government led by the National Party had been installed (see below, Chapter 12). The previous government, a coalition headed by Muhammad Nazir of the Muslim Masjumi Party, had shown greater inclination for Muslim solidarity than for any regional organization.[30] The National Party, together with its junior partner in the coalition, the Socialist Party, led by Sjoetan Sjahrir, were much more militantly anti-Western than the Masjumi, and it was they who now set the tone.[31] Pan-Islamic aspirations were laid aside. They were replaced by a policy calling for a banding together of countries with neutralist[32] tendencies, coupled with an activist foreign policy in favour of anti-colonialist movements struggling for independence. [33]

As a result of this policy shift Dr. Subarjo, the Indonesian foreign minister, left in October 1952 for a tour of the Arab countries and Iran in order, in his own words, to examine the possibility of establishing a neutralist bloc with the twin purpose of working for the reduction of world tension and initiating economic cooperation among the members of the bloc. Subarjo told a correspondent of the Cairo daily *al-Ahrām* that both India and Indonesia believed that economic cooperation should precede political cooperation, for a strong economy was an essential prerequisite to gaining complete independence from the West. Economic independence, he stressed, was the efficient weapon against imperialism, which was the prime cause for wars. Such a bloc, he added, need not be limited to Muslim countries only, but should include Burma, India, Thailand, Ethiopia and others with whom close cooperation had already been established in the United Nations.[34] Although nothing tangible emerged from this first effort, relations between Indonesia and the Arab countries were greatly strengthened as a result of Subarjo's tour, and the idea of a neutralist bloc was implanted in the Middle East.

The new government in Indonesia of Dr. 'Ali Sastroamidjojo, which was formed in the summer of 1953, continued the foreign policy of its predecessor; in the opening speech in Parliament of the new prime minister, on August 24, 1953, one of the points stressed was the need to pursue a policy of close cooperation with Asian and Arab countries. Two days later the Indonesian ambassador in Cairo declared his country's willingness to boycott France in all spheres, as a countermeasure to the French decision to exile the Moroccan Sultan. He also supported the idea put out by the Arab League for an Arab-Asian conference on governmental level—similar to the 1949 New Delhi conference on Indonesia—to discuss the North African question. But, apart from its support by the Arab countries, the reaction to this idea remained lukewarm.

In the meantime another confrontation with a colonialist power, much nearer to Indonesia than North Africa, was reaching its climax. The French in Indochina were being increasingly hard pressed by the Vietminh, and the possibility of US intervention was causing disquiet, not only in Indonesia, but notably in India, Burma, and, to a lesser extent, Ceylon. In January 1954 the Indonesians made a discreet proposal for holding a conference of the heads of government of Egypt, Pakistan, India, Burma, Ceylon and Indonesia to discuss the situation in Indochina and North Africa. Two months later, the chairman of the Foreign Affairs Committee of the Indonesian Parliament, citing the urgency of the Indochina situation, called for a full-scale Afro-Asian conference.

In the event, however, it was not the insistent Indonesian attempts but the initiative taken by the prime minister of Ceylon which brought about a conference of Asian leaders. Side by side with the Indonesian efforts, and without any coordination, the Ceylon premier, Sir John Kotelawala, had also been working for an Asian entente. According to him, the idea had been taking shape in his mind for about seven years, and "was first given expression by me in a broadcast talk in Rangoon in 1948."[35] Just how little contact existed between the countries of Asia can be seen from the fact that Sir John's original intention had been to confine the talks to Burma, Ceylon, India and Pakistan—the four Asian members of the British Commonwealth. He decided to extend an invitation to Indonesia, as well, because she was of the "same cultural area" and because "she, too, had shaken off the shackles of colonialism at about the same time as ourselves"[36] but not because of Indonesian efforts to convene a similar conference, of which evidently nothing was known in Ceylon.

The overriding thoughts of Sir John Kotelawala as he sent the invitations were, in his own words, to do something to stop possible war over Indochina, and to make the voice of Asia heard.[37] In the event, his initiative came at a most opportune moment, for these two aims had been occupying the thoughts of other Asian leaders, notably U Nu and Nehru.

Nehru, in particular, had been becoming increasingly alarmed at the possibility of US intervention in Indochina. On March 29, 1954, US Secretary of State John Foster Dulles had made an important policy statement, which spelt out in clear terms the probability of imminent American intervention. "Under the conditions to today," Dulles had stated, "the imposition on Southeast Asia of the political system of Communist Russia and its Chinese Communist ally, by whatever means, would be a grave threat to the whole free community. The United States feels that that possibility should not be passively accepted but should be met by united action. This might have serious risks. But these risks are far less than those that will face us a few years from now if we dare not be resolute today."[38] At the beginning of April the French, under siege at Dienbienphu, requested American aid in the form of a carrier-strike against the Vietminh forces pressing on the beleaguered French garrison. Dulles was in favour of a more general intervention, but he wanted an international task force, similar to the Korean operation. On April 10 he left for London and Paris in order to coordinate action with his allies; the British, however, after initial acceptance of the plan, backed down.[39] Even if these behind-the-scenes preparations were, at the time, unknown to Nehru, the imminence of a possible war between the US and China in Indochina was plain. It was underlined by the dispatch to the South China Sea of two US aircraft carriers, the *Boxer* and the *Philippine Sea*, with tactical air groups armed with atomic weapons on board. Belatedly, Nehru woke to the dangers of a more general conflict inherent in the Indochina situation, and now wished to make India's influence felt in much the same way as it had been felt over the Korean issue. In a speech in the Lok Sabha on April 24, Nehru voiced his apprehensions, and put forward a six-point plan for solving the Indochina conflict.[40] Two days later, the Geneva conference on Korea and Indochina was opened. That neither India, nor any major Asian country apart from the participants in the two wars, including

China, was invited to attend this major international conference devoted to purely Asian issues was considered an insult to the newly won independence of so many Asian states. Thus Sir John Kotelawala's twin aim of doing something to avert war and to make Asia's voice heard was sympathetically received, and even Nehru overcame his suspicion of regional conferences and hastened to Colombo.

The Colombo conference opened on April 28, 1954, two days after the beginning of the Geneva conference. Those attending were Nehru of India, U Nu of Burma, Muhammad 'Ali of Pakistan, Dr. Sastroamidjojo of Indonesia, and the host, Sir John Kotelawala. Of all the pre-Bandung conferences this one was the most cantankerous. The participants refused to heed Nehru's plea that they should devote themselves to one issue only—Indochina, "the most important issue before the world today"[41]—and ranged over a wide number of subjects. Not surprisingly, the Pakistani premier hastened to raise the question of Kashmir: so long as that problem remained unsolved, it was a little presumptuous for the Asian powers represented to teach peace to others. First "our own differences" must be resolved, he declared.[42] If this blast against India had been expected, however, the proposal by Ceylon that the conference should declare itself against "Communist aggression and infiltration" took the Indians completely unawares.[43] The resolutions on Communism on the one hand, and Western colonialism on the other, became the main stumbling block: Ceylon and Pakistan were determined not to accept one without the other. Nehru, however, insisted that a resolution condemning Communism was tantamount to taking sides in favour of the West in the cold war, and was therefore incompatible with India's policy of non-alignment. He flatly refused to accept the draft resolution put forward by Ceylon, which declared inter alia that international Communism was the biggest potential danger in South and South-East Asia. This argument was to be repeated, no less fiercely, at Bandung, but there, as at Colombo, a compromise formula was eventually found. The five premiers expressed their "unshakeable determination to resist interference in their countries by external Communist, anti-Communist or other agencies."[44]

These were, inevitably, side issues. The burning problem, as Nehru had pointed out, was Indochina, and it was around this question that the major part of the conference revolved. Nehru's six points formed the basis of the discussion, with Pakistan leading the opposition, mainly to the fifth point, which called for non-intervention by the great powers. Once more prolonged—and often acrimonious—discussion produced a compromise formula, which called for a cease-fire without delay, negotiations between the parties concerned, a declaration by France that she was committed to the independence of Indochina, and agreement between China, Britain, the United States and the Soviet Union on the steps necessary to prevent a resumption of hostilities.

In the midst of these discussions on Indochina, the Indonesian premier Dr. Sastroamidjojo put forward his proposal to hold an Asian-African conference. It was this initiative which directly set in motion the machinery which was to lead to Bandung. His proposal was not greeted very enthusiastically. Dr. Sastroamidjojo "was very keen on it, but the others were not so sure how it would work out," noted the prime minister of Ceylon,[45] while *The Times* commented: "This afternoon the conference transferred its attention to suggestions made by Burma for economic cooperation and joint planning and by Indonesia for an Afro-Asian conference. The other prime ministers appear to be preoccupied with other issues, notably Indochina and Communism. . . ." *The Times* continued: "Pan-Asianism is not a telling factor, although of course Asian countries are generally and vaguely sympathetic towards each other."[46]

Thus preparations for Bandung were begun on a muted note. Out of the fifteen articles of the final communiqué at Colombo, the one dealing with the Afro-Asian conference appeared as article 15, and read: "The prime ministers discussed the desirability of holding a conference of African-Asian nations and favoured a proposal that the prime minister of Indonesia might explore the possibility of such a conference."[47] Other articles dealt with colonialism—"a violation of human rights and a threat to peace"—the hydrogen bomb, the seating of China in the UN, Palestine, and, of course, Indochina to which the greater part of the communiqué was devoted. The fact that Sir Anthony Eden, the British foreign secretary, had set up direct radio contact between Colombo and Geneva during the Colombo conference, and that the great powers had paid so much attention to the deliberations at Colombo, had given an international importance to the conference which would otherwise have been absent.

It was this attitude of the great powers, more than the statesmanlike quality of the discussions at Colombo, which created the term the "Colombo Powers" which later gained currency. "The cease-fire and the fact that the great powers had so openly angled during the conference for the support of the uncommitted nations were seen as a vindication of non-alignment, a tribute to India's diplomatic activities, and a proof of the vitality of its policy," wrote F.C. Jones of the Royal Institute of International Affairs in London.[48] This sentiment was heightened when India accepted the chairmanship of the Armistice Supervisory Commission for Indochina.

Thus, at the time when the idea of an Afro-Asian conference was formally launched, the prestige of the uncommitted nations of Asia had reached new heights. Moreover, the fact that a series of highly political resolutions had been passed unanimously at Colombo strengthened the hands of the Indonesians who were now able to claim that the same subjects could be discussed, with equal unanimity, in the wider context of an Afro-Asian conference, thus strengthening these resolutions by giving them the greater weight of a larger number of nations. As Sir John Kotelawala pointed out in a talk at the Overseas Club in Manila in December 1954, "there is no reason at all why what we have been able to do amongst the five Colombo Powers should not happen amongst all the democratic countries of Asia. All that is necessary is to come together and talk."[49]

All the same it was not quite so simple as that. Sir John had inadvertently put his finger on one of the problems with his qualifying adjective "democratic." The question of China's participation in the proposed conference loomed large from the very beginning, with Indonesia, Burma and India insisting on her inclusion. The Colombo talks had taken place at the time of the final assault on Dienbienphu. As the talks ended, the headlines in London's *The Times* were: "Third Major Assault Begun on Dien Bien Phu. French Posts Overrun in Fierce Fighting."[50] The Communist victory had an enormous psychological impact on the peoples of Asia, comparable perhaps to the Japanese victory over Russia in 1905. It placed the Chinese presence in Asia in completely new perspective. Nehru, in particular, had reached the conclusion that peace in Asia was bound very largely to the degree that China was accepted into the Asian community. He was determined that India and China, as the two largest countries of Asia, should live in peace and harmony with each other. This determination is reflected in the *Panch Sheel*, or five principles, which formed the preamble to an Indian-Chinese trading treaty on Tibet, signed on April 29, 1954, a day after the Colombo conference began. These five points, which were only named *Panch Sheel* later in the year,[51] contained the following principles:

(1) mutual respect for each other's territorial integrity and sovereignty;
(2) mutual non-aggression;
(3) mutual non-interference in each other's affairs;
(4) equality and mutual benefit;
(5) peaceful coexistence.

A great deal has been written and has been made of the *Panch Sheel*, not least by the Indians themselves. It is, therefore, enlightening to read the remarks of one of the major architects of India's foreign policy, Krishna Menon, on this subject:

> When we were discussing the Tibetan Treaty the way we should conduct ourselves came up willy-nilly. After all, what is the Tibetan Treaty? Tibet, including the various trade agreements involved, was the only problem we had with China which called for regularization. . . . The five points, as you can see, are not very well drafted. It was not as though it was a prepared formula. It emerged out of the conversations—that is all there was to it.

He continued in a later passage:

> When I saw the drafting of the Five Principles I thought it had been rather badly written. I said so to the prime minister, and he said, 'what does it matter; it isn't a treaty or anything, its a preface to this Tibetan business.' Quite frankly it was only afterwards that the Five Principles emerged as a *mantra* (dictum), a slogan, a sop.[52]

Krishna Menon further pointed out that "the five points really contained nothing new," that they were "merely a restatement of those principles which we call non-alignment—what else!"[53] Thus, at the time, not too great importance was attached by the Indians to the five points. Indeed, it was the Chinese premier Chou En-lai who suggested in an exchange of letters after the agreement that the five principles could be made the basis of a reasonable settlement of any outstanding questions.[54] The points were elevated to a rank of outstanding importance when Chou En-lai visited New Delhi on June 25 on his way home from Geneva and the two leaders affirmed their agreement with the five principles as the basis of their intentional conduct.

For the Indians these principles now became the foundation-stone of their foreign policy. They sought adherents to the *Panch Sheel* with a crusading zeal; it was almost as if they considered it the universal panacea to all evils in international relations. Above all, they saw it as a basis for friendly relations with China, to which Nehru attached supreme importance. In a letter sent to the Indian Congress Party leaders after his meeting with Chou En-lai, Nehru wrote that the meeting indicated a historic change in the relationship of forces in Asia. No one could guarantee peace for a given number of years, but even a few years gained was worth striving for. If the great powers declared their adherence to the policy of non-intervention there would be an immediate change for the better. "Even if such declarations are not sincerely meant the result will be to create a force in favour of peace and non-interference," Nehru wrote.[55] Speaking in a foreign policy debate in the Council of States a month later he declared that India and China would have to play important roles in Asia and the world, and it was necessary that they should understand and cooperate with each other. Their contacts should be friendly because of the five principles to which both had agreed.[56]

Thus India based her Asian and foreign policy increasingly on friendship and cooperation with China. On the evidence of Krishna Menon the first storm clouds that were already gathering in 1954 in relations between India and China were considered of no significance by the Indian leaders. They accepted unequivocally Chinese suzerainty over Tibet[57]; they considered Chinese probings at the frontier at Barahoti and at the North East Frontier Agency to be "smaller territorial disputes, not the prelude to aggression,"[58] and they evidently sincerely believed that the *Panch Sheel* agreement with the Chinese committed China to espousing the same foreign policy objectives as those of India, above all, non-intervention in the affairs of other countries, peaceful coexistence, and broadening the "area of peace."

The orientation towards China was all the greater because of the vehemence with which India opposed the efforts of the Western great powers to set up a military alliance which, in Indian eyes, was directed overtly against China. This can be seen from India's reaction to the invitation sent to the "Colombo Powers" to attend the talks at Baguio, Philippines, which led to the establishment of SEATO.[59] Commenting on the invitation, Nehru declared that collective peace was the only alternative to war preparedness, and understanding between India and China contained the nucleus of collective peace. The proposed South-East Asia Collective Organization, he added, would do more harm than good.[60] Krishna Menon was more outspoken: the proposed organization was a modern version of the protectorate, designed to defend an area against its will, he declared.[61] This point was taken up by Nehru, in a speech in the Lok Sabha: "It seems to me that this particular Manila Treaty is inclined dangerously in the direction of spheres of influence to be exercised by powerful countries." Nehru was particularly afraid of the intervention by the powers in the internal affairs of countries:

> One can understand the mention of external aggression in a defence treaty, but there is reference also to 'a fact or situation created within this area' which might entitle them to intervene. Observe these words. They do not refer to external invasion. It means that any internal development in that area might also entitle these countries to intervene.[62]

The growing apprehension of India in the face of SEATO was summed up in the *Statesman* of New Delhi in the following words: SEATO had brought India and the Asian countries closer to China. An Asian entente based on coexistence and distrust of the West could become a reality.[63]

It was precisely for such an Asian entente that the Indonesians were striving so hard. The key to the wider Asian-African conference that Dr. Sastroamidjojo envisaged lay in New Delhi, and it was to the Indian capital that the Indonesian premier first made his way in order to finalize arrangements for the proposed conference. Nehru, however, was constantly blowing hot and cold on the idea. It was his desire to lead China into the Asian fold and to strengthen the hands of Asian countries still being pressurized by the US to join the Manila pact,[64] but his experience at Colombo, the long and often acrimonious arguments with the premiers of Pakistan and Ceylon, made him draw back from the idea of yet another general conference. In his discussions with the Indonesian premier he evidently expressed the belief that the only acceptable outcome of the conference could be the extension of the Afro-Asian bloc in the UN, "a loose organization which would agree not to discuss controversial subjects."[65] Sastroamidjojo, however, was indefatigable in his efforts; he also phrased the objectives of the conference in such a manner that Nehru found it difficult to oppose them. Thus, in a speech to the Indian Council of World Affairs, Sastroamidjojo said, "This conference . . . will enable us to strengthen our cooperation, to expand our efforts for peace, whilst it will also convince the world that this enormous area does not want in its affairs any interference in the realization of its peaceful policies."[66] Nehru could hardly object to such lofty aims. The outcome of Sastroamidjojo's visit was a joint statement with Nehru, in which, inter alia, it was stated that they "were agreed that a conference of this kind was desirable and would be helpful in promoting the cause of peace and the common approach to their problems."[67] It was decided that another meeting of the Colombo Powers should be held first, "preferably at Jakarta," to decide upon the agenda and the list of invitees.

The second meeting of the Colombo Powers was held at Bogor, at President Sukarno's summer palace on the outskirts of Jakarta, on December 28, 1954. The main problem, from the outset of the talks, was not what was to be discussed but who was and who was not to be invited. The neutralist criterion could not be applied, for China could, by no stretch of the imagination, be termed neutralist in cold-war terminology, and both India and Burma were adamant on procuring China's presence at the conference. An automatic geographical criterion was equally untenable, for this would entail an invitation to Chiang Kai-shek's National government at Taiwan and would thus lead to the exclusion of the Chinese Peoples' Republic. Exceptions, therefore, had to be made, and Nehru forthwith proposed "certain variations and minor modifications" of the application of the geographical rule.[68] The debate on China versus Taiwan was a protracted one, and threatened at one point to bring to an end all the preparations for the conference. But the five premiers had, by then, gone too far. Neither Pakistan's Muhammad 'Ali or Ceylon's Sir John Kotelawala wished to be accused of "desolidifying" Asian solidarity. As a consolation prize to Pakistan for agreeing to the inclusion of Peking, the others agreed to her demand to exclude Israel, though this was done with great reluctance by Burmese premier U Nu, who, before his departure for Bogor, had assured the Israeli ambassador in Rangoon that Burma would only participate at the Afro-Asian conference if Israel was invited. Sir John Kotelawala also strongly opposed the Pakistani demand, asserting that such a decision would be tantamount to racism.[69] It was Nehru who finally tilted the balance against Israel. Although he opposed her exclusion, he declared, an invitation to Israel would automatically close the door to Arab participation. It was preferable, therefore, that Israel should not be invited.[70] This surrender to an implied threat of boycott by the Arab states was to be a precedent often followed later in Afro-Asian conferences.

In addition to Taiwan and Israel, the Union of South Africa was excluded for its racialist policies, and so were North and South Korea. Invitations were sent out to twenty-five countries of which only the Central African Republic declined to attend. The interesting point in these discussions was that none of the five Colombo Powers raised the question of Soviet participation. The question whether the Soviet Union was part of Asia or not, which was to bedevil Afro-Asian conclaves in the future, was not even broached at Bogor. Nobody was to defend the "Soviet Union belongs to Asia" thesis more vigorously than the Indians in the future, but their silence on this subject at Bogor was to have far-reaching effects on the Afro-Asian Movement.

On the question of what was to be discussed at the conference there were fewer divergences in opinions. In effect the premiers agreed to the Indian point of view that the agenda should be determined at the time of the conference itself, and should be within the framework of four stipulated objectives:

1. to promote goodwill and cooperation among the nations of Asia and Africa, to explore and advance their mutual as well as common interests and to establish and further friendliness and neighbourly relations;
2. to consider social, economic and cultural problems and relations of the countries represented;

3. to consider problems of special interest to Asian and African peoples—for example, problems affecting national sovereignty and of racialism and colonialism;
4. to view the position of Asia and Africa and their peoples in the world today and the contribution they can make to the promotion of world peace and cooperation.[71]

The five prime ministers agreed that the conference be held in Indonesia during the second half of April 1955, each country being represented by its prime minister or foreign minister. Largely to allay the fears of those countries which had not granted diplomatic recognition to China, it was agreed that any country's acceptance of the invitation "would in no way invoke or even imply any change in its view of the status of any other country."

The prime ministers dispersed as the year drew to a close. The final preparations for the Asian-African conference were left to a small international Secretariat. The site chosen for it was the town of Bandung, in the hills of Java, and it is to there that we must now turn.

NOTES

[1] Those participating were delegates from: Afghanistan, Armenia, Azerbaijan, Burma, Butan, Cambodia, Cochin China, Ceylon,China, Egypt, Georgia, India, Indonesia, Iran, Kazakhstan, Korea, Laos, Malaya, Mongolia, Nepal, Palestine (Jewish community), Philippines, Siam, Tadzhikistan, Tibet, Turkey, Turkmenistan, Uzbekistan, Vietnam.

[2] Nehru, *India's Foreign Policy*, p. 248ff.

[3] See, *Asian Relations*, p. 2.

[4] "Indian National Congress," *Congress Bulletjn*, Allahabad, 1.11.1945.

[5] Bright (ed.), *Before and After Independence*, pp. 381–2.

[6] Nehru, *Independence and After: A Collection of Speeches*, New York, 1950, p. 341.

[7] The subjects selected for discussion were: the national movements for freedom, migration and racial problems, economic development and social services, cultural problems, and women's problems. A proposal to discuss defence and security questions was rejected as being too controversial and political—see *Asian Relations*, p. 4.

[8] Nehru, *India's Foreign Policy, loc. cit.*

[9] Also quoted in Norman, *Nehru*, p. 270.

[10] See Poplai (ed.), *Asia and Africa in the Modern World*, App. II, pp. 195–6.

[11] (a) to promote the study and understanding of Asian problems and relations in their Asian and world aspects;

(b) to foster friendly relations and cooperation among the peoples of Asia and between them and the rest of the world;

(c) to further the progress and well-being of the peoples of Asia.

See Poplai, *ibid.*, App. II., p. 196.

[12] Quoted by Norman (ed.), *Nehru, The First Sixty Years*, Vol. 2, pp. 89–90.

[13] Poplai (ed.), *Selected Documents on Asian Affairs: India, 1947–50*, Vol. 11, Section VII, New Delhi: Conference on Indonesia, Proceedings of First Plenary Session; see p. 663.

[14] *Ibid.*, p. 672.

[15] *Ibid.*, p. 673.

[16] *Ibid.,* pp. 684–5.

[17] Thus, the Arab League Council, in a special resolution in 1949, encouraged its members to increase their cooperation with the countries of Asia—see Resolution 241, Session No. 10, Arab League Council, 21.3.1949.

[18] According to Jansen, the group was formed on December 5, 1950; see his *Afro-Asia and Non-Alignment,* p. 102. On the other hand, according to the former secretary-general of the Arab League, 'Abd al-Rahman Azzam, the group came into being over the question of Indonesian independence, i.e., in 1949. "We rallied round India to support Indonesia, and that was the birth of the Arab-Asiatic group. There was then India, the Philippines and China—Nationalist China—and the Arab states. Turkey was always hesitating and never took it seriously." 'Azzam is quoted in Carnegie Endowment for International Peace, *Egypt and the U.N.,* p. 74.

[19] Thus, in 1953, for example, the Ethiopian delegate failed to sign a petition of the group to the Security Council on the ground that the head of the delegation was not in New York; in June 1953, the Ethiopians again absented themselves from the caucus meeting, and in July they refused to sign a petition to the UN secretary-general on the subject of Tunisia and Morocco.

[20] *Al-Ahrām,* Cairo, 23.12.1952. According to the Israel daily *Haaretz* one of the items on the agenda was German Reparations for Israel, a subject which the non-Arab delegates refused to discuss, see *Haaretz,* Tel Aviv, 24.12.1952.

[21] Cairo Radio, 23.12.1952, 14.30.

[22] The draft resolution on Tunisia which was finally brought before the UN General Assembly was so mildly worded that the French could raise no objection to it—see United Nations General Assembly, official records, 8th Session Annexes, Agenda item 56, p. 3.

[23] *Al-Ahrām,* Cairo, 19.2.1954.

[24] *Ibid.,* 1.10.1954.

[25] *Ibid.,* 6.11.1954.

[26] See Chapter 5, p. 91 ff.

[27] Nehru, *Independence and After,* pp. 229–44.

[28] *U.S. News and World Report,* New York, 15.6.1956.

[29] One of the reasons for this Chinese orientation was economic: China rapidly became an important market for Indonesia's raw materials, and, in particular, for her rubber, for which she paid prices higher than the accepted world prices.

[30] Its full name is Madjelis Sjuro Muslimin Indonesia, or Council of Indonesian Muslim Associations (see also below, Chapter 12). In 1950 the

party canvassed actively for the establishment of a Muslim university in
South-East Asia, and proposed to hold a regional Islamic conference in
Indonesia. In February 1951 the Masjumi took an active part in the World
Islamic Conference in Karachi, and one of its leaders declared that his
party was in full accord with the idea of a "Muslim bloc" and for inter-
Muslim cooperation on the political, economic and cultural planes.

[31] The Socialists and Masjumi quit the coalition in July 1953 when a new
government under Dr. Sastroamidjojo of the National Party was formed
(see also below, Chapter 12).

[32] "Neutralist" is a word covering many shades of meanings. It is used in
this context in the Indonesian sense, i.e., neutralist with regard to the
great-power conflict, but, at the same time, militantly anti-colonialist.

[33] Mainly those in North Africa. With the Arab countries, Indonesia was
the most active campaigner in the Arabo-Asian group in the UN in favour of independence of the North African territories.

[34] *Al-Ahrām*, 10.10.1952.

[35] Kotelawala, *Asian Prime Minister's Story,* p. 117.

[36] *Ibid.,* p. 118.

[37] It was not only Indochina that he had in mind when he proposed the conference in late 1953. The growing friction between Pakistan and India
over the possibility of Pakistan receiving American military aid was another subject he thought should be aired—see *Hindu,* 14.1.1954.

[38] *New York Times,* 30.3.1954. See also a statement by Vice-President
Richard Nixon, made on April 16, that in the event of a French withdrawal the US would have to send troops to Indochina.

[39] For an account of those brink-of-war manoeuvrings, see article by James
Shepley "How Dulles Averted War," in *Life,* 16.1.1956, based on a series
of interviews with Dulles. See *Survey of International Affairs,* 1954,
Royal Institute of International Affairs, London, 1957, p. 21 ff., for a full
account of the April crisis on Indochina.

[40] These points were:
the creation of an atmosphere of peace and negotiations;
immediate cease-fire;
a French declaration bestowing independence on Indochina;
direct negotiations;
guarantee of non-intervention by the great powers;
the use of the United Nations as a means for reaching a solution and not
as a threat of sanctions—See *Hindu,* 25.4.1954.

[41] *The Times,* 29.4.1954.

[42] *Ibid.*

[43] *The Times,* 1.5.1954.

[44] For the Colombo resolutions, see Poplai (ed.), *Asia and Africa in the Modern World*, App. V, pp. 202–5.

[45] Kotelawala, *op. cit.*, p. 174.

[46] *The Times*, 1.5.1954.

[47] Poplai, *Asia and Africa*, p. 205.

[48] In *Survey of International Affairs, 1954, op. cit.*, p. 288.

[49] Kotelawala, pp. 151–2.

[50] *The Times*, 3.5.1954.

[51] They were referred to as *Panch Sheel* by Nehru for the first time on September 23, 1954, at a state banquet he gave in honour of President Sukarno—see Rajan, *India in World Affairs*, p. 51.

[52] Brecher, *India and World Politics: Krishna Menon's View of the World*, pp. 142–3.

[53] *Ibid.*, p. 143.

[54] *Hindu*, 3.5.1954; see also *Survey of International Affairs*, 1954, *op. cit.*, p. 245.

[55] *The Times*, 8.7.1954.

[56] *Ibid.*, 27.8.1954.

[57] Thus, Menon, "we had never questioned Chinese suzerainty over Tibet," etc.; see Brecher, *op. cit.*, p. 139.

[58] Brecher, *ibid.*, p. 144.

[59] SEATO, or the South-East Asia Treaty Organization, was the name given to the South-East Asian Collective Defence Treaty signed at Manila on September 8, 1954. For details see *Great Britain Foreign Office, South-East Asia Collective Defence Treaty, Manila, September* 8, 1954 (.9282), London, H.M.S.O., 1954.

[60] *The Times*, 26.8.1954.

[61] *The Times*, 28.8.1954.

[62] Speech in the Lok Sabha, 29.9.1954, quoted in Nehru, *India's Foreign Policy*, p. 89.

[63] *Statesman*, New Delhi, 12.9.1954.

[64] Speaking before the Foreign Relations Committee of the Senate in November 1954, Dulles declared that efforts to persuade India to join the Manila defence pact had been virtually abandoned, but inducements were still being held out to Burma and Indonesia—see *The Times*, 12.11. 1954.

[65] *The Times*, 23.9.1954.

[66] *Asian-African Conference Bulletin*, Ministry of Foreign Affairs, Djakartá, March 1955, No. 1. The speech was made on 24.9.1954.

[67] *Ibid.* See also *The Times*, 27.9.1954, whose New Delhi correspondent commented on the joint statement: "There is still remarkably little evi-

dence here of any enthusiasm for the proposed conference. Indian diplomacy is tending more and more to be concerned primarily with specific issues."

[68] See Conte, *Bandoung*, p. 34.

[69] *Ibid.*, p. 34; see Kotelawala, p. 175, on the discussions on Israel at Bogor.

[70] The Indian change came only after complete impasse had been reached. Krishna Menon describes the scene: "The Burmese were difficult at first. They said 'we won't come without Israel.' We said our position is the same but we have got to carry the Arabs with us. We will do whatever the Conference agrees but we will vote for an invitation to Israel. And we were three to two, Ceylon, Burma and India for, and Pakistan and Indonesia against; but Pakistan was the leader. They made propaganda against us and issued leaflets terming us a pro-Jewish country." See Brecher, *India and World Politics*, p. 52.

[71] See *The Times*, 30.12.1954, for the text of the full communiqué of Bogor.

4 BANDUNG

The stage was now set for Bandung. The date had been fixed and the invitations sent out. Yet there were many of the organizers who still had misgivings, not least among them Nehru himself. He did not expect any far-reaching results from the conference, and he made this very clear when he addressed the Lok Sabha two months after Bogor.[1] Two factors had helped to make up Nehru's mind regarding the need for having the conference at all. One was the policy of military defence pacts pursued by the U.S. Secretary of State John Foster Dulles; the other was the lengthening shadow of Communist China over Asia.

Both these factors were interrelated. The American policy of containment of the Communist bloc had been largely directed by events in the Far East. The US had, in the two preceding years, gone to the very brink of war three times over Asian questions—in Korea in June 1953, in Indochina in April 1954, and in the Formosa Straits in the autumn of 1954.[2] The tense international situation had given added urgency to the US policy of welding together the non-Communist nations of the world into a chain of countries bound to each other and to the US by military pacts which would give her the right to intervene in the event of any Communist threat or encroachment. By the mid-1950s the US had created a vast system of alliances throughout the world which included forty-two sovereign states.[3] As tension increased, so did the pressure which Dulles brought to bear on the non-committed nations, especially of Asia. In such circumstances the holding of a conference of Asian and African countries assumed a new significance for Nehru. The conference would be the reply of the non-committed to the efforts of the West to establish a system of military alliances. By endorsing the *Panch Sheel*, the five articles of peaceful coexistence, the leaders of Asia and

Africa would proclaim their rejection of Dulles' collective defence system, and would rally to the ranks of the non-committed those nations which were hesitating about joining one of the military pacts. Thus, from the outset, Nehru saw the unanimous acceptance of the *Panch Sheel* as a prime objective at Bandung.[4]

The policies of Dulles were not the only concern of Nehru. Coupled with the increased presence of the US in Asia was the growing might of Communist China which gained new significance after the Vietminh victory at Dienbienphu in 1954 and the creation of the Democratic Republic of Vietnam. This Communist encroachment into South-East Asia created new political tensions. China, in Nehru's view, should no longer remain in isolation. Asia must come to terms with the most powerful country in the continent. The best way of attaining this objective was by holding a conference of the Asian countries with the participation of China. This, then, became the second main aim of Nehru, and throughout the preliminary discussions on Bandung he made it plain that India would not participate unless China was invited. The Indians wished to see the same rapprochement between the Asian countries and China as they themselves had achieved with China in the early 1950s. They evidently hoped to strengthen the ties of China with Asia at the expense of her links with the Soviet Union and international Communism.[5]

These aims of the Indians (and of the Burmese and Indonesians) fitted in fully with China's own aspirations in the Far East at the time. Communist China wanted to be accepted and recognized by Asia—only eight of the twenty-eight countries which were to convene at Bandung (apart from China herself) had recognized China—and at the same time she wished to reassure non-Communist Asia that it had nothing to fear from her, despite the Communist victory in Vietnam. This aim emerged clearly during Chou En-lai's visit to India in June 1954, and his enthusiastic adherence to the *Panch Sheel*. Speaking at a press conference after signing the agreement, Chou En-lai declared that cooperation among Asian countries could be increased if the *Panch Sheel* were adhered to. Asked if "big and small, strong and weak nations" could exist peacefully together, he replied that they could, "no matter what kind of social system they had," if they observed the five principles.[6] The final communiqué signed by Chou En-lai and Nehru stressed that adoption of the five principles would help to create an area of peace which could be enlarged as circumstances permitted, thus lessening the chances of war. The preparations for the Asian-African conference were hailed enthusiastically by the Chinese. Commenting on the Bogor preparatory conference, the *Peking Daily* wrote: "The Chinese people have always advocated peaceful coexistence, without excluding any country. They hold that the Asian-African conference should not create any exclusive regional bloc, but work for the extension of the area of peace and for collective security. The Chinese people endorse the objectives and are convinced that its efforts will be most helpful to the relaxation of tensions."[7]

This conciliatory attitude of the Chinese before Bandung did much to convince Nehru, U Nu and Sukarno that their efforts to bring China and the Asian countries together would help to lessen tension in the world in general and in Asia in particular.[8] This, and the acceptance of the *Panch Sheel,* would be the main achievements of Bandung, in the opinion of Nehru. The Indian premier did not want the conference to deal with controversial issues, and this attitude was reflected in the Indian press.[9] Nehru's views were generally shared by U Nu, the Burmese premier. Indeed, the opening words of the speech U Nu had prepared for the inaugural session at Bandung, but which he did not deliver, were: "Meeting as we do for the first time, it would indeed be surprising if we were to reach dramatic or epoch-making decisions."[10]

What were the motivations of the other leading participants in going to Bandung and their expectations from the conference? The attitude of the Arabs was much more complex than that of Nehru or U Nu. The secretary-general of the Arab League 'Abd al-Khāliq Ḥassūna announced on December 12, 1954, that the meeting of the Arab League Council had approved the participation of the Arab countries. Three weeks prior to this announcement the Indian ambassador in Cairo had been summoned to the Egyptian foreign minister who told him that Egypt would refuse to participate if Israel was invited. Egypt reserved her final answer, which would only be given in the affirmative if the membership and the agenda of the conference were acceptable to her. The conference, the foreign minister told the ambassador, should not form a bloc either by itself or with others. The subjects Egypt wished to be put on the agenda were

Lt.-Col. Abdel Nasser, as prime minister of Egypt, visits New Delhi to be greeted by the Indian Premier Pandit Nehru.

Dr. Subandrio, Indonesian foreign minister—seen with Pres. Nasser and Dr. Maḥmud Fawzi the Egyptian minister of foreign affairs—when they met in Cairo, in 1959.

Palestine, North Africa, racial discrimination, and arms and atomic energy control.[11]

Indeed, the initial Arab reaction to Bandung was decidedly cool. The Arabs had no wish to play second fiddle to either the Communists or the neutralists, and they feared that their own divergences might be brought before the limelight of the world public media. Egyptian President Jamāl Abdel Nasser had to be persuaded by Nehru to go to Bandung. The Indian premier spent two days in Cairo at the end of February 1955 during which he brought all his skill and charm to work on a recalcitrant Abdel Nasser. Significantly, the joint communiqué after the visit was composed almost entirely of pet phrases of Nehru. It spoke of the destructiveness of war, of tensions arising from power blocs, and of the need to expand the "area of peace." By this time, Iraq's open adherence to a Western military pact, coupled with Pakistan's success in keeping Israel out of the list of invitees to Bandung, helped to make up Abdel Nasser's mind for him.[12] His decision to go personally to Bandung was to be a turning point in his career.

The talks that Abdel Nasser had had with Nehru before Bandung were not entirely successful. The five principles of coexistence did not have much appeal for the Egyptian leader, and his insistence that Palestine be discussed at the conference "was accepted grudgingly by Mr. Nehru," according to *The Times* in London.[13] When Abdel Nasser, while in India on his way to Bandung, was asked by Indian correspondents what he thought of the five principles, he replied that Egypt had her own principles of the revolution which inspired faith in independence. He added that he did not know much about the *Panch Sheel*, but was for the complete independence of all countries.[14] It was not the sort of reply to endear the Egyptian president to his Indian hosts, especially as it was assumed in the Indian press that Nehru had endeavoured to persuade Abdel Nasser to endorse publicly the five principles.

Other Arab countries differed widely from the Egyptians in their attitude to the forthcoming conference. Both the Iraqis and the Lebanese held talks with the Turkish premier, Adnan Menderes, before the conference was held, and they agreed to make common cause against the Communists and against the neutralists led by Nehru.[15] At the conference itself they were joined in this stand by Pakistan, Thailand and the Philippines, while, of the Arab countries, Libya and the Sudan generally supported them.[16] The Turks and the Iraqis, in particular, disliked Nehru's views on neutrality, and Fadhil Jamali of Iraq went so far as to say that the "principle of neutrality advocated by five principles" was not in conformity with the UN Charter.[17]

There can be little doubt that these and other pro-Western nations in Asia and Africa were urged by the United States to attend the Bandung conference in order to defend Western positions and prevent the conference from becoming a propaganda springboard for the Communists, or even the neutralists. US policy underwent a change in the months immediately preceding the conference, inasmuch as the first reaction of calling on all allied countries to boycott it was superseded by the decision to counter-attack at Bandung itself. But US suspicions remained unchanged right up to the inaugural meeting on April 18, 1955. Dulles appears to have been persuaded by his British and French allies that it was preferable for the pro-West nations to attend Bandung than otherwise. The French foreign minister Antoine Pinay declared:

> Il serait inopportun et vain de s'opposer à une telle réunion, qui constitue un grand évènement; si la participation de certain pays africains semble peu souhaitable, celle des pays asiatiques non communistes doit être considérée comme désirable: leur présence fera contrepoids à celle de la Chine populaire et prouvera que leur politique étrangère n'est pas dictée par les puissances occidentales.[18]

Sir Anthony Eden, the British foreign secretary, sent cabled instructions to his ambassadors on January 19, 1955, that "no efforts should be spared to persuade all anti-Communist governments of Africa and Asia to be represented at Bandung."[19]

Thus the pro-Western countries of Asia and Africa went to Bandung ready to defend Western interests vigilantly, not only against Communist machinations but also against any attempt to transform the conference into a neutralist bloc under Nehru's aegis. The pro-West group was led by the members of the North Atlantic Treaty Organization (NATO) and SEATO who were present: Turkey, Pakistan, Thailand and the Philippines. The states "more or less friendly to the West," according to the head of the Philippines delegation, General Carlos Romulo, included Ethiopia, Liberia,

Libya, Iraq, Lebanon, Iran and Ceylon.[20] Romulo might have added Japan, Sudan, and South Vietnam to this list. Opposing them were the Communist regimes, China and North Vietnam, and, again in the words of Romulo, "the aggressively neutralist states: India, Indonesia, Burma and most of the remaining Arab countries."[21]

Thus, as the date of the conference drew near and the first delegations began arriving at the steamy-hot airport of Jakarta on their way to Bandung, the crystallization of opposing stands was already becoming apparent. The Bandung correspondent of the *Times of India* wrote, three days before the conference opened:

> Beneath the pleasant façade of Afro-Asian amity here, there are already some rumbling notes of mounting discord on the vital issue of coexistence, which might erupt into a highly unpleasant debate. Even before the Bandung conference has begun, the voice of Washington has started extending to this Asian-African forum its global game of shadow boxing with world Communism. The advance parties of some pro-Western Asian-African delegations are openly lobbying here against the Nehru–Chou–Nu doctrine of 'five principles,' dubbing them as Coumunist-inspired.[22]

If the stand taken by Washington and the pro-Western delegations was clear, that taken by Moscow was far more complex. The Russians, as already mentioned, were not invited to Bandung; indeed, nobody even proposed inviting them. This situation left them in somewhat of a quandary. They could hardly condemn the conference organizers as "lackeys of imperialism" after Communist China had been invited. On the other hand, they could hardly accept that they had been excluded from the world of Afro-Asia. Their solution to this dilemma was to play up to the Asian conference of "peace fighters" meeting in New Delhi less than a week before the Bandung conference was convened, in which the Soviet delegates were playing a prominent role,[23] and, at the same time, to laud the aims of the Bandung conference itself. The Soviet press gave more space to the New Delhi conference than it did to Bandung, but what it did say on Bandung was laudatory.[24] The Soviet deputy foreign minister A.E. Kuznetsov issued a statement in which he pledged the full understanding of the Soviet people for the struggle of the Asian and African countries against all forms of colonial rule and for political and economic independence.[25] On the eve of the conference, Marshal Voroshilov, the president of the USSR, together with the presidents of the Soviet Socialist Republics of Uzbekistan, Kazakhstan and Turkmenistan, sent warm greetings. There was no similar gesture of goodwill from the US or other Western powers.

At the conference itself a number of subjects—and personalities—dominated the proceedings from the outset. The subject which occupied the time of a large number of those present was the tension existing between China and the United States over the question of the Formosa Straits and the offshore islands. The initiative on this question was taken by Ceylon's premier, Sir John Kotelawala, who offered to act as mediator between China and the US, but it was Chou En-lai's statement in the Political Committee on April 23 which, to use the expression of General Romulo, "electrified" those present. "The Chinese people are friendly to the American people," Chou En-lai declared. "The Chinese people do not want to have a war with the United States of America. The Chinese government is willing to sit down and enter into negotiations with the US government to discuss the question of relaxing tension in the Far East, and especially the question of relaxing tension in the Taiwan area."[26]

This, as far as the hundreds of journalists covering Bandung were concerned, was the sensation of the conference. However, in the broader issue of attaining Afro-Asian solidarity at Bandung, the question of US-Chinese tension was a side affair, and will not be gone into here.

The main issues at Bandung were the attempt of the pro-Western delegations to condemn Communism—an attempt which brought forth a particularly heated debate on the question of colonialism—and the clash between the aligned and the non-aligned. There were, in addition, differences in tactics, mainly over organizational questions. The two most controversial figures at the conference were undoubtedly Chou En-lai and Nehru.

The first clash came over procedural questions. Twenty-two of the twenty-nine delegates had arrived by noon on April 17—a day early—and, mainly at the suggestion of Nehru, they immediately convened to decide on questions of procedure and agenda, in order to save time. Nehru proposed a highly informal procedure, similar to the one used at meetings of the Commonwealth prime ministers. He also proposed to do away with the preliminary speeches of the heads of delegations, and thus save two days. These proposals were accepted by the twenty-one other delegations, but when the Pakistanis arrived shortly afterwards, and learnt of these decisions at an evening meeting of the five "Colombo" sponsors, they denounced them as illegal, and the following day succeeded in reversing them.[27] The delegates were forthwith divided among three committees— political, economic and cultural—and a five-point agenda was de- decided upon: economic cooperation; cultural cooperation; self- determination and human rights; problems of dependent peoples; and promotion of world peace and cooperation.[28]

The conference was formally opened on April 18, 1955, by Indonesia's president Ahmad Sukarno and her premier 'Ali Sastroamidjojo. Their opening addresses were followed by the long line of speeches—many almost identical with each other—which Nehru had tried so hard to avoid. In the event, only India, Burma and Saudi Arabia waived their right to speak. However, in these opening speeches the seeds of controversy were already sown. The Iraqi delegate, Fadhil Jamali, made a violent attack on world Communism and Soviet colonialism, an attack which was echoed in less extreme terms by the delegates of Iran, Pakistan, the Philippines and Turkey, while both Cambodia and Thailand made direct reference to Chinese threats to their countries. The Pakistani delegate, Muhammad 'Ali, in the words of the *Times of India*, "tried his very best to have the Palestine issue put on the agenda as an independent item, but when he found that even the Arab countries were not very enthusiastic about it, he reluctantly agreed to have it listed under human rights and self-determination."[29] In the subsequent debate on Palestine both Pakistan and China were to outdo the Arabs in their attempts to condemn Israel.[30]

It was not, however, the Palestine issue but the attacks on Communism which held the attention of the onlookers. Everyone awaited the reply of Chou En-lai, to see how he would react. When he eventually delivered his speech it was a model of moderation and conciliation, and set the tone for Chinese conduct throughout the conference. "On the basis of the five principles, China is prepared to have normal relations with all African and Asian countries," he declared, and continued: "We are Communists. We believe in Communism. There is no need to publicize one's ideology here. The Chinese delegation has come to this conference to seek common ground rather than emphasize our differences." [31]

The next attempt to "get at" China, if indirectly, took place on the third day of the conference, when its delegates went into closed session. The first item on the agenda of the Political Committee was "Human Rights and Self-Determination" with the subheading "Palestine, and Racial Discrimination." The Indian delegate opened the discussion, claiming that the issues should only be dealt with in broad terms. "We have no right to criticize others for violating human rights if we ourselves do not observe them. Palestine and racialism are important but they must come later." [32] The delegate of the Philippines concurred. Whereupon the Lebanese delegate proposed the committee should support the Universal Declaration of Human Rights of the UN Charter, a proposal which was immediately backed by Turkey, Iran and Pakistan, but opposed by India, North Vietnam and China. Here again was a challenge thrown down before China by the pro-Western delegates, who assumed that the Chinese would retaliate by a strong attack on the United Nations. They were to be disappointed. Taking the stand, Chou En-lai declared that if they liked they might refer to the UN Charter, but they must not expect those countries which were not members of the United Nations Organization to express opinions about anything done by the organization. Why stir up a controversy? the Chinese premier asked. [33] This neat sidestepping of an issue on which delegates had expected a major clash to develop won the approbation of all present. It was one more victory for the Chinese premier, who had become the central figure at the conference. *The Times* in London commented: "The guns which had been trained ready to oppose the expected Communist manoeuvres have somewhat misfired against the bland refusal of Mr. Chou En-lai to invoke any Communist line as such." [34]

It was, however, in the debate on colonialism that the most serious clash took place between the pro-Western delegates and China, supported by the neutralists. The discussion was set in train by an unexpected attack by Sir John Kotelawala of Ceylon on what he termed Soviet colonialism. Sir John describes the scene in his autobiography in the following words:

It was nearly five in the evening, and in the loud and confused eloquence I had not been able to catch the Chairman's eye or reach his ear. I very nearly gave up, but by one last effort I succeeded. In the course of my observations I said: 'There is another form of colonialism, however, about which many of us represented here are perhaps less clear in our minds and to which some of us would perhaps not agree to apply the term colonialism at all. Think, for example, of those satellite states under Communist domination in Central and Eastern Europe—of Hungary, Rumania, Bulgaria, Albania, Czechoslovakia, Latvia, Lithuania, Esthonia and Poland. Are not these colonies as much as any of the colonial territories in Africa or Asia? And if we are united in our opposition to colonialism, should it not be our duty openly to declare our opposition to Soviet colonialism as much as to Western imperialism?' I finished and silence. Then the silence broke. Chou En-lai got up in marked agitation and said that, as I had made references to Communist colonialism, he reserved the right to make a statement and that he would do so the following morning. Nehru was even more agitated . . . . [He] asked me in some heat, 'Why did you do that, Sir John?' Why did you not show me your speech before you made it?' I have no doubt the remark was well meant, but the only obvious reply I could make was: 'Why should I? Do you show me yours before you make them?'[35]

The following morning Chou En-lai took the floor to answer Sir John's remarks. Once more he presented a picture of moderation. "Countries participating in this conference do have different ideologies but we prefer not to enter into arguments on this subject in this conference room," he declared. "However, we are prepared to discuss the subject outside the conference."[36] Chou En-lai's appeal for harmony was accepted by Sir John Kotelawala, who abstained from introducing his remarks as a formal proposal. But this was not the end of the debate. Taking the rostrum after Chou En-lai, Pakistan's Muhammad 'Ali insisted that it was unrealistic and wrong not to mention Soviet imperialism: "If we are prepared to accuse and mention friendly countries like France, there is no reason why we should not mention the USSR," he maintained. The Syrian delegate whereupon sought to persuade the delegates that the subject of Soviet imperialism fell outside the scope of the conference, but the Iraqi delegate disagreed: freedom should be championed the world over, he insisted. Turkey thereupon submitted, in the names of Iran, Iraq, Lebanon, Libya, Pakistan, the Philippines, Sudan and Liberia, a proposal condemning "all types of colonialism, including international doctrines resorting to the methods of force, infiltration and subversion. . . ."[37]

In the ensuing debate, which was held under great tension, India made a counter-proposal of a general nature while South Vietnam and Japan supported the Turkish proposal. Egypt, surprisingly, took no part in the debate. A full-scale crisis was warded off when a drafting committee, consisting of Burma, Ceylon, China, India, Lebanon, Pakistan, the Philippines, Syria and Turkey, was called upon to find a compromise formula which would satisfy all.

In the meantime the second great discussion was already under way. This took in the questions of aligned versus non-aligned, *Panch Sheel* and peaceful coexistence, war and peace. The gauntlet had first been thrown down by Pakistan's Muhammad 'Ali who proposed "Seven Pillars of Peace" in lieu of India's five principles. The controversial "fifth pillar" proposed by the Pakistani premier was the right of all nations to self-defence collectively or individually, thus justifying the alignment of his own and other countries within the framework of military pacts. These Seven Pillars were formally proposed in closed session after Burma's premier U Nu had suggested that all present should adopt the five principles of coexistence as the basis of their international behaviour.[38] Pakistan's Seven Pillars were countered by seven other principles put forward by the Egyptian leader, Abdel Nasser.[39] But when Zorlu, of Turkey, made a speech upholding the principle of military alliances, Nehru, according to those present, virtually "exploded" and delivered one of the toughest speeches he had yet made.[40] It contained many of Nehru's basic views and deserves to be quoted. The third world war was going to be catastrophic, he said. This must be understood. It must, therefore, be avoided. Asia and Africa could not prevent the big powers from going to war, but they could help in lessening international tensions. They should make their views clear that they would not join either bloc in war. If the world was divided into two blocs, the danger of war increased, but if there was an area of non-aligning countries, the danger was reduced. Moral force counted, and the Asian and African countries could exert their moral force. Their leaders should not now become camp followers of one or another big country or merely be anti-Communist. They should be something positive. Nehru's speech brought a storm of protest. Notable was the speech of Fadhil Jamali, the Iraqi ex-premier, who asked whether as an alternative to the smaller nations joining one of the two great power blocs India was prepared to bring them together as a third bloc which would give them the protection they needed. Nehru replied that the stage had not yet been reached where they could help each other. Such a bloc would involve its member states in a common danger.

Once more, however, it was not Nehru but Chou En-lai who was to deliver the key address.[41] As Professor Kahin has pointed out[42] the Chinese premier stepped in not only to demonstrate the reasonableness and peacefulness of China, but also, ironically, to bridge the widening gap between the positions of India and of the Western-aligned states. If the term "peaceful coexistence" was objected to it could be replaced by the expression used in the Preamble of the UN Charter, "live together in peace." The important thing was to establish a set of principles with a view to safeguarding collective peace, and he thereupon proposed a new set of seven such principles.[43] The speech was, once more, one of moderation and reasonableness. It was followed shortly afterwards by Chou En-lai's statement, mentioned earlier, regarding his willingness to enter into negotiations with the United States over reducing tension in the Taiwan area. By now even the most sceptical were becoming convinced by his show of sincerity. *The Times* in London had this to say of his performance:

> From Turkey to the Philippines, Mr. Chou has spread his apparent reason and tolerance . . . . It has been Mr. Chou En-lai's week. On Monday he gently shook his sleeves and showed they were empty; on Tuesday his pockets, and there were still some who said how clever all this was. Yesterday the doves fluttered out from the box behind, to settle on the heads of as many delegates as had questioned his performance.[44]

By now the deliberations were nearing their end. The real work of the conference was left in the hands of the drafting committees, whose members worked round the clock in an effort to find a formula which would be acceptable to all. They were aided by the fact that no one present wanted to take the blame for wrecking the conference. There was thus no stand or principle which could not be sidestepped. Compromise became the order of the day, enabling the deadlock to be broken. The conference came to an end on a note of unanimity, for the articles were so generally and vaguely formulated that all sides of the various disputes could read into them the points they wished to see. As the *Times of India* points out: "This impressive measure of unanimity was achieved at a heavy price by diluting principles to accommodate cold-war politics." It continues: "The emphasis on unanimity unfortunately led to a patchwork picture of Asian-African solidarity without the underlying spirit of accord and oneness of purpose."[45] Thus the problem of Soviet imperialism was solved by declaring that "colonialism in all its manifestations is an evil which should be speedily brought to an end,"[46] while, at the insistence of Pakistan, Turkey and several other delegations, the right of collective self-defence was recognized ("respect for the right of each nation to defend itself singly or collectively, in conformity with the Charter of the UN"). It was, however, heavily qualified by a sentence, proposed by President Abdel Nasser, which called for "abstention from the use of arrangements of collective defence to serve the particular interests of any of the big powers."[47]

Thus the conference came to an end. What had it achieved? Had a genuine Afro-Asian solidarity emerged from it, as was later claimed?

Two points are immediately apparent from the previous survey. One is that the conference was really a misnomer: Africa, at least Africa south of the Sahara, played virtually no part in what was to all intents and purposes an Asian conference. The second point is that the conference was, in effect, engulfed by the very cold war it had sought to remain above, causing divergences which were papered over only with the greatest difficulty by the final communiqué.

In regard to the first point, the Ethiopians and Liberians generally followed the pro-West camp, while the delegate from the Gold Coast was hardly heard at all. Specific African problems received only scant attention (with the exception of the issues of Tunisia, Algeria and Morocco, which were brought up by both the Arab and Muslim delegates, and of South Africa), and whereas the conference saw fit

to single out for specific mention in the final communiqué the problems of Palestine, of West Irian (Netherlands New Guinea) and of
Aden and the South Arabian Protectorates, no particular reference
was made to any of the numerous colonies south of the Sahara.

The most striking feature of Bandung, however, was the enormous diversity of views on some of the most basic subjects raised at
the conference. Far from having obtained the unanimous approval for
the *Panch Sheel* that Nehru had hoped for, the majority of those
present declared themselves opposed to the five principles of coexistence; indeed, the word coexistence does not even appear once
in the final communiqué.

On the purely political level it would be safe to say that there
was no Afro-Asian solidarity at Bandung. The alignments within
the context of the cold war proved stronger than any feeling of Afro-
Asian togetherness; indeed these cold-war ties were so strong that
they cut across closer affiliations, as was demonstrated by the differences which emerged among the members of the Arab League or
among the five sponsoring "Colombo Powers." Again, these cold-war
alignments were so strong as to cloud over the unanimity of feeling
for the subject most close to the hearts of Asians and Africans, namely
that of colonialism. The discussions on this subject were so tinged
with cold-war colours that Latvia, Esthonia and other East European
"satellites" were mentioned more than the non-independent territories
of Africa. The equation of Afro-Asian feeling with non-alignment,
as Nehru had envisaged, manifestly did not happen at Bandung.

Despite all that has since been written and said about Bandung,
a careful perusal of the speeches and discussions that took place in
that small, mountain-resort town in central Java in April 1955 reveals that there was, at that time, very little to show for any Afro-
Asian, or even Asian, solidarity or ideology. The tone of the conference was to a large extent set by the delegates of India, China,
Burma and Indonesia on the one hand, and the group of Western-
aligned delegations, led by Pakistan, Turkey, Iraq, the Philippines,
Lebanon, Iran and Thailand on the other. Between these two groups
there was very little agreement on any subject. Of the other delegates,
those representing Afghanistan, Ethiopia, Gold Coast, Jordan, Laos,
Liberia, Libya, Nepal, Saudi Arabia, Sudan and the Yemen had
very little to say, except on specific subjects affecting them, such as

Palestine, North Africa or Aden. The Egyptian president, Jamāl Abdel Nasser, though considered one of the major figures on the side of non-alignment, kept surprisingly quiet. His speeches were few and short,[48] and he only made his mark at the end of the conference as chairman of the key drafting committee on coexistence.

Manifestly, therefore, no Afro-Asian ideology emerged from Bandung. Perhaps for that reason no greater efforts were made to assure some sort of organizational continuity. It was decided, significantly perhaps on a proposal by China, that the five sponsors should consider convening another such meeting. Indonesia's delegate suggested that it should take place within a year, and Abdel Nasser, even before the conference got properly under way, began putting out feelers for a second conference to be held in Cairo.[49] No definite organizational framework was decided upon, however, no secretariat or secretary-general appointed. Afro-Asianism was not institutionalized. When Nehru was asked whether he thought that Bandung was the first step in the direction of a more cohesive group of states in Asia and Africa, he replied: "Well, it is too widespread for it to develop into a cohesive group. . . . But you may say that it may develop into something which holds togeth ."[50]

Yet the balance-sheet of Bandung was not entirely negative. For one thing, one of the main objectives of at least some of the participants, to draw China more into the Asian orbit, was fully achieved. The attacks of the pro-Western delegates had been against Communism in general, or against the Soviet Union, but rarely against China. The Chinese, for their part, were very clearly on a peace offensive in Asia. The only questions interesting Chou En-lai at Bandung were Afro-Asian solidarity, and the community of interests of the underdeveloped. It was he, far more than Nehru, who worked for an Afro-Asian solidarity, and the unanimity achieved was due primarily to his willingness to compromise. There can be little doubt that China was convinced at Bandung that she had much to gain by cultivating the good will of fellow Asians. The result was a considerable relaxing of tension in Asia, which was to last for four years until the Chinese invasion of Tibet.

If this was a concrete gain of Bandung, there were also more intangible results. Nehru declared to journalists after the final communiqué was announced that it was "a very good conference," and that "we have made history" and have acted as "agents of historic destiny."[51] Perhaps he understood better than most that, when the squabbles and arguments were long forgotten, the fact would remain, written in history, that twenty-nine nations of Asia and Africa had assembled together to discuss their common future. For Nehru, the lifelong fighter against the European colonialist, it was the fulfillment of a dream. Without anyone having consciously intended it that way—except, perhaps, the perspicacious Chinese premier—Bandung created a sense of *racial* solidarity which far surpassed any conscious political solidarity. This was the real significance of Bandung. For this reason the decalogue of Bandung—the ten principles of the final communiqué—became the Ten Commandments of Afro-Asia, the political creed of all people of colour.

NOTES

[1] "By its very nature, a conference of this type is hardly likely to discuss controversial issues as between the countries represented there. Also, if I may express my own opinion, I hope it will not function as if it was setting up a group in rivalry to the others. It is essentially an experiment in coexistence, for the countries of Asia and Africa . . . are meeting together in a friendly way and trying to find out what common ground there is for cooperation in the economic, cultural and political fields"—Nehru in a speech in the Lok Sabha, 25.2.1955.

[2] According to Dulles himself. See his article in *Life Magazine*, 11.1.1956.

[3] See speech by Dulles on 9.6.1955, in which he mentions this number. For an excellent analysis of alliances, see Henry A. Kissinger's classic, *Nuclear Weapons and Foreign Policy*, New York, 1958, his chapter on "The Impact of Strategy on Our Allies and the Uncommitted."

[4] Speaking on the forthcoming conference on January 11, 1955, Nehru said he thought everybody would accept the five principles. "A gathering like this does not meet to reach formal decisions, but it can lay down a basis for a common approach to problems." This basis for a common approach was, very obviously in the eyes of the Indians, the *Panch Sheel*.

[5] As one of the leading Indian newspapers put it, " . . . much will depend on whether Peking considers itself more Asian than Communist or vice-versa"—*Times of India*, Delhi, 28.12.1954.

[6] *The Times*, London, 28.6.1954.

[7] *Peking Daily*, 5.1.1955.

[8] This view was not, however, shared by many of those invited. A typical reaction was that of the Philippines. Commenting on the invitation of China, *Manila Times* wrote: "The mere fact that the proposal for a 'neutral peace strip' from Egypt to the Philippines, which is to be the main purpose of the Afrasian conference contemplated by the Colombo-Power Premiers, has the endorsement of Red China should make it suspect to all men of decent minds"—*Manila Times*, 1.1.1955.

[9] For example, *Times of India*, 10.4.1955: "while the countries attending the Bandung conference have different ideologies and some of them have different commitments and affiliations, this experiment in coexistence . . . is not expected to raise any controversies."

[10] The speech was later published by the Director of Information, Rangoon, 19.5.1955.

[11] *Statesman*, Calcutta, 22.11.1954.

[12] See Stevens, "Arab Neutralism and Bandung," *Middle East Journal*, Spring 1957.

[13] *The Times*, London, 30.4.1955.

[14] *Times of India*, 13.4.1955.

[15] There was, however, a strong opposition in the Lebanon led by Kamāl Jumblāt, which supported the neutralist attitude at Bandung. As far back as March 1953, the congress of Arab socialists in the Lebanon convened a "Third Bloc" conference whose aim was to establish a neutralist bloc together with the Asian countries and to forestall attempts to link Middle East countries with the Western defence system—see *Jerusalem Post*, 2.3.1953.

[16] The Iraqis were reportedly extremely angry with Jordan at Bandung for having veered to the neutralist camp.

[17] According to *Times of India*, 15.4.1955.

[18] Quoted by Conte, *Bandoung, tournant de l'histoire*, p. 39.

[19] *Ibid.*, p. 38.

[20] Romulo, *Meaning of Bandung*, pp. 3–4.

[21] *Ibid.*, p. 4.

[22] *Times of India*, 15.4.1955.

[23] The New Delhi conference was called the Asian Conference for the Easing of International Tension. See Chapter 7, p. 126 f., for details.

[24] Thus, for example, *Literaturnaya Gazeta,* Moscow: "The convening of the Bandung conference will mean the practical implementation of peaceful coexistence"—6.1.1955.

[25] Quoted fully in *Times of India*, 18.4.1955. See also Sergeyeva, in *New Times*, No. 17, 26.4.1965, pp. 3–4.

[26] Quoted by Romulo, p. 18.

[27] Backing Pakistan in her demands were Turkey, Lebanon, Iraq, Thailand, South Vietnam and Ceylon—see *Times of India*, 19.4.1955.

[28] *Times of India, ibid.;* see also the excellent summary of the Bandung conference in Kahin, *Asian-African Conference,* pp. 9–11, and the chapter on Bandung in Jansen's *Afro-Asia and Non-Alignment,* which contains much fascinating material.

[29] *Times of India*, 19.4.1955.

30 The debate on Palestine is not considered by the writer to be relevant to the main subject of this book, and will not be gone into fully here. The full discussions on this subject which took place in closed session are recorded in conference documents AAC/SR/2 and AAC/C.R./3.

31 *Times of India*, 20.4.1955.

32 Doc. No. AAC/SR/1. Asian-African Conference. Meeting of Heads of Delegations, 20.4.55, 9.30 am–12.30 pm, p. 2. These protocols of the conference were issued by the Conference Secretariat, which distributed them to the participants. One of them, who prefers to remain anonymous, lent his copy to the writer. As the discussions were held in closed session, these documents were naturally never published.

33 *Ibid.,* p. 5.

34 *The Times*, London, 21.4.1955.

35 Kotelawala, *An Asian Prime Minister's Story*, p. 187. For full speech of Sir John, see conference doc. No. AAC/C.R./4–21.4.1955, pp. 7–11.

36 Doc. No. AAC/SR/5—22.4.1955. Conference Room No. 2, in Dwi Warna Building, p. 2.

37 *Ibid*, pp. 4–5.

38 Conference Doc. No. AAC/SR/6—22.4.55, pp. 3–4.

39 These were: disarmament; adherence to the UN Charter; ending of power politics and its using of small nations as its tools; liquidation of colonialism; respect for the political independence of other countries; recognition of the right of every country to choose freely its political as well as its economic system—*ibid*, pp. 8–9.

40 According to *Times of India*—23.4.1955. For full text of speech, see Conference Document, *ibid.,* p. 10ff. The speech is also brought in full by Kahin, *op. cit.*, pp. 64–72.

41 See *New York Times*, 25.4.1955. The full text can be found in Kahin, *op. cit.*, p.56ff.

42 Kahin, *ibid.*, p.25.

43 Respect of each other's sovereignty and territorial integrity; abstention from aggression and threats against each other; abstinence from interference or intervention in the internal affairs of one another; recognition of the equality of all nations; respect for the rights of all countries to choose freely a way of life as well as political and economic systems; abstention from doing damage to one another.

44 *The Times*, London, 25.4.1955.

45 *Times of India*, 25.4.1955.

46 This phrase was put forward to the drafting committee by India's Krishna Menon. See his account of the deliberations in Brecher, *India and World Politics: Krishna Menon's View of the World*, p. 53.

[47] For full text of the final communiqué, see appendix in Kahin, *op. cit.*

[48] It is, perhaps, indicative that his name is not mentioned once in the book by Romulo on the Bandung conference.

[49] On April 18, 1955, an Agence France Presse dispatch reported that, according to Radio Cairo, Abdel Nasser would propose at Bandung that the next Afro-Asian conference should be held in Cairo. After his return to Accra from Bandung, the Gold Coast delegate, Kojo Botsio, told a mass rally that Abdel Nasser had offered to be host to the next conference —see *Ghana Evening News,* Accra, 17.5.55. *Ghana Evening News* of 26.4.55 reports that Abdel Nasser told the Bandung delegates on April 22 that he would like to invite them to the second Afro-Asian conference in Cairo "before the end of this year. Col. Nasser hopes to announce the date before the end of the current conference." In the event, no more mention was made of Abdel Nasser's intentions on this subject.

[50] Brecher, *New States of Asia*, Appendix: Talks with Nehru, p. 210.

[51] *Times of India,* 25.4.1955.

5 POST-BANDUNG: THE OFFICIAL FOLLOW-UP

Within months of the Bandung conference memories of the disagreements were already becoming blurred, and the myth of the spirit of Bandung was fast taking shape. There were a number of reasons for this development, to be found both within the framework of Afro-Asia and in international developments. One was undoubtedly due to the fact that the conference had succeeded in ending in unity despite the wayward winds which had blown so fiercely throughout its deliberations. Once that unity had been attained, it became, in itself, a power factor in the foreign policies of all the participants. The sense of "belonging" and of "solidarity" which Bandung gave to the twenty-nine nations which took part in the conference was, perhaps, one of its most significant results. This new-found solidarity provided an alternative to adherence to the world blocs, and, in itself, contributed largely to the rapid spread of non-alignment after Bandung. The sense of solidarity was, to the majority of participants, far more important than the disagreements and squabbles which had marked the conference proceedings. Indeed, there was hardly a delegate, on his return home, who did not call the conference a resounding success. The concrete evidence of this success were the ten principles, soon dubbed the Declaration of Bandung and the Bandung Manifesto. It did not matter that of these ten principles, two were self-contradictory,[1] and the gist of the remainder could be found in the preamble to the Charter of the United Nations. The UN Charter had been written by Europeans, and Americans, and Russians whereas the principles of Bandung had been drawn up by the Afro-Asians only. It was a question of colour, but much more than that. In this consciousness of *we* and *they* merged a number of emotion-charged sentiments: the colour difference, the solidarity of the underdog, the assertion of the colonized, the banding together of the poor and destitute, the freeing from the psychological chains of inferiority, the aggravation of having others decide one's own future, the craving for a new solidarity of equals. All the pent-up frustrations, the result of generations of living under colonial rule, now found some release in the myth of the spirit of Bandung. For the common aspiration of the vast majority of Afro-Asians was to shake off the vestiges of colonialism and make their own weight felt in world affairs. Bandung, they felt, was a step in the right direction.

Nehru, on his return home, reported to the Lok Sabha in the following words:

> The most important decision of the conference is the declaration on world peace and cooperation. The nations assembled set out the principles which should govern relations between them and indeed the countries of the world as a whole . . . it would be a misleading of history to regard Bandung as though it was an isolated occurrence and not part of a great movement of human history.[2]

Nehru also told Parliament that the "recommendations wisely avoided any provision for setting up additional machinery for internation cooperation, but, on the other hand, sought to rely on existing international machinery in part, and, for the rest, on such decisions as individual governments may, by contact and negotiation, find it possible to make." He was making it plain by this statement that, in his view, Bandung had been enough of a good thing, and that he did not want to see any institutionalization of a formalized Afro-Asian Movement.[3] Even on non-political subjects no definite machinery for cooperation was prepared. Article 11 in the chapter on Economic Cooperation in the final communiqué called for the appointment of liaison officers in participating countries for the exchange of ideas on matters of mutual interests. Nothing came of this proposition. The similar nature of the economies of the countries concerned made the practical possibilities of promoting trade and economic contacts between them extremely limited.[4] This is, indeed, borne out by the fact that in the two years following Bandung India's total volume of trade with Asian countries dropped by 28 per cent!

Nevertheless Bandung was hailed as a resounding success throughout the Afro-Asian world. Abdel Nasser returned home to banners reading "Welcome, hero of Bandung, champion of peace and liberty! Welcome, champion of Africa and Asia!" His role at the conference was acclaimed by the Egyptian press as marking "the emergence of Egyptian diplomacy from its old shell into the wide world." "Jamāl Abdel Nasser's voice will echo everywhere in Asia and Africa as a new symbol of hope," wrote Anwar as-Sādāt in the Cairo daily *al-Jumhūriyya,* "the peoples of Egypt, Palestine, Tunisia, Morocco, as well as those oppressed in the jungles of Kenya, will for ever be proud of him."[5] Abdel Nasser himself told an Indian journalist on his way home from Bandung that he appraised the Bandung conference "as one of the two most important events of modern history"—the other being the discovery of atomic energy![6] There can be little doubt that the Bandung conference marked one of the crucial turning points in Abdel Nasser's political thinking, and indeed of Egypt's foreign policy.

Certainly, Bandung appears to have affected the Egyptian leader most strongly of all the participants.[7] His contact with the leaders of the Afro-Asian world, in particular with Nehru, U Nu, Sukarno, and, in a different sense, Chou En-lai, opened up new vistas in international relations and brought Abdel Nasser fairly and squarely into the camp of the militantly non-aligned. It was Abdel Nasser's full conversion, and his subsequent activities, far more than Nehru's, which were to transform the policy of non-alignment into the dominant trend in Africa and Asia. In the years following Bandung, it was he who set the pace of militancy and who gave birth to the new concept of positive neutralism. Nehru was supremely the man of peace, the pacifist who believed he could serve as world arbitrator and at the same time serve the interests of his country. His overriding aim was to widen the "area of peace" in the world and thus lessen the chances of a third world war which would spell disaster for his people. Abdel Nasser did not set his sights so high; his advocacy of non-alignment was much more a matter of national expediency, and the ideological overtones came only later, after he had decided that this was the most profitable policy he could take up in terms of Egyptian self-advancement. As Fayez A. Sayegh has pointed out, "the roots of Egyptian neutralism—as indeed of Arab neutralism as a whole—lay not in the relationship between Egyptian (or Arab) society and the cold war, but in the national experiences, problems, struggles and aspirations of Egypt and the Arab world."[8]

Thus, after Bandung, Nehru turned all his attention to the struggle for peace. This was, for him, far more important even than the anti-colonial struggle. A new war, which he still considered imminent, could bring chaos and disaster on India and the other countries of Asia even if they did not participate in it; their economic advancement would be halted, to say nothing of the terrible threat of mass destruction by atom and hydrogen bombs. "Nothing counts more than the prevention of war between East and West! What is the emancipation of a number of additional peoples, when entire humanity is in danger of annihilation," he is reported to have declared.[9] His avowed aim was to enlarge the number of countries subscribing to the *Panch Sheel*. When the Soviet Union, during his visit to Moscow in June 1955, recognized these five principles, he felt that this was a crowning achievement.

Abdel Nasser, however, did not see it that way. Indeed, he never accepted the five principles. He had little patience for Nehru's pacifist outlook, nor for his desire to act as world mediator. The Egyptian leader was far more of a pragmatist. "The major element in the Arab conception of neutralism is neither peace nor international responsibility but the primacy of national independence, self-determination, and non-intervention," wrote Professor Leonard Binder.[10] This was very different from the Indian outlook, but it was this attitude, far more than the universal pacifist conception of the Indians, which was to colour the political thinking of the Afro-Asians.

Yet the political orientation of the nations of Asia and Africa in the immediate post-Bandung period obviously did not take place in a vacuum. It was governed largely by developments in the international arena, and above all, by the state of conflict between the two world blocs. A number of issues affected the position of the Afro-Asians and indirectly contributed to the consolidation of the Bandung spirit. None was more important than the atmosphere of détente which began to be felt in the world during 1955. The new government of the Soviet Union, headed by Nikita Khrushchev and N. A. Bulganin, which took over power in February 1955, had a lot to do with this new atmosphere. Their emphasis on peaceful coexistence, which now became a fundamental concept in Soviet foreign policy, coincided with the spirit of the Bandung principles. The lessening of tension in the Far East which came about immediately after Bandung, the new

signs of concern over nuclear weapons, and the signs of a rapprochement on disarmament were also well in line with the thoughts
expressed in the Bandung declaration. By 1955 it had become clear
that the two world blocs had become deadlocked in an atomic stalemate; any direct military confrontation could lead to disastrous
consequences for both of them, and indeed for the entire world. From
that year on the cold-war conflict shifted increasingly to spheres in
which the dangers of a thermonuclear war were more remote—above
all to competition for support of the uncommitted nations of Asia, the
Middle East and Africa. And it was the Russians who took the initiative.

One of the outstanding events at that time was the rapprochement
between the Soviet Union and Marshal Tito's dissident Communist
regime in Yugoslavia. The visit of Messrs. Krushchev and Bulganin
to Belgrade in May 1955, ending the rupture between the two countries, led to immediate repercussions in the Afro-Asian world. It was
interpreted by Nehru[11] and others as a major factor leading to an
improvement of the international climate in 1955. There can be little
doubt that among the reasons that led the Russians to renew their
relations with Yugoslavia was their concern to curry favour with the
nations of Asia and Africa, with whom the Yugoslavs were already
on the best of terms. One of the points in the joint declaration which
the heads of the two countries signed on June 2, 1955, was that both
governments welcomed the results of the Bandung conference as a
significant contribution to the idea of international cooperation and
support of the efforts of the peoples of Asia and Africa towards the
strengthening of their political and economic independence, and
considered that all this contributed to the strengthening of world
peace.

There was, however, another aspect of the Yugoslav-Soviet
rapprochement which was not lost on the Afro-Asians. Tito had
successfully played off one super-power against the other, gaining
from both, and both the Russians and the Americans heaped economic
aid on Yugoslavia. Here was the proof that non-alignment could be
a successful, indeed, a profitable policy. This point, together with the
advantages of the controlled socialist economy and of the political
structures existing in Yugoslavia, were forcefully brought home to
Abdel Nasser during his meeting with Tito at Brijoni in July 1956. The

idea of the Nasser–Nehru–Tito axis, leading a non-aligned Afro-Asia, became a prime objective of the Egyptian president after that meeting. Nehru, it should be added, was needed more for the tremendous prestige his name still conjured up and for the special place India held in the two continents than for his views against force and against any teaming up into what might be construed as a Third Force.

Tito had been the first Communist leader to visit countries of Asia and Africa. He had visited India and Burma in 1954 and then gone on to Egypt and Ethiopia. Like the Russian leaders, Tito had been none too happy at the geographical definition limiting the participants at Bandung, which automatically excluded Yugoslavia. After Bandung he made great efforts to change this definition to an ideological one. From a mere question of belonging either to Africa or to Asia, he wanted to build a grouping of the non-aligned, which would include the vast majority of Afro-Asian states and also Yugoslavia. He worked on this aim with a will, and no one was influenced more than Abdel Nasser.

Thus Tito's activism in Asia and Africa, his gospel of militant non-alignment, had a marked effect on the direction the Afro-Asian Movement was to take. Coupled with the influence of Yugoslavia was the official blessing by the Communist bloc of the Afro-Asians, as expressed in the Belgrade communiqué, and their condonance of Tito's policy of non-alignment, which could be construed from the new Yugoslav-Soviet détente.

The Communist attitude to the non-Communist countries of Asia and Africa had begun to change after Stalin's death in 1953, a change which was to receive official recognition at the twentieth Communist Party Congress in Moscow in 1956, when the "two camps" formula was scrapped and the notion of a "zone of peace," of socialist and non-aligned countries, was added. The old Stalinist anathema of the "national bourgeois" leaders, such as Nehru, was officially negated, and the congress welcomed friendly relations between the Soviet Union and India, Burma, Afghanistan and Egypt, and other countries aspiring to national independence. But the rehabilitation of Nehru and other non-Communist leaders of Afro-Asia actually took place long before the twentieth Congress. An invitation to Nehru to visit the Soviet Union was extended as early as November 1954; in February 1955 agreement was reached between the Soviet Union and

India on Soviet assistance in building the Bhilai Steel Works; a month later an article appeared in *Pravda* warmly praising Nehru, a fact which threw confusion into the ranks of the Communist Party of India which had previously strongly denounced the Indian premier.[12] The apogee of this new Soviet-Indian entente came in June 1955 with Nehru's visit to Moscow and the Russian acceptance of the five principles, and with the return visit paid later in the year by Khrushchev and Bulganin to India.

Thus, despite Soviet preoccupation with domestic affairs in that year of crucial developments in the Soviet Union, the Soviet leaders were already showing heightened interest in the Afro-Asian countries. In the same month that the Russians offered India economic assistance, G. M. Malenkov fell from power and the efforts of Khrushchev to oust his other rivals reached their climacteric. At the same time European problems were playing a large part in Soviet foreign policy considerations. The Warsaw Pact was created to be followed by Khrushchev's all-important visit to Belgrade. However, far from leaving Asian affairs to China, as was widely believed to be the Soviet position after the Chinese performance at Bandung, the Russians were laying a solid foundation for their new orientation to the Afro-Asian countries. Indeed, in retrospect, it appears as if the USSR was building up her relations with India as a possible counter-weight to China.[13]

The emphasis of Soviet foreign policy was now increasingly placed on the Afro-Asian world. With not too great finesse, the Russians did their utmost to ingratiate themselves with the Africans and Asians; trivial but significant instances were the dinner offered in Moscow to the ambassadors of the Bandung participants during the visit to Moscow of Premier U Nu of Burma in November 1955,[14] or the meeting at the Academy of Sciences in Moscow of these diplomats on the second anniversary of the Bandung conference, at which Bobodjan Gafurov, the party expert on Asian affairs, lectured on the solidarity between the Soviet Union and the new countries of Afro-Asia.[15] On every possible occasion the Bandung principles were warmly praised, and the Bandung conference was upheld as the beacon of light in the struggle of the Afro-Asian peoples against colonialism and Western imperialism.[16]

At the same time, in the years immediately after Bandung, there existed a similarly favourable Chinese approach to the "Bandung spirit." The Chinese had their own reasons for this policy. In their eyes the Bandung nations could become part of a "united front" centred around China which, in time, would participate in a massive war of liberation against the major enemy of China—the United States.[17] In speeches made by Chinese leaders after Bandung, the conference was invariably described in terms of the struggle against colonialism and for national independence and world peace[18]; Bandung served as an inspiration for the assault against imperialism, while, at the same time, furthering the cause of world peace. The relationship between the Chinese and the other countries of Afro-Asia was seen as one of mutual benefit. One of the most active Chinese leaders in Afro-Asian affairs, Kuo Mo-jo, stated this quite clearly:

> . . . our people have done everything possible to support every struggle waged by the peoples of the different Afro-Asian countries for gaining and safeguarding their national independence. At the same time the people of the countries of Asia and Africa have equally supported energetically the struggle waged by the Chinese people against American aggression and for the safeguarding of national sovereignty and territorial integrity. Socialist China remains faithful to the struggle against imperialism and for the maintenance of world peace, faithful to the five principles of peaceful coexistence and to the spirit of Bandung.[19]

The Chinese, at least until 1965, made great efforts to broaden their ties with the countries first of Asia and then of Africa.[20] They were among the most vociferous in insisting on the existence of a strong Afro-Asian solidarity, though, as they gradually became disillusioned with the Afro-Asian leadership, they increasingly switched their descriptions of solidarity from the Afro-Asian states to the Afro-Asian peoples, and to the Afro-Asian Peoples Solidarity Organization which they considered a natural continuation of the Bandung spirit.

This attitude of both the Soviet Union and China led to several results. It furthered the myth of Bandung, not only in declaring its success, but also in emphasizing its anti-Western character; it encouraged the militantly non-aligned among the Afro-Asians to draw closer to the Soviet bloc, a tendency accelerated by offers of economic aid; and it correspondingly deterred the more conservative regimes in Africa and Asia from having anything to do with the Afro-Asian Movement.

Compared with the impact that this new Soviet policy had on the Afro-Asian nations, Western policy during the same period was weak and vacillating. There were some signs from the West of a reappraisal of its position, a reappraisal made all the more urgent by the obvious Soviet inroads into regions which had previously been monopolized by the West, but no clear-cut policy emerged. While US President Eisenhower, on April 21, 1956, declared that "we must accept the right of each nation to choose its own path to the future,"[21] Secretary of State Dulles, less than two months later, was saying in effect the exact opposite, when he condemned neutrality as "an obsolete conception and except under very exceptional circumstances, it is an immoral and short-sighted conception."[22]

The Russian position was even further enhanced in Afro-Asian eyes in 1956 after the military intervention by France, Great Britain and Israel at Suez. The sympathies of most of the Afro-Asian leaders were plainly on the side of the Egyptians. This was clearly expressed in a meeting of the premiers of Burma, Ceylon, Indonesia and India in New Delhi on November 12, 1956. The Afro-Asians approved whole-heartedly the stand taken by the Soviet Union throughout the Suez crisis. At the same time, only a few of them condemned the Soviet Union for her intervention that year in Hungary,[23] and, naturally enough, none were more conscious of the part the Russians had played than the Egyptians themselves.

By 1957 the Egyptians, with the active backing of Marshal Tito, had moved into the forefront of the militantly non-aligned states. They had powerful means to transmit their call to non-alignment. By that time, Cairo was becoming a major centre for African political activity. African political exiles found a ready haven in the Egyptian capital, and many among them were employed in the radio network, which, beamed to all parts of Africa, was technically among the most powerful in the world. In the late 1950s a total of thirteen political "offices" had been established in Cairo under the direction of African political exiles; these directed political and subversive activity against the ruling regimes in their home countries which generally were still governed by colonial powers.[24] Through these media the Egyptians emphasized the need for Afro-Asian solidarity in the anti-colonialist struggle, and, at the same time, stressed the advantages of a policy of non-alignment and "positive neutrality."[25] Bandung and Afro-Asian solidarity were mentioned in most of Abdel Nasser's speeches on foreign policy. He quoted the Bandung principles in his speech at the UN General Assembly in 1960, and, in his speech at the Casablanca conference held in January 1961, expressed the wish that a second Afro-Asian conference would in the near future be held on African soil. "We sincerely wish that such a conference and such a step in the struggle of Asia and Africa will produce the same creative effects as those of the Bandung conference in 1955," he declared.[26] On his return from Casablanca he addressed the Egyptian National Assembly in the following terms:

> The Arab struggle has extended on a broad Arab line from Bandung to Casablanca and events and experiences have proved that this broad line is the Arab safety line, also the Peace line. . . . If we consider the battle of Suez a turning point in the liberation of the African continent, then we can say that the call for Afro-Asian liberation came from Bandung.[27]

Similarly, at the first conference of independent African states, held at Accra in 1958, the only speaker to refer to an "Afro-Asian existence" was the Egyptian foreign minister, Dr. Muhammad Fawzi,[28] and, at his behest, the conference expressed its "unswerving loyalty" to the "Declaration of the Asian-African Conference held at Bandung."

Thus although at the Bandung conference the group of non-aligned nations was in a minority, the concepts of Bandung and "Afro-Asian solidarity" were becoming increasingly identified with non-alignment. This dualism is evident in the speeches of Sékou Touré of Guinea[29]; it also emerges clearly in the declaration of the 1958 Accra conference which proclaimed at one and the same time the need to forge a common foreign policy for Africa, based on the Bandung declaration and the UN Charter, and the necessity to opt for non-commitment, i.e., disengagement from the two world blocs.[30] It is stated implicitly in the charter of the 1961 Casablanca conference, which both affirms the will of the participants "to reinforce peace in the world by adopting a policy of non-alignment" and reaffirms their "unshakeable adherence" to the Bandung declaration.

The legitimatization of the policy of non-commitment, or non-alignment, by the eight participants[31] at the Accra conference was to set the tone for other African states as they became independent. Thus the Bandung declaration coupled with a policy of non-alignment gradually became part of the political stock-in-trade of the nations of Africa and Asia. In 1961 non-alignment was still the official creed of the "Casablanca Powers" only; it was not mentioned in the charter of Monrovia. But ten of the twenty-eight independent African states attended the conference of non-aligned states held at Belgrade that year (see below), including two of the moderate, West-leaning Monrovia group states.[32] True, different heads of state read different meanings into the term "non-alignment," and for some, at least, it was more of a lip service to a slogan than a new foreign policy orientation. Yet the fact that such a declaration of non-alignment was incorporated into the most solemn and binding of all political documents to have emerged from independent Africa, namely, the charter of the Organization of African Unity (OAU), demonstrates the extent to which non-alignment had become fashionable among the emergent states of Afro-Asia. The ideological reasoning for this attachment to non-alignment will be gone into more fully later on; in practice there existed a cleavage between the *political* attitude of African leaders to cold-war issues, which often expressed itself by open alignment with one or other of the two super-power blocs, and the *psychological* adherence to non-alignment as an expression of freedom and independence to conduct their own affairs despite the inherent weakness of the African states as expressed in lack of economic and military power.

This attraction to non-alignment, and the dichotomy of terms between its principles and the Bandung declaration, were encouraged by Nehru, the veteran of the non-aligned Afro-Asians, by Jamāl Abdel Nasser, and by African militants; it also received the benign approval of the Communist bloc.

Thus, in the years immediately following the Bandung conference a significant reorientation occurred in the concept of a unified Afro-Asian camp. Whereas at Bandung there had been a vague, undefined urge to get together to discuss problems common to the

Afro-Asian world, there now developed a more cogent formulation of a political ideology to be subscribed to by all those wishing to remain within the Afro-Asian fold. It was a political creed formulated by the militantly charismatic leaders of Asia and Africa—Nehru, Sukarno, Abdel Nasser, Ben Bella of Algeria, Sékou Touré, Nkrumah of Ghana —to which the lesser dynamic leaders had to give lip service. The pillars on which this creed rested were non-alignment with either of the two world blocs, coupled with self-assertion and militant anti-colonialism.

The new orientation found concrete expression in two different channels: in the activities of the Afro-Asian group at the United Nations, and in the organizing and holding of a conference of Heads of State and Government of Non-Aligned Countries in Belgrade in 1961 and its aftermath in Cairo in 1964. It is to these two manifestations of the new Afro-Asian policy orientation that we must now turn.

We have followed in Chapter 3[33] the first steps taken by the Afro-Asian group at the United Nations. In the post-Bandung period the activities of the group were transformed. It changed its character, both numerically and ideologically. In 1955, after five years in which not a single new member had been admitted to the UN, sixteen countries joined the world organization, of which six immediately joined the Afro-Asian group. In 1956 four new countries were admitted, all from Africa and Asia. In 1957 two—Ghana and Malaya—joined the UN, and in 1958 Guinea was admitted. The great flood of new members, all Afro-Asian, occurred in 1960 and in 1961. In those two two years nineteen African and two Asian countries (Cyprus[34] and Mongolia) swelled the ranks of the UN, completely transforming its composition. In 1945 there had been twelve countries from Africa and Asia[35] in the UN as against thirty-nine others. In 1955 the Afro-Asians had increased to twenty-five[36] as against fifty-one others. In 1961 there were fifty-three members from Africa and Asia, with only fifty-one members from the other continents. Not only the United Nations was transformed by this influx of newly independent countries. The composition and power structure of the Afro-Asian group itself were completely altered. Before Bandung it had largely been an Arabo-Islamic body. Of the pre-1955 group six countries were Arab, four were non-Arab Muslim, four were Asian non-Muslim and two were Black African. Of the Arab members, Egypt and Syria could be considered non-aligned, and Iraq and Lebanon Western-oriented, while Saudi Arabia and the Yemen took a stand veering towards the West except on issues dealing with Muslim and Arab questions. Of the non-Arab Muslim members, only Indonesia was truly non-aligned, Pakistan and Iran voting generally with the West, and Afghanistan taking a stand similar to that of Saudi Arabia. The non-Muslim Asian members were evenly divided: India and Burma well in the non-aligned camp, and Thailand and the Philippines staunchly pro-Western. Both the African countries—Liberia and Ethiopia—could be generally expected to take a pro-Western stand. The pre-1955 group could, in fact, be defined as Arab-Muslim dominated (ten out of sixteen) with only five out of the sixteen following a consistently non-aligned policy. These five were, however, the most active members of the group: India, Burma, Indonesia, Egypt and Syria. Their representatives took up by far the most of the talking time in the sessions of the group and made most of the proposals.[37]

By 1961 Arab-Muslim supremacy had been completely inundated by the African element. The Arab countries now counted eleven, the non-Arab Muslim six (Malaya and Mauritania having joined the previous four), the Asian non-Muslim countries had increased to ten, while the Black African states now numbered twenty-two.[38] Such a heterogenous group, embracing within its fold such diverse regimes as the Mongolian Peoples Republic and Liberia, could obviously not be expected to work in unison. Already in 1958, at the meeting of independent African states in Accra, a separate African caucus in the UN was decided upon[39]; the Arabs, from the very beginning of the UN, had been meeting separately. Above all, however, cold-war alignments prevented an Afro-Asian alliance; no unity of action on any cold-war issue was ever obtained. A breakdown of voting figures during the sixteenth UN General Assembly in 1961 clearly reveals this lack of homogeneity: on issues where the United States and the Soviet Union voted differently, 26.1% of the Afro-Asian members voted with the US and 29.2% with the Soviet Union, while only in less than one-third of the votes—31.3%—did their voting differ from that of either the US or the Soviet Union.[40] Significantly, before the massive entry of Africans into the UN in 1960 the Afro-Asian group did succeed in maintaining a united stand in two-thirds of the votes.[41] A fairly sound indicator of Afro-Asian alignment was the yearly vote on the seating of Communist China in the UN. In 1961, for example, the vote of the Afro-Asian group was divided with twenty-five in in favour of China's admittance, twenty-three against and five abstentions.

With such a wide range of diversity, the entire concept of an Afro-Asian group becomes questionable. It could also be expected that the group would exist in the shadow of continuous tension, and that the danger of its falling apart would be ever present. That this has not occurred is due to the informal, almost casual manner in which the affairs of the Afro-Asian group in the UN have been conducted. It has held regular meetings throughout the year, not only during Assembly session, each member having the right to convoke a meeting. It was decided to install a president by monthly rotation, and a Secretariat has been established. However, subjects connected with the cold war or with great-power alignments have been studiously avoided; they have never been brought before the Afro-Asian forum. Nor have inter-group controversies, such as the Kashmir question, to mention only one. No formal vote has ever been taken; the chairman sums up the consensus of opinion after discussion, and freedom of voting has been left to all members. There is thus no question of there being a bloc, and a semblance of unity has been observed only when the particular interests of the member states were not involved. Additionally, despite common belief, the group per se cannot be considered unaligned in cold-war issues, as the voting habits described above demonstrate. The most vociferous of its members, however, have been the spokesmen of the non-aligned, and for this reason, the Afro-Asian group in total has erroneously been considered generally to take a non-aligned stand. This is not to say that the group as a whole has not had any influence on world issues. In matters affecting its members as a whole, there had been a united front. This has been particularly conspicuous on questions related to world disarmament, to aid to emergent countries—the entire Afro-Asian group voted for the creation of SUNFED—and, to an almost similar degree, to the entire complex of anti-colonialism. When the question of independence of Tunisia and Morocco was finally brought before the UN General Assembly, the entire Afro-Asian group voted in favour; the same occurred on the Algerian question, with the exceptions of Laos, Cambodia and the Philippines which refused to support an extreme anti-French resolution. Afro-Asian activity on this subject reached its climacteric during the fifteenth UN General Assembly in 1960. The Assembly had never seen such a concentration of heads of state. Khrushchev was there, with all the Communist leaders of Eastern Europe; so were the British premier Harold Macmillan and numerous other heads of government from Western Europe. Fidel Castro of Cuba attended and so did Tito of Yugoslavia. Prominent among the leaders of the Afro-Asian countries who came to New York were Nehru, Nkrumah, Abdel Nasser and Sukarno. It was in the presence of this illustrious gathering that the Afro-Asians scored their greatest success yet: a resolution condemning colonialism which was put forward by forty-three African and Asian states, and was accepted by eighty-nine countries without a single delegation voting against it.[42] In his speech before the vote, Abdel Nasser quoted largely from the Bandung declaration, stressed the importance of non-alignment, and called for a summit meeting of heads of state and the cessation of the cold war.

These gains of the Afro-Asian group in the UN should not be overemphasized, however. There is no evidence that on a single issue of importance any of the great powers has yet been forced to change its policies because of Afro-Asian pressure. As an observer of the Afro-Asian performance in the UN has put it:

> The progressive disillusionment with the capacity of the UN to act in the political arena invited the tendency to adopt abstract proclamations more adapted to evasion of concrete issues than to the facing of them, and to the setting of noble but distant goals that every country is free to interpret in the light of its own national interests. The very fact that the organization is today more representative than it was has contributed to the lessening of its political effectiveness.[43]

This lack of effectiveness was never so dramatically illustrated as by the fifteenth General Assembly itself, and in the months immediately following it. The Afro-Asian call for a meeting of the two world leaders had been rejected by both; an attempt to get the disarmament talks going on a practical note failed completely. The UN itself "was in a state of disarray and frustration unparalleled in history," the proceedings of the past three months having been "a rare example

of futility, which had created widespread disillusionment."[44] Far
from there having been any relaxation of world tension after the
Assembly, as the Afro-Asian leaders had hoped, the cold war reached
a new intensity, The first months of 1961 witnessed the rupture of
diplomatic relations between the US and Cuba, to be followed three
months later by the abortive US invasion at the Bay of Pigs; that year
saw also the escalation of the war in Vietnam, a dangerous rise in
tension in Laos which became one of the potential flash-points for a
new war, the assassination of the Congolese premier Patrice Lumumba
and the deepening of the Congo crisis, the failure of the US–USSR
summit meeting between John F. Kennedy and Khrushchev at Vienna,
and, in August, the construction of the ill-famed Berlin Wall, after a
summer of mounting tension over the German issue.[45]

It was in this atmosphere of increased tension that the decision to
hold a conference of non-aligned nations was taken, significantly
enough, not by Nehru nor by Sukarno, the two primary architects of
Bandung, but by Tito and Abdel Nasser. The subject was discussed
lengthily by them during a visit of Tito to Cairo in April 1961; the
joint communiqué they issued on April 22 declares that "the two presidents held the view that consultations between the non-aligned
countries are indispensable for the purpose of consolidating world
peace, safeguarding the independence of all nations and eliminating
the danger of intervention in their affairs."[46] Four days later, joint
letters signed by Tito and Abdel Nasser were sent to the heads of
state of twenty-one countries suggesting the conference "in view of
recent world developments and the dangerous increase in international tension." The following month President Sukarno visited
Cairo and added his sponsorship to the conference; Sékou Touré and
Modeibo Keita of Mali also arrived in the Egyptian capital in the same
month and voiced their unqualified support of the idea. But Nehru's
attitude was totally different. He had stopped over in Cairo in February 1961 on his way to a Commonwealth conference in London,
and Abdel Nasser had broached the subject. Nehru had been less than
enthusiastic, claiming that the UN was the proper forum for such
moves. India later also objected to the exclusive nature of the list of
invitees; in Nehru's opinion, at least fifteen more countries should
have been invited. In the event, Nehru only gave his consent to
attend the Belgrade conference a mere three weeks before it was held.

He had little choice. A conference of the unaligned nations without the participation of India was unthinkable and would have been construed as a hostile act by the sponsors. Moreover, a conference at Belgrade of the unaligned nations, which automatically precluded the participation of Pakistan and China, was preferable to a "second Bandung" conference of Afro-Asian nations, for which Sukarno had been pressing with increasing insistance, with both Chinese and Pakistani support.[47]

On June 5, 1961, delegations from twenty countries convened in Cairo for a preparatory meeting prior to the full-dress conference. The meeting was important in that, for the first time, an attempt was made to define the term non-alignment. The definition emerged in the wake of sharp discussion between the Indian and some of the Asian delegates, who sought to enlarge the number of invitees, and the Yugoslav and Egyptian representatives with the "Casablanca" group, who wished to keep the number limited to those attending the preparatory meeting. The criteria for "non-aligned," as presented at Cairo, were composed of four points: an independent policy based on peaceful coexistence; non-participation in multilateral military alliances; support of liberation and independence movements; and non-participation in bilateral military alliances with great powers.[48]

The first conference of Heads of State and Government of Non-Aligned Countries subsequently held in Belgrade in September 1961 has been described by one observer as a "Bandung without China and with the addition of Yugoslavia and Cuba."[49] The differences, however, were far greater. Of the twenty-five participants only fifteen had attended Bandung; on the other hand, some of the most active and prominent delegates at Bandung—such as those from China, Pakistan, the Philippines, Thailand and Turkey—were absent from Belgrade. But it was in the content of the two conferences that the main difference lay: at Bandung the non-aligned were in a minority, and the accent had been placed on the solidarity and problems of the emergent countries of Asia and Africa. At Belgrade, on the contrary, the accent was placed on world affairs, with European problems, such as the German issue, well in the lead. There was a question of priorities. Nehru, and to a lesser degree, Tito and Nasser insisted that world peace and peaceful coexistence were more important than any other issue, while Sukarno and a number of African leaders placed as top priority the question of anti-colonialism. Nehru, in the typical form of understatement which so characterizes his style of speech, declared that "imperialism, colonialism, racialism and all the rest" were "somewhat overshadowed" by the crisis in the world, which could so easily lead to war. "First things must come first," Nehru insisted, "and nothing is more important and has more priority than this world situation of war and peace. Everything else . . . has a secondary place."[50] But for Sukarno peace "based on a world order of social justice and prosperity" was not possible "without the eradication of colonialism and imperialism in the world."[51] Nkrumah put it even more sharply when he declared that the problem of disarmament came second to "colonialism, overt or covert."[52]

Despite the views of the militant Afro-Asians, as they may be called, it was the approach of Tito and Nehru which prevailed at Belgrade. The accent in the final "declaration" issued by the conference was placed on the need to prevent war, on peaceful coexistence, on disarmament, and on general international questions. A special statement on the danger of war and an appeal for peace preceded the declaration; emissaries[53] brought letters to Kennedy and Khrushchev urging them to resume negotiations.[54] Colonialism was, as could be expected, denounced in the declaration, but did not receive the pride of place which the militants had wanted. There was thus at Belgrade a widening-out of the horizons of Afro-Asia, or, as some felt, a diluting of the aims which had been set by some of the more militant subscribers to the Afro-Asian camp. The argument was increasingly heard that the Afro-Asian framework had outlived its usefulness, and that its place had now been taken by the grouping of non-aligned states which embraced not only the emergent nations of Asia and Africa but also countries from Europe and Latin America. This might not be a third bloc, as it was coming to be called, but its sponsors saw it "as a like-minded group that could act together in the UN and elsewhere when the occasion demanded," to quote the American expert on contemporary Middle East affairs Charles Cremeans.[55] Abdel Nasser, speaking of the Belgrade conference, called it "the conscience of the world and its moral spirit,"[56] and his words were echoed by Emperor Haile Sellasie of Ethiopia ("cumulative moral influence"), President Nkrumah of Ghana ("moral force"), and others.

There were several heads of state who refused to accept this proposed change in the direction of their movement. They felt the solidarity of the "have-nots" of Asia and Africa to be stronger than the political affinity of nations following a policy of non-alignment. They began to clamour with increasing insistence for a new Afro-Asian summit conference, a "second Bandung." There was nothing new in this call; as we have seen, there had already been talk of a "second Bandung" while the first conference there was still in progress, and since then the idea had been intermittently brought up. The Indonesians had been the main initiators. At a press conference in Geneva in June 1956, President Sukarno announced that talks were proceeding among the "Asian Powers" on holding another "Asian" conference. [57] It had been proposed to hold the conference in Cairo in the second half of 1956 and the Egyptians had already given their consent. [58] The proposed conference was postponed, however, mainly because of the tension existing between Egypt and Iraq at the time and because of the lack of enthusiasm displayed by Nehru. In 1957 there was again talk of a conference, but once more the idea was shelved. [59]

At the same time the prime minister of Ceylon called for the holding of an Afro-Asian conference on economic questions proposing Colombo as its venue. In a letter addressed to thirty-one heads of state, sent on October 15, 1958, Premier Solomon Bandaranaike wrote the following:

At the Colombo Power conference on the Suez crisis held in New Delhi in November 1956 [see above, p. 88] the question was mooted whether another conference on the lines of Bandung should be held early in pursuance of the decision of the Bandung conference that it should meet again in two years' time. It was felt in the circumstances then prevailing that it would be desirable to postpone the holding of such a conference. However, it was decided on my suggestion that a consultative committee representing the five Colombo Powers be set up to deal with certain economic problems arising out of the Suez situation. The committee was set up and met once in Colombo in June 1957. This is practically all that has been done in this important field. . . . I feel that even if it may be still considered not opportune to call a second conference on the Bandung lines dealing with political and other similar issues, a conference consisting generally of countries represented at Bandung and dealing purely with economic problems would be very desirable and would be likely to produce useful results. . . . I would suggest that the conference might be held at some convenient time in 1959, with Colombo as the meeting place.[60]

Writing of this initiative the Ceylon press, on February 5, 1959, claimed that twelve countries had answered favourably, including Ghana, Japan, Turkey, the UAR, Malaya, Indonesia, Pakistan and China. Significantly, India was not on the list. Nehru adopted a "wait and see" policy; the idea was eventually buried in the wider-embracing UN initiative which led to the establishment of SUNFED.

Immediately after the Belgrade conference, the Indonesians again broached the subject with the Indian premier, only to be answered once more in the negative. This time, however, the Indonesians persevered and in 1962 they issued a tentative agenda for a "second Bandung." The conference, they claimed, would help solve bilateral disputes in Afro-Asia and was necessary owing to the intensification of the East-West arms race and the emergence of new Afro-Asian countries.[61] By now India, in conjunction with the UAR, agreed in principle to the holding of the conference provided it was convened on the demand "of a large majority of the Bandung Powers."[62] However, their proposal to hold a preparatory conference in December 1962 came to nothing because of the Sino-Indian conflict. Instead, a totally different Afro-Asian conference was held in the same month —the representatives of six Afro-Asian countries met in Colombo to seek ways of bringing to an end the military action on the Sino-Indian frontier. Relations between China and India had already begun to deteriorate as early as 1957, but the conflict took on the character of an open military clash in 1962. The whys and wherefores of the Sino-Indian crisis fall outside the scope of this book; so do the byzantine manoeuvrings of the parties involved, and notably the six countries at Colombo, to reach some sort of compromise. But the conflict as such between the two largest countries of Afro-Asia—both of which had been the first signatories to the concept of *Panch Sheel*, the five principles of coexistence, and among the most active participants at Bandung—shattered the brittle façade of Afro-Asian unity and solidarity as no other single event succeeded in doing. In the words of C.S.

Jha, one of the leading Indian delegates at Bandung and later at Algiers, the conflict "drove a hard nail into the body of Afro-Asian solidarity and from that date the whole fabric of Afro-Asian solidarity was damaged."[63] The December 1962 deliberations at Colombo, and the attempts of President Abdel Nasser to mediate, only aggravated the situation, for the Indians felt that they had been betrayed by their Afro-Asian friends, a feeling which increased their growing isolation and enlarged the gap between their policy and that of the Afro-Asian militants.[64]

The Sino-Indian crisis had an additional effect: it served to harden the lines of division which had already been becoming apparent within the Afro-Asian world. Roughly the lines followed those created by the Sino-Soviet split: between Afro-Asian leaders who placed the emphasis, with the Russians, on peaceful coexistence, and others who considered, with the Chinese, that the endeavour of the liberation movements against colonialism, by means of armed struggle if need be, deserved their undivided support even at the sacrifice of peaceful coexistence. The Sino-Indian crisis helped to cement a Soviet-Indian axis at all Afro-Asian confabulations, an axis bound as much by negative factors—hostility towards China—as by the more positive desire for peaceful coexistence. Around this axis a number of countries, notably the UAR, Lebanon, Cyprus—to mention a few—grouped themselves. Similarly, the more militant Afro-Asians, as well as those like Pakistan, Ceylon, and even Iran which were particularly hostile to India and the Soviet Union, gathered in an opposing camp. These two groupings crystallized in the demand for a "second Belgrade" conference of the non-aligned states on the one hand, and the continued demand for a "second Bandung" on the other. From 1963 there developed a race between the promoters of these two conferences, with both sides doing their utmost to enlist support from the recalcitrants in the Afro-Asian camp.

According to Jha, the idea of a "second Belgrade" was born "sometime towards the end of 1963."[65] But it is virtually certain that the project was discussed between presidents Tito and Abdel Nasser on Brijoni Island in May 1963. In November the Ceylon premier Mrs. Sirimavo Bandaranaike declared her support during a visit to Cairo—she later changed her mind—and so did Ethiopia and India. By February 1964 preliminary discussions had become sufficiently advanced for formal invitations to have been sent out to all those who had participated at Belgrade in 1961 to take part in a preparatory meeting at ambassadorial level to be held on March 23, 1964, in Colombo, to prepare a conference to take place—this time in Cairo—in the autumn of 1964. The invitations were answered in the affirmative by all states except Mali, Burma and Ecuador. The Indonesians, who attended Colombo, attempted delaying tactics and called for a conference of Emergent Forces instead of non-aligned countries. Their efforts were not successful, and the ambassadors decided instead to hold another conference of non-aligned countries at Cairo. This time it was to be a much larger affair. In addition to the invitees to Belgrade, all countries of the OAU and of the Arab League were to be invited, and also Argentina, Bolivia, Brazil, Chile, Mexico, Uruguay, Venezuela, ex-British Guiana, Jamaica, Trinidad and Tobago, Laos, Austria, Finland and Sweden. The list was once more arbitrary; no one attempted to explain, for example, why Sweden should be considered more non-aligned than the Irish Republic.

The Colombo meeting of 1964 set the date and also formulated an agenda for the projected Cairo conference. Significantly, Moscow Radio gave it wholehearted approval.[66] The Russians were very evidently backing the Yugoslav–Egyptian–Indian initiative against the Chinese-supported call for a "second Bandung." The renewed Soviet support of non-alignment emerged clearly in a leading article entitled "non-alignment, not neutralism" which appeared in *Pravda* on October 5, 1964. "The non-aligned countries defend the principles of peaceful coexistence also because this will aid the final victory of the national liberating forces," *Pravda* stated, and continued:

The non-aligned states are taking part in a decisive offensive against the forces of war and a no less important role is being played by them in the struggle for the elimination of colonialism in all its aspects. . . . As for the Soviet Union it supports the policy of non-alignment, deeming that such a policy limits the sphere of activity of the aggressive blocs, broadens the zone of peace and lessens the risks of war.

Never had a more unequivocal statement been made in the Soviet press in favour of non-alignment.

While these preparations for the Cairo conference were under way, the sponsors of a "second Bandung" were not being inactive. The race was still on. In April 1964, a month after the preparatory meeting held in Colombo, a similar preparatory conference, of Bandung invitees, took place in Jakarta. A bad omen for the ill-fated second Afro-Asian conference could already then be seen: only twenty-one countries sent delegates to the Jakarta meeting. Among Bandung participants who declined the invitation were Burma, Japan, Jordan, Laos, Lebanon, Libya, Saudi Arabia, Sudan, Thailand, the two Vietnams and Yemen. The participants at Jakarta, in discussing the raison d'être for a new Afro-Asian conference, touched on the most basic tenets of Afro-Asian solidarity. Their discussions therefore provide a valuable clue to the attitude of their governments to this question. The conference was opened by the president of Indonesia Ahmad Sukarno who, in his usual ringing terms, called on the conference to smash and crush the last vestiges of colonialism. "Our best weapon in this struggle against domination lies in preserving Afro-Asian solidarity." The Afro-Asian nations should pool their ideas at a second conference, he said, and decide themselves "what our new world is to be." [67] His theme was taken up by his foreign minister, Dr. Subandrio, who chaired the first session, and emphasized that a second conference was necessary to preserve the cohesion and solidarity which had existed earlier and which was most vital to fight the common foe, colonialism, and neo-colonialism. Afro-Asian solidarity was also needed for the domestic development of these countries, Subandrio declared. [68] But the ghost of Bandung was riding high. In the second session the following morning the delegate of Turkey spoke—no doubt to the consternation of those present—of the right of countries to join together in common effort for defence purposes against aggression. [69] He felt that the principal objective of the second conference should be the same as that of Bandung, namely to review the present position of Africa and Asia in the world and the contribution they could make to world peace and cooperation. For the Ghanaians the main subject for discussion was to be colonialism, economic cooperation and measures for promoting world peace and security, [70] while the Algerians believed that the conference of non-aligned countries and the Afro-Asian conference should have the same objective: liquidation of all sorts of domination and the promotion of equality among nations as prerequisites for eternal peace.[71] It was, however, left to the Indian representative to retreat from the rarified air of high principles back to the charged atmosphere of controversial issues: by proposing that the Soviet Union and Malaysia be invited, he threw the conference into confusion. In a thinly veiled action against the Indonesians, who hoped that the conference would once more convene in Bandung at as early a date as possible, he proposed that the conference be held in an African country in April 1965 "to commemorate the tenth anniversary of the first Bandung conference."[72] The inference of the date was clear: by that time the conference of non-aligned countries could be held, drawing the wind out of the sails of the second Bandung. The Indian proposals were lengthily debated. Guinea formally opposed the invitation of the Soviet Union[73] while the Chinese once more produced their familiar argument that there was no place for the Soviet Union in an Afro-Asian conference as she was not an Asian power. In the end, the issue remained unresolved. According to the *Times of India*[74] only Ceylon supported the Indian proposal unreservedly regarding the Soviet Union and Malaysia. The Arabs, wrote the *Hindu,* kept "their diplomatic silence" on all controversial issues, and failed to make a stand regarding the Soviet Union as well as on Malaysia. The "troika" working against the Soviet Union were China, Indonesia and Pakistan, according to this report.[75]

If the Jakarta meeting did not succeed in resolving the vexed issue of Soviet and Malaysian participation, it did succeed in formulating the objectives of the second Afro-Asian conference, based partly on a working paper which the Indonesian delegation produced.[76] These objectives were declared to be:

to strengthen mutual acquaintances and friendship;
to attain common understanding of the basic problems arising out of the revolutionary changes which have taken place in all fields in Afro-Asia in their common struggle against imperialism, colonialism and neo-colonialism to achieve full national independence;
to search for appropriate methods of cooperation;
to make policies for the peaceful settlement of disputes;
to revive the spiritual heritage of the Afro-Asian peoples and

to exploit fully their natural resources;

to formulate guiding principles (*a*) to inspire against colonialism, (*b*) to secure restoration of lawful rights of domicile of populations evicted, (*c*) to ensure complete emancipation of countries still under foreign domination;

to strengthen economic, social and cultural cooperation.[77]

It was decided that the conference be convened on March 10, 1965, in an African country decided on by the OAU.

One of the interesting features to emerge from the Jakarta documents is the lack of any clear stand, or indeed much activity, by the Arab delegates in general and the Egyptians in particular.[78] The Egyptians, like the Indians, did not hide the fact that they were lukewarm to the whole idea of a second Bandung. A month before Jakarta, Abdel Nasser openly declared that he did not think the time for a second Bandung to be opportune. "We cannot go to a second Bandung conference unless we ensure unity and common positions," he told a *Tanyug* official Yugoslav news agency correspondent. The time was not now suitable "chiefly because of conflicts between many Asian countries." In a pointed criticism of the entire concept of Afro-Asianism, he declared that he would give priority to the problems of world peace as being common to all nations, and "not to a single region."[79]

The Egyptian president made his point of view clear to President Sukarno in a letter, the gist of which was later published by Muhammad Ḥasanayn Haykal, in *al-Ahrām*.[80] Priority should be given to the conference of non-aligned countries for the following reasons, the Egyptian president was reported to have written to Sukarno:

The Afro-Asian entity is situated in a geographical framework; it covers a span of territory despite the contradictions existing within it;

Bandung succeeded because the idea of independence was at the basis of its objectives. It was limited then to twenty-nine participants. Today, in Africa alone there are thirty-six independent countries; therefore, that base is not suitable for a second Bandung. The social and economic conditions existing in these countries can be better be discussed in an ideological framework than in a geographical one; Afro-Asians are involved in conflicts among themselves—e.g. India–Pakistan, India–China;

Gigantic forces in quest of development have been born in Latin America and even in Europe. To confine the conference to Afro-Asia would break the contacts with these forces which should be incorporated;

The problem of neo-colonialism is to be tackled in unified manner.

Haykal commented: China and Indonesia believed in the continuation of Bandung, "to encourage the national liberation movements and to establish the strategy of the struggle against old-fashioned colonialism." India and Egypt thought otherwise, as non-alignment included "all the free forces in the Afro-Asian solidarity movement, and because the struggle against old and new forms of colonialism had passed from the two continents to others as well, notably Latin America."

Many of the Afro-Asian countries, and particularly African ones, very obviously did not share Abdel Nasser's viewpoint. As one of the leading papers in Ceylon pointed out, "many of these countries see the non-aligned talks as a 'Lonely Hearts Club,' referring to the enthusiasm of India and Yugoslavia for the conference. They speak of India's nervousness at its diplomatic isolation and of its diminishing image as a non-aligned country. . . ."[81] Ceylon had veered sharply to the pro-Bandung camp.

As the two preparatory meetings came to an end, both sides stepped up their efforts to enlist support. As early as December 1963 Chou En-lai had visited Cairo to enlist Abdel Nasser's blessing for the second Bandung, but with no great success.[82] The Pakistanis were no less active. The Pakistan president Ayub Khan visited Ceylon in December 1963 and mobilized Mrs. Bandaranaike's support. It was better to have a second Bandung than a second Belgrade, he declared during his visit, for there were a number of problems, such as the Indian–Chinese conflict, which could be aired at an Afro-Asian meeting but not at a Belgrade-type conference. In mid-June the deputy foreign minister of Indonesia toured African capitals to canvass support,[83] following on the heels of the general secretary of the Indian Foreign Office, Desai, who sought to persuade the African leaders to postpone the conference until after the non-aligned conference was held. The issue of precedence had really been already settled, however. By having had to agree to an African venue for the second Bandung there was no possibility, apart from holding it in Cairo, of making the technical preparations before October 1965, the date set for the second Belgrade. It is, therefore, to that conference that we must first turn.

NOTES

1. This is admitted by one of the main participants in the subcommittee which formulated the ten points, Krishna Menon of India. See Brecher in an interview with Menon, in *India and World Politics—Krishna Menon's View of the World,* p. 53.

2. Statement in Lok Sabha, 30.4.1955, quoted in Nehru, *India's Foreign Policy—Selected Speeches 1946–1961.* For Nehru's first speech at Bandung and his statement in the Lok Sabha, see p. 269 ff.

3. This point was made even more bluntly by Krishna Menon: "We were always against repeating 'Bandung' in a hurry as some wanted, because we were afraid we would undo the good done there. It was the high point of Asian unity"—see Brecher, *ibid.,* p. 55. Krishna Menon speaks, significantly, of Asian but not of Asian-African unity.

4. According to Rajan, India did appoint a liaison officer to pursue the policies conforming to these resolutions, but, apparently, with no great success. See his *India in World Affairs—1954–1956,* p. 629.

5. *Al-Jumhūriyya,* Cairo, 2.5.1955.

6. Dewan Berindranath in *Caravan,* New Delhi, November, 1957.

7. Abdel Nasser admitted as much himself in a speech he made much later: "We all remember the doubts raised in 1955 with regard to the non-aligned policy and the harm that that policy might cause to the country. We all remember also what followed when we opened the way to the East . . . we passed successfully through the armament crisis and through other operations such as the policy of neutrality." See Abdel Nasser, *Speeches and Press Interviews,* (1962), p. 377.

8. Sayegh (ed.), *Dynamics of Neutralism in the Arab World,* p. 165.

9. Conte, *Bandoung,* p. 291. Thus, also, Nehru's message to Dr. Sastroamidjojo, on the first anniversary of the Bandung conference: "World peace and cooperation was the keynote of our conference. Its achievement stood and continues to be menaced by the Hydrogen Bomb, the symbol of fear, suspicion, of the outdated belief in the balance of power and of peace based on fear"—*News and Views on Indonesia,* Indonesian Embassy, Canberra, Vol. 7, No. 16, 17.5.1956.

[10] Binder, *Ideological Revolution in the Middle East*, p. 241.

[11] *Hindu*, 8.7.1955.

[12] The party was forced to reverse its policy and support Nehru's foreign policy, which led *The Times* to comment: "The Communist party of India has again been sacrificed for the benefit of Soviet foreign policy!"—*The Times*, London, 6.7.1955.

[13] That the seeds of conflict between the Soviet Union and China already existed at that time, and had even begun to germinate in the days of Stalin, is beyond doubt. A number of works have appeared on this subject; particularly commendable are Fejtö, *Chine-URSS: La fin d'une hégémonie;* Zagoria, *Sino-Soviet Conflict;* and Crankshaw, *New Cold War: Moscow v. Peking.*

[14] U Nu's visit to Moscow did not prevent him declaring after his return to Burma that he did not think that the Soviet Union should take part in "a purely Asian conference (sic!) such as Bandung," as she was European— *The Times*, 10.11.1955.

[15] See Fejtö, p. 101.

[16] Thus, the British Communist expert on Africa described Bandung in the following terms: "The independent nations of Asia and Africa came together at Bandung in April 1955 to affirm their solidarity in the fight to end colonialism." Bandung gave "to each and every nation in Asia and Africa an immense confidence in the strength of the anti-colonial forces and in the certainty of victory in the struggle for national independence" —Woddis, *Africa—The Roots of Revolt*, p. 250. There are dozens of similar examples.

[17] For an excellent résumé of Chinese foreign policy objectives in the immediate post-Bandung period, see W.A.C. Adie's "China's Foreign Policy," *World Review*, March 1968. One of the reasons why the Chinese were later to attach such importance to AAPSO was because they became disillusioned with the possibility of creating a United Front with the Afro-Asian heads of state, and prefered to act "from below."

[18] Thus Lieou Tchang-cheng, president of the Association of Friendship of the Peoples of China and Africa and vice-president of the Federation of Trade Unions of China: "Five years ago the leaders of twenty-nine countries of Asia and Africa met at Bandung to discuss important problems regarding the struggle against colonialism and for the conquest and the safeguarding of national independence, as well as the defence of world peace and the reinforcing of the solidarity of the peoples of Asia and Africa. . . ."—*"Documents relatifs sur l'assemblée organisé par les différents milieux de Pékin pour commémorer le Ve annivérsaire de la conférence de Bandoeng et pour célébrer le fondation de l'Association*

d'Amitié des Peuples de Chine et d'Afrique"—supplement to *La Chine Populaire*, No. 6, 1960, p. 3.

[19] Kuo Mo-jo, *"Documents,"* p. 9.

[20] China's attention was increasingly drawn to Africa after Bandung, and by 1960 this had become a major preoccupation of Chinese foreign policy. By that time Chinese delegations had already paid visits to twelve different African countries, while, according to Lieou Tchang-cheng, Africans from "thirty-five countries and regions" had visited China. The Chinese efforts in Africa after 1960 were increasingly channelled through the Association of Friendship of the Peoples of China and Africa, which was composed of seventeen of the largest organizations in China, including the Federations of Trade Unions, the Federation of Women, of Youth, the Union of Writers, of Journalists, etc.

[21] American Documents, 1956, p. 30, quoted in *Survey of International Affairs*, 1955–56, Royal Institute for International Affairs, p. 200.

[22] *Ibid.*, p. 201.

[23] India's refusal to condemn the Soviet Union over Hungary is explained at length by Krishna Menon in Brecher, pp. 85–97.

[24] The "offices" received financial aid from the Egyptian presidency, and were run by exiles from Kenya, Uganda, South Africa, South-West Africa, Southern Rhodesia, Northern Rhodesia, Basutoland, Zanzibar, Nigeria, Cameroons, Equatorial Africa, Ruanda-Urundi and Eritrea. Foremost among them was the Uganda Office, led by John Kale (killed in an aircrash in the Soviet Union in 1961), and the Kenya Office, directed by Wera Ambitho.

[25] The term "positive neutralism" was, according to Binder, first used by the Egyptians in September 1956, after the Brijoni conference—see Binder, p. 240.

[26] Abdel Nasser's speech at the Casablanca conference, 4.7.1961. See *Speeches and Press Interviews*.

[27] Speech to the National Assembly, 23.1.1961, *ibid.*

[28] For a concise summary of the proceedings at Accra, see Legum, *Bandung, Cairo and Accra*.

[29] See for example speech by Sékou Touré reproduced in *Political Awakening of Africa*, London, 1965, p. 161.

[30] "All the participating Governments shall avoid being committed to any action which might entangle them to the detriment of their interests and freedom"—Legum, *Bandung, Cairo and Accra*, p. 18.

[31] Ethiopia, Ghana, Liberia, Libya, Morocco, the Sudan, Tunisia and the United Arab Republic. Among those eight were two states—Ethiopia and Liberia—whose regimes were generally considered to be conservative and pro-Western.

[32] The ten were: Congo (Kinshasa), Sudan and Tunisia which had been adherents to neither Casablanca nor Monrovia; Somalia and Ethiopia, both members of the Monrovia group; Ghana, Guinea, Mali, Morocco and the UAR, all signatories to the Casablanca charter.

[33] P. 48 ff.

[34] Despite its Greek majority and its anomalous geographical position Cyprus had been admitted to Afro-Asian organizations.

[35] Including Turkey and Nationalist China, but not including South Africa.

[36] Including Israel, which, because of Arab pressure, was not admitted to the Afro-Asian group.

[37] According to one of the participants—who wishes to remain anonymous—interviewed by the writer.

[38] In percentages, the Afro-Asian states increased from 25 to 47% of the UN membership between 1947 and 1961, while the African alone increased from 3 to 20% during the same period.

[39] See Legum, *Bandung, Cairo and Accra.* The African group works through a coordinating body of the leaders of delegations and a Secretariat of four, elected for two years.

[40] This breakdown of the voting was done by Francis O. Wilcox, in Martin (ed.), *Neutralism and Non-Alignment,* pp. 127–8. Wilcox further analysed the voting pattern according to groupings and found that the eleven Arab states voted 11.6% times with the US and 40.5% with the Soviet Union, the twenty-three African 30.7% with the US and 24.4% with the Soviet Union, and the Asian 19% for the US and 34.2% for the Soviet Union. According to Miller, the Arab members were most successful at maintaining "formal unity"; on approximately 90% of the votes they voted together compared with the 60% of the Africans—see his *Politics of the Third World,* p. 19.

[41] Hovet, *Bloc Politics in the United Nations,* also J.B. Duroselle and J. Meyriat (ed.) *Les Nouveaux Etats Dans les Relations Internationales;* P. Gerbet, "Les Nouveaux Etats et les Organizations Internationales," Paris, 1962, pp. 4–57.

[42] The US, however, with eight other Western countries abstained, incurring the wrath of the Afro-Asians. For details see General Assembly Official Records, 15th session, 947th meeting, p. 1273 ff.

[43] Rossi, *Third World,* p. 167.

[44] *Survey of International Affairs, 1959–1960,* p.569.

[45] Tito indirectly admitted this lack of effectiveness in three paradoxical sentences in his opening speech at the Belgrade conference that year. Speaking of the efforts made by the non-aligned nations at the UN General Assembly to ease international tension, he declared: "No one can deny

the fact that this first concerted action of non-aligned countries was successful. In the first place, a tremendous moral victory was achieved." He then continued: "However, today, one year later, we must, unfortunately, note that the situation is much worse, as the cold war has assumed proportions liable to lead to the greatest tragedy at any moment"—see *Conference of Heads of State and Government of Non-Aligned Countries* (A Collection of Documents), Belgrade, p. 17.

[46] *Gamal 'Abd el-Nasser's Speeches,* 1961, issued by the Ministry of Information, Cairo. It appears evident that the main initiator of the idea was Tito, and not Abdel Nasser, for the earlier joint communiqué he made on his African tour especially with presidents Habib Bourguiba of Tunisia and Sékou Touré indicate his line of thought regarding the contribution of non-aligned countries to achieving a relaxation of world tension.

[47] Thus, Zulficar Bhutto, the Pakistani foreign minister, in a public speech at Hyderabad, called for a second Bandung, declaring, "All Afro-Asian countries, from Algeria to Japan, should converge in a great congress for reassessment of their current problems." The Chinese declared their support for an early second Bandung during a visit of Chen Yi to Jakarta in April 1961—see the joint communiqué issued after his visit.

[48] *Observer,* London, 18.6.61. Jansen, in his *Afro-Asia and Non-Alignment,* mentions five points, pp. 285–6. It was decided to invite Bolivia, Ecuador, Cyprus, Nigeria, Togo and Upper Volta.

[49] Miller, *The Politics of the Third World,* p. 33.

[50] See Belgrade Conference, *op. cit.,* p. 108

[51] *Ibid.,* p. 38.

[52] *Ibid.,* p. 99.

[53] The emissaries were presidents Sukarno and Keita to the US, and President Nkrumah and Premier Nehru to the Soviet Union.

[54] For the special statement, see Belgrade Conference, *op. cit.,* p. 252; for the full text of the declaration, see pp. 253–61; for the text of the letters sent to President Kennedy and Nikita Khrushchev, see pp. 264–5.

[55] Cremeans, *Arabs and the World,* p. 263.

[56] Abdel Nasser in speech on 22.7.1961 commemorating the ninth anniversary of the Egyptian revolution. He used the term "conscience of the world" in his Belgrade speech, as well. The attitude of the Egyptian president had, it should be noted, undergone a subtle change since his first conversion to non-alignment.

[57] *The Times,* London, 30.6.1956.

[58] According to the prime minister of Ceylon in an interview with journalists in Sidney, Australia, 8.11.1955. *Forum,* Bombay, of January 1956 also announced that the conference would be held in Cairo in 1956.

[59] This was revealed by Indonesian Foreign Minister Subandrio, in his opening speech at the Jakarta meeting of ministers in preparation of the second Afro-Asian conference, see conference document B/PC/conf. 2/PI. 1, 10.4.1964.

[60] Personal information.

[61] *Times of India,* 24.7.1962.

[62] *Times of India, ibid.*

[63] Jha, "The Algiers Conference," *India Quarterly,* Vol. XXI, No. 4, Oct.– Dec. 1965, p. 379.

[64] For a full account of the Colombo meeting, see "Conference of Six Afro-Asian non-aligned countries," *Ceylon Today,* Vol. XI, No. 12, December 1962, pp. 1–13. See also Jansen, *op. cit.,* who dealt very fully with the political moves in regard to the Sino-Indian conflict.

[65] Jha, *op. cit.,* p. 380.

[66] Moscow Radio, 1330 GMT, 29.3.1964, in BBC Monitoring Report SU/1516/A4/1.

[67] *Times of India,* 12.4.1964.

[68] Proceedings of Meeting of Ministers in Preparation of the Second Afro-Asian Conference, Djakarta (Jakarta), 10–15.4.1964. Issued by the Organizing Committee. Summary Record of the First Meeting of the Plenary Session. Doc. B/PC/conf. 2/PI.1, 10.4.1964, p. 3.

[69] *Ibid.,* Doc. B/PC/conf. 2/PI.2, p. 8.

[70] *Ibid.,* pp. 13–14.

[71] *Ibid.,* Doc. B/PC/conf. 2/PI.3, p. 31.

[72] *Ibid.,* Doc. B/PC/conf. 2/PI.2, p. 12; see also *Times of India,* 12.4.1964 and 18.4.1964.

[73] *Ibid.,* Doc. B/PC/conf. 2/PI.3, pp. 41–2.

[74] *Times of India,* 18.4.1964.

[75] *Hindu,* Madras, 22.4.1964.

[76] Proceedings of Meetings of Ministers, *op. cit.,* Doc. B/PC/Conf. 2/3— 9.4.1964. The first three objectives endorsed by the meeting are exact copies of the Indonesian proposal.

[77] *Ibid.,* Doc. B/PC/Conf. 2/2.—14.4.1964. Objectives of the Second Asian Conference.

[78] The Iraqis, who were not averse to scoring against the Egyptians, were an exception. As early as January 1964 the Iraqi foreign minister had welcomed the idea of a new Afro-Asian conference and had declared his willingness to be one of the sponsors—Baghdad Radio, 5.1.1964, 1700 GMT.

[79] *Hindustan Times,* 20.3.1964.

[80] *Al-Ahrām,* Cairo, 5.11.1965.

[81] *Ceylon Observer,* 20.2.1964.

[82] Thus, *Hindustan Times,* 24.11.1963: "Chou virtually demanded Nasser to support the Second Bandung, but Nasser reaffirmed his intention to go ahead with the second non-aligned conference. . . ."

[83] The reaction of the Nigerians was interesting. According to one of the ambassadors in Lagos, they replied that they were trying to develop a framework for African unity and settle inter-African problems by peaceful means. They suggested that the Asian states should do the same and only after that could there be proper coordination in an Afro-Asian conference.

6 CAIRO AND ALGIERS: THE DEMISE OF AFRO-ASIANISM

The second conference of non-aligned countries convened in Cairo in October 1964 in very different circumstances from those of the first conference held three years earlier in Belgrade. In the intervening period there had been a marked relaxation of international tensions. The division of the world into two opposing world blocs had become less pronounced, with the Sino-Soviet split and the independent policy followed by France blurring the sharp lines of division. There was thus much less urgency in the confabulations. At Belgrade, there had been a great deal of talk of the non-aligned countries serving as the conscience of the world, and of the need to stand between the two world giants and save the universe from mass destruction by preventing a head-on collision between them. There was much less talk of that nature at Cairo. Non-alignment as a peace-maker had lost much of its force and urgency; new and additional reasons were needed to hold the group together. This, in part, accounts for the return to the theme of anti-colonialism as the dominant subject at Cairo, despite the secondary role it had played at Belgrade. But there were additional reasons for this different approach. There was the hardening US attitude in Vietnam and Congo, in marked contrast to the benign encouragement of non-alignment displayed by the Soviet Union, backed by the Moscow accord for the cessation of nuclear tests. Above all, the Cairo conference took place under the shadow of the death of two world leaders, one who would have wielded a moderating influence on the conference and the other who had inspired grand thoughts for a better future: with the death of Jawaharlal Nehru in 1964 India, to all intents and purposes, ceased to be predominant in Afro-Asian or non-aligned conclaves, while the assassination of President Kennedy removed a widely felt hope among the non-aligned nations that under his administration the US would move closer to their points of view on world affairs.

Thus at Cairo the moderates were largely in disarray. The Indians without Nehru were reduced to near impotence.[1] Tito, and his insistence that non-alignment meant "respect for peace and active coexistence among the peoples and states,"[2] was listened to impatiently by many of those present; his emphasis on peaceful negotiations, disarmament and coexistence was considered too European an approach. The Egyptians demonstrated their militancy from the very beginning by refusing to allow the Congolese premier, Moise Tshombe, access to the conference building.[3]

In contrast to the speech of the Indian premier, Lal Bahadur Shastri, who declared "first and foremost we believe in peace, in the settlement of all disputes through peaceful means,"[4] there was the statement of Kwame Nkrumah, the Ghanaian president, who stated flatly that "as long as oppressed classes exist there can be no such thing as peaceful coexistence between opposing ideologies."[5] Against Tito's definition of non-alignment was a very different one put forward by Sékou Touré when he said that "non-alignment perfectly expresses the wishes of our states to free themselves from the domination of centuries."[6]

Nkrumah, Sukarno, Sékou Touré, Modeibo Keita, Ben Bella, Premier Milton Obote of Uganda, and most of the African delegates concentrated almost exclusively on the struggle against colonialism, leaving the Asians, such as Shastri, Mrs. Bandaranaike or King Mahendra of Nepal, as well as the delegates of the UAR and Yugoslavia, to defend the tenets of peaceful coexistence and nuclear disarmament. There was, however, an additional undercurrent apparent in some of the speeches by the Africans. Thus Joseph Murumbi, prime minister of Kenya, delivered a speech heavily slanted against the US but declared that "the division among the peoples of the world may not, after all, be due to ideological differences but to the economic disparity between the developed Military Powers, who still wish to dominate the world, and the developing nations. . . ."[7]

This lumping together of the "developed Military Powers" could hardly have pleased the Soviet Union. However, it typified a growing African feeling that the détente between the great powers, as characterized inter alia by the Moscow test-ban treaty, could have an adverse effect on them, both in the domain of great-power aid and in the role they would be able to play in the international arena. This point was made to this writer most strongly by Oscar Kambona, the former foreign minister of Tanganyika. It also finds expression in a penetrating leading article in *Jeune Afrique* which states:

> Depuis la conclusion des accords de Moscou sur la céssation des expériences nucléaires, on a de plus en plus le sentiment qu'une convention tacite ou sécrète a été conclue entre Russes et Américaines pour diviser le monde en zones d'influence ou les intérêts de chacun sont préservés . . . *ce n'est plus une détente, c'est une complicité de grandes puissances.*[8]

This sentiment accounts in part for the scepticism displayed by some of the Africans at Cairo for the tenets of peaceful coexistence. The idea was all but repudiated by the delegates of Ghana, Tanganyika, Burundi, Mali, Congo (Brazzaville), and in particular by Ahmad Sukarno of Indonesia, who declared that "there will be peaceful coexistence between the developing countries and the imperialist states only when we can face them with equal strength, and that equal strength we can obtain only through solidarity among us." For Sukarno the solidarity should be one of the New Emergent Forces, which included countries like China, but not India. Yet, largely through Egyptian, Indian and Yugoslav insistence, a resolution on coexistence was adopted by the conference and an attempt was made to define it. The repeated Yugoslav demand for a codification of its principles by the UN was also accepted. The final declaration of the conference contained the following major points:

> concerted action for the liberation of the countries still dependent;
> elimination of colonialism, neo-colonialism and imperialism;
> a call for aid of freedom movements, *including military aid*;
> respect for the right of peoples to self-determination[9];
> condemnation of racial discrimination, and of military pacts and the stationing of foreign troops and bases in any country;
> the upholding of peaceful coexistence and the codification of of its principles in the UN.

The fundamental principles of peaceful coexistence were laid down by the conference.[10]

The all-embracing definition of coexistence aroused no great enthusiasm among many of the delegates, but it was so worded that no one could really object to it. The main sentiment at the conference, however—in contrast to that voiced at Belgrade—was that colonialism and not the cold war was the main cause for international tension. The German problem, which had figured so prominently at Belgrade, was not even mentioned at Cairo. The Soviet Union was not criticized once in the final declaration, which repeatedly brought the US to task. The conference also remained silent over India's proposal to send a delegation to China to protest the nuclear tests being carried out there. Despite the resolution on peaceful coexistence, the New China Agency was able to comment triumphantly: "India and Yugoslavia failed in their efforts to impose the so-called peaceful coexistence line whose aim is to liquidate the struggle against colonialism and imperialism."[11] In spirit, if not in substance, the Chinese claim was correct.

In content if not in form the Cairo conference was more a continuation of the metamorphosis of the Bandung spirit than that of Belgrade. But in contrast to Bandung it was Africa which took pride of place at the Cairo conference and the African delegates who set the tone. One of the prominent features of the foreign policies of many African states was the search for alliances and allies, to shore up internal weakness and keep off the spectre of isolation in the international sphere. Both Afro-Asianism and the grouping of non-aligned nations served this policy aim well. It was reflected in a number of speeches by African leaders at Cairo, some of whom all but advocated the formation of a third bloc. Thus, Alphonse Massemba-Debat, the president of Congo (Brazzaville), demanded that "periodic as well as extraordinary consultations should be held among the non-aligned countries to formulate a joint attitude in the face of any crucial problem arising on the international scene"[12] and even Sékou Touré declared that the non-aligned countries must solve political problems "in a concerted action."[13]

However, although the composition of the Cairo conference was overwhelmingly Afro-Asian in character—forty-five out of the forty-seven delegations[14] being Afro-Asian—the Africans, or at least the more militant among them, preferred to look to the particularistic Afro-Asian framework than to the universal one of the gathering of the non-aligned. This, in part, accounts for the fact that once again no effort was made to set up an organizational structure or to institutionalize non-alignment. The delegates at Cairo were also acutely conscious of the impending "second Bandung" by now, scheduled to be held in Algiers in March 1965. [15]

The Jakarta preparatory conference had appointed a standing committee of fifteen countries to make arrangements to hold the second Afro-Asian conference and to assist the host country. But the committee was largely bypassed. Instead, from the end of 1964 until the final postponement of the conference in October 1965 there occurred an unprecedented coming and going of African and Asian statesmen between the two continents, embracing all the sixty-one countries invited.[16] The immediate cause for these early confabulations was the demand of several participants to postpone the conference from March 1965 till at least May. This early postponement proved to be a bad omen; it marked the beginning of a long rearguard action to save the conference against the continued sniping of its detractors. The president of the Ivory Coast Republic Félix Houphouët-Boigny persuaded nearly all the ex-Afro-Malagasy Union (UAM) countries not to participate, while the Senegalese conditioned their participation on a clear definition of the conference's aims and a prepublished agenda. The moderate Africans felt there was little chance of their being able to curb the more extremist elements, and it was therefore preferable that they stay away altogether.

The real problem facing the conference organizers, however, was not the hesitations of the African moderates, but the Sino-Soviet quarrel over Soviet participation. The battle had begun at the Jakarta preparatory conference when the Indian proposal to invite the Soviet Union had been strongly opposed by China, Indonesia, Pakistan and Guinea, with most other delegates tending to agree with the Chinese. Immediately after Jakarta the Soviet government issued a statement which accused the Chinese, inter alia, of harping increasingly on race as a factor to "determine the community of political interests."[17] The Chinese reply was not long in coming: Afro-Asianism was not a racial concept; what most of its adherents had in common was the experience of oppression by Western imperialism and a common desire to defend their independence against colonialism and imperialism. This was the basis of Afro-Asian solidarity, the Chinese insisted.[18]

The conference had been postponed till June 1965, and throughout the intervening months the interested parties campaigned for their various points of view. The Indians were anxious to prevent the conference from being dominated by China and Indonesia, in league with Pakistan. The Algerians, who had invested $30 million in the preparations for the conference,[19] were anxious that it be a success and sent out emissaries far and wide to assure maximum attendance. The Indonesians lobbied against Soviet, and particularly against Malaysian, participation, threatening to boycott the conference if representatives of the latter were invited. The UAR attempted to impose certain conditions, namely that the foreign ministers should meet immediately before the conference and decide on Soviet participation, and that regional conflicts—such as the Indian-Chinese dispute—should not be raised.[20] The ubiquitous Chinese themselves spared no efforts to prevent a decision to invite the Soviet Union. The Russians, for their part, sent Deputy Foreign Minister Kuznetsov to Asia and Africa to muster support. The Soviet government appeared to have decided that it must make a determined effort to gain admission to the conference. Failure would be a major triumph for the Chinese, and would close the door to the Afro-Asian world. Yet these pressures brought no results except a perceptible increase in tension as the date of the conference drew nearer.

The decision regarding the agenda and the participants to be invited was to be taken, as the Egyptians had proposed, by the foreign ministers, who were to meet in Algiers on June 25 and deliver their recommendations to the heads of state, who were to convene on June 29, 1965. But these decisions were never taken. Six days before the foreign ministers were due to meet, Ahmad Ben-Bella, president of Algeria and host of the conference, was deposed and imprisoned, and his place was taken by Houari Boumedienne. For those who had viewed the entire project of the conference with reluctance, the event must have appeared a heaven-sent opportunity for delay. Thirteen Afro-Asian members of the British Commonwealth, in conference in London, sent a cabled appeal for postponement. The Indians especially sought to gain support for the postponement plea. The Algerians themselves, however, were equally determined to go ahead, and they demanded support from the other twelve Arab delegations. The Arabs and the pro-Chinese together could muster a majority. But it was not to be. On the morning of June 26 a small bomb exploded in the conference hall. It did not do much damage but was sufficient to provide the pretext for the reluctant Arabs and Africans, and in particular the UAR, to back down from their support of Algiers. The enraged Algerians went so far as to suspect the Egyptians of having engineered the bomb attack in order to ensure a postponement of the conference.[21]

On June 26 the foreign ministers convened for exactly one minute, when, in the words of the Indian delegate C. S. Jha, "the delegates were told that the meeting of the foreign ministers would not take place; that the Standing Committee would meet instead. We rushed back 20 kilometres to the city to attend the Standing Committee meeting which lasted about seven hours and in the end produced the resolution postponing the conference: 28 October was fixed as the date for the Foreign Ministers' Conference and 4 November for the Summit."[22]

Not only the postponement but the new dates were a severe blow to the new regime in Algeria, for the summit conference of the OAU was due to convene in Accra on October 21, 1965, an event which could take the wind out of the sails of the Algiers conference. President Nkrumah refused to consider a postponement of OAU for the sake of Algiers. In Africa itself, and to a lesser extent in Asia, opposition to the new Algerian regime and to the conference was hardening despite desperate Algerian attempts to gain support.[23] Burma was the first country to decide not to attend because of the Boumedienne coup. The presidents of Dahomey and Upper Volta publicly harangued against the conference. Much graver for the Algerians was the decision of presidents Sékou Touré and Julius Nyerere of Tanzania to support postponement of the conference.

On October 30, forty-four delegates convened in Algiers for the first meeting of the Foreign Ministers' Conference.[24] But by October the international climate had changed considerably from that of June. The foreign ministers were meeting under different circumstances. Steady pressure by the Soviet Union on Afro-Asian countries made it virtually assured that the foreign ministers would decide on her invitation. The Chinese, on the other hand, had been thrown on the defensive, a fact exacerbated by the anti-Chinese coup d'état in Indonesia on September 30 which neutralized China's principal

ally. The Chinese, sensing their probable defeat at the foreign ministers' meeting, stipulated virtually unattainable conditions for their
participation at the summit: neither the Soviet Union, nor UN Secretary-General U Thant nor Malaysia would be invited, and India
should be condemned as an aggressor.

The tables were thus turned, and the roles reversed. The Chinese,
who had previously insisted on holding the conference, now became
the champions of its postponement. The Indians, sensing victory at
the expense of the Chinese, became its chief protagonists. The roll-
call of those absent at the October Foreign Ministers' conference is,
in itself, indicative of the changed circumstances. The African
moderates continued to stay away, which was hardly surprising, but
the pro-Chinese, including China herself, North Vietnam and
Pakistan, were conspicuous by their absence.[25] The meeting was
opened by the Algerian foreign minister, 'Abd al-'Azīz Bouteflika,
who had been the most insistent among the Algerians in pressing for
the holding of the conference. Bandung had been the starting point
for national liberation, he declared, Algiers must be the starting
point for the solidarity of all progressive peoples struggling for peace.
In the half-empty conference hall these words must have sounded
hollow indeed. In the second session that evening the Uganda delegate
declared that the heads of state meeting at Accra had not yet decided
whether to come to Algiers or not; they wished first to see the reports
of the Preparatory Committee. The Indian delegate C. S. Jha then
proposed that the Soviet Union, Malaysia and Singapore be invited,
a proposal which was backed up by fifteen other delegates.[26] No one
had yet mentioned the possibility of a postponement, but on the
following day Indonesia raised the question whether the conference
should take place; those absent could not be ignored, he declared. That
day the deliberations continued until three o'clock in the morning,
when a clear majority crystallized in favour of inviting the Soviet
Union, and also a majority for postponing the conference. The
Arab states, which had voted in favour of holding the conference at
the Arab summit meeting at Casablanca, were now wavering. On
November 1 the Algerians themselves decided in favour of postponement, and that, to all intents and purposes, decided the issue.

Bearing heavily on the delegates was a message that Chou En-lai
had sent to all Afro-Asian heads of state, which was made public on

October 26. Such a conference at the present time, the message ran, "would not help to achieve common aims but, on the contrary, would harm Afro-Asian solidarity and friendly relations between Afro-Asian states and would lead to a split." It became patently obvious that if the Soviet Union was invited and China and her allies stayed away, this indeed would lead to a split which would gravely undermine Afro-Asian relationships. A conference in such terms was almost unthinkable, and the majority, who had been unenthusiastic about the conference in the first place, decided against it. The resolution stated simply that "in the present situation, with many heads of state and government probably declining to attend the conference, the foreign ministers have come to the conclusion that the present moment is not conducive to the holding of a second Afro-Asian conference." The Algerians had issued an official communiqué a day earlier declaring that postponement "will not signify a victory of the Chinese position, but rather a victory for the imperialists who have all along banked on division among the progressive forces." Yet the Chinese did see the outcome as a victory for them, although Bouteflika had stated in the final declaration that there was "a general tendency for the Soviet Union to participate at the conference." The postponement was decided, on the condition that the conference take place at a future date in Algiers, and that the Standing Committee continue to act. It soon became, however, a moribund body.

In this manner the efforts to revive Bandung and Afro-Asian solidarity petered out. The delegates dispersed amidst a general sigh of relief, coming not only from most of the Afro-Asian countries themselves but also, for different reasons, from the West, from the Soviet Union and from China. Seldom had there been such an ill-conceived conference and such relief to see its demise. The reactions were quick to follow along expected lines. Whereas the Chinese spoke lengthily of a new victory for Afro-Asian solidarity, the *Indian Express* wrote pithily that "Algiers has torn the mask off Afro-Asian solidarity, which is a myth and a farce. The moment has come for India . . . to say good-bye to all that."[27] The more staid *Times of India* commented simply, "one can say that the era opened by the Bandung conference has come to an end,"[28] while Muḥammad Ḥasanayn Haykal, writing in *al-Ahrām,* declared more cautiously that it was good the conference had not taken place, for if it had

Afro-Asian solidarity "would have become a myth." "To have held the conference in such conditions," he wrote, "would have shattered Afro-Asian solidarity and would have transformed it, at the Club des Pins, into ruin and ashes."[29]

Thus Afro-Asianism, in its official guise, left the scene. But it was still flourishing in its unofficial, militant capacity, in the form of the Afro-Asian Peoples' Solidarity Organization, to which we must now revert.

NOTES

1 Krishna Menon had some very harsh things to say of the Indian performances at Cairo: "We became camp followers there," "Our personalities did not make an impact on the conference or on the delegates," etc. See Brecher, *India and World Politics*, p. 226.

2 Belgrade Home Service, 1400 GMT, 6.10.1964, in BBC Monitoring ME/1678/E/1–7.

3 The "Tshombe incident" dominated the accounts in the international press of the conference proceedings. They will not be gone into here. The fullest account of the "incident" can be found in *West Africa*, London, 10.10.1964, p. 1131.

4 Cairo Radio in English, 0700 GMT, 8.10.1964, quoted in BBC ME/1679/E/4–8.

5 *Ibid.,* in BBC ME/1678/E/12–16.

6 Cairo Radio in French, 0722 GMT, 9.10.1964, in BBC ME/1682/E/3.

7 Cairo Radio in English, 0700 GMT, 9.10.1964, in BBC ME/1682/E/11.

8 *Jeune Afrique,* 23.3.1964. (Present writer's italics.)

9 This article did not include a provision demanded by Shastri who, in his speech, had declared that "there can be no self-determination for different areas and regions within a sovereign and independent country, for this would lead only to fragmentation and disruption."

10 For the full definition, see Cairo Home Service, 1000 GMT, 11.10.1964, in BBC ME/1681/E/2–17.

11 Quoted in *AFP* Special, No. 5501, 12.10.1964.

12 Cairo Radio in French, 0700 GMT, 8.10.1964, in BBC ME/1682/E/1.

13 Cairo Radio in French, 0722 GMT, 9.10.1964, in BBC ME/1682/E/3.

14 Afghanistan, Algeria, Angola, Burma, Burundi, Cambodia, Cameroon, Central African Republic, Ceylon, Chad, Congo (Brazzaville), Cuba, Cyprus, Dahomey, Ethiopia, Ghana, Guinea, India, Indonesia, Iraq, Jordan, Kenya, Kuwait, Laos, Lebanon, Liberia, Libya, Malawi, Mali, Mauritania, Morocco, Nepal, Nigeria, Saudi Arabia, Senegal, Sierra Leone, Somalia, Sudan, Syria, Togo, Tunisia, Uganda, UAR, United

Republic of Tanganyika and Zanzibar, Yemen, Yugoslavia and Zambia. Twenty-nine out of the forty-seven were African. There were also ten observers—nine from Latin America, and one, Finland, from Europe.

[15] The Political Committee of the OAU chose Algiers as the site for the conference at its meeting on July 17, 1964.

[16] Thirty-four African countries, eighteen from east and south Asia, seven from west Asia, and two Euro-Asians (Cyprus and Turkey).

[17] *New Times,* No. 19, 1964, pp. 31–2.

[18] *Peking Review,* No. 23, 1964, pp. 6–8.

[19] According to Muḥammad Ḥasanayn Haykal, in *al-Ahrām,* Cairo, 4.11.1965.

[20] *Al-Ahrām, loc. cit.*

[21] *New York Times* wrote on 28.6.1965: "Privately Algerian officials have spoken freely of their suspicion that it was the work of the Egyptians and they have encouraged Arab newsmen to carry such accusations without attribution to Algerian sources." Even before the bomb had exploded Muḥammad Ḥasanayn Haykal had written that postponement was virtually inevitable. Opposition to Boumedienne was mounting, he wrote. There might be bloodshed during the conference. Supporters of the new regime admitted that 70% of the population supported Ben-Bella—see *al-Ahrām,* 24.6.1965. Haykal's article caused extreme annoyance in Algeria. These and other incidents made a leading French commentator conclude that "Nasser played a double game—openly supporting Boumedienne, while behind his back doing everything possible to make the Algiers conference a failure"—see *Figaro,* Paris, 2.11.1965.

[22] Jha, *op. cit.,* p. 383.

[23] In the month of August alone Algeria sent fifteen missions to Afro-Asian countries to explain the conference—see *Revolution Africain,* Algiers, No. 135, 28.8.1965, pp. 12–13.

[24] With the arrival of the Yemeni delegate two days later, the number became forty-five. Significantly among these were only twenty-two foreign ministers; the other countries were represented either by their ambassadors or by high officials of their foreign ministries.

[25] Absent were: Afghanistan, Burundi, Cambodia, China, Congo, North Korea, Ivory Coast, Dahomey, Zambia, Guinea, Upper Volta, Pakistan, Sierra Leone, Tanzania, Togo, and North Vietnam.

[26] Representing Egypt, Iran, Iraq, Japan, Jordan, Kenya, Laos, Malawi, Mali, Mongolia, Nepal, Nigeria, Rwanda, Tunisia, Uganda.

[27] *Indian Express,* 3.11.1965.

[28] *Times of India,* 3.11.1965.

[29] *Al-Ahrām,* Cairo, 5.11.1965.

7 THE MILITANTS TAKE OVER

In June 1954, two months after Dr. Sastroamidjojo had proposed the convening of an Asian-African conference, a resolution was passed by the World Peace Organization (WPO) which was to be the first step towards the establishment of the Afro-Asian Peoples' Solidarity Organization (AAPSO). The fact that this step was taken neither in Asia nor in Africa is itself significant. That it was taken by a Communist front organization is doubly so.

The WPO had convened in Stockholm in a "Meeting for the Lessening of International Tensions." Asian problems were high on the agenda. The Indochina war was reaching its climax; the Sino-American confrontation across the Formosa Straits was threatening to lead to armed conflict; the first feelers for an anti-Communist South-East Asian defence pact had already been put out by the US. The delegates at Stockholm decided that these problems should be discussed at an all-Asian conference of peace fighters. Subsequently, the Asian Conference for the Relaxation of International Tension (ACRIT) met at New Delhi on April 6, 1955, less than two weeks before the opening of the Bandung conference. The timing of the conference was significant. Whether deliberately intended so or not, ACRIT was construed by many as an attempt of the Communists to set a frame of reference for Bandung. Some even believed that it was intended to steal the thunder from the Asian-African conference. If this had been the aim of the organizers, they failed miserably, for the ACRIT conference at New Delhi passed almost unnoticed in all but the Communist countries. Prime Minister Nehru was reputedly annoyed at both the timing and the venue of the conference, and refused to attend the meetings.

Prominent among the eighteen countries which sent delegates to New Delhi was the Soviet Union, whose delegation was headed by

Nikolai Tikhonov.[1] The Russians, not invited to Bandung, were already making it clear that they considered themselves part of Asia, and this point was emphasized in the Soviet press which reported the proceedings of the conference. The Chinese sent Kuo Mo-jo, president of the Academy of Sciences, to head their delegation; he later became a leading figure in Afro-Asian conferences and one of the major spokesmen of the Chinese on their policy towards the Afro-Asian Movement. Most of the other delegates present were either Communists or fellow-travellers, and this was reflected in the resolutions they passed. These included the demand for the elimination of all vestiges of colonialism, the liquidation of military and naval bases of "non-Asiatic governments" in Asia, the condemnation of SEATO, support for China in her demand for a seat in the United Nations and over the issue of Taiwan. These demands were repeated at Bandung by some of the more militant delegations. Another resolution called for the formation of a permanent organization, to be known provisionally as the Asian Solidarity Committee, which aimed at extending its activities throughout Asia by the establishment of national solidarity committees.

By October 1956, fourteen such committees had been established in Asian countries.[2] These were not necessarily headed by Communists; but the executive bodies of the committees were generally Communist controlled.[3]

At a meeting of the Asian Solidarity Secretariat in New Delhi in December 1956, it was decided to extend the organization to Africa, and to persuade the Egyptians to be hosts to an Afro-Asian Solidarity Conference.[4] A goodwill mission was subsequently sent to Cairo in February 1957, composed of delegates from India, China, the Soviet Union, Indonesia and Japan.[5] The delegation included Anatoly Sofronov, who was later to represent the Soviet Union in most such conferences, and Dr. Anup Singh, the extreme left-wing secretary-general of the Indian Solidarity Committee. The delegates met with the Egyptian president, who gave his approval to holding the conference in Cairo.[6]

By late September 1957 the Egyptian committee had become sufficiently organized to call for a twenty-country preparatory committee to convene in Cairo to put the finishing touches to the preparations. The agenda was fixed, invitations were sent out, and budgetary problems were solved. The preparatory committee sent emissaries to tour the countries of Asia and Africa to explain the aims of the forthcoming conference, to mobilize support and to ascertain that those invited would attend; brochures calling for "Afro-Asian Solidarity" were distributed in their thousands; a special "Solidarity Week" (December 1–7, 1957) was devoted to propagating the conference aims, while stressing that it would remain faithful to the principles and spirit of Bandung.

By mid-December the proposed conference had already attracted world attention and was arousing a great deal of comment. To the diplomatic correspondent of *The Times,* the Cairo conference was "pretty clearly a Communist masquerade in the borrowed colours of Bandung." He added: "although the delegates are by no means all Communist, the conference is heavily slanted to take an anti-Western line, and to serve the Communist line, just as well as — or better than — if all the delegates were Communist."[7] Most of the Western comment took a similar line. The press comment in African and Asian countries, however, was far less uniform, and depended largely on the political colour of the paper concerned. Some of the Asian newspapers in particular were extremely critical. The Rangoon daily *Nation,* for example, wrote:

> Lest the unwary be misled by the term Afro-Asian, which is being applied to a conference to be held shortly in Cairo, we think it timely to point out that this conference has nothing to do with the famed Afro-Asian conference held in Bandung in 1955 . . . . The Cairo conference is in no way a true successor to the Bandung conference, and if its name implies that it is a parallel of any kind, it is a misnomer. The use of the same name is, of course, a clever move on the part of the fellow-travellers who are sponsoring the meeting and hope to cash in on the prestige of Bandung.[8]

Similar views were expressed by a number of other newspapers in various countries of Asia and Africa.[9]

Not surprisingly, the Communist press, on the other hand, denied that the Cairo conference was being manipulated in any way by the Communists,[10] while the Chinese daily *Jen min Jih Pao* wrote:

"The solidarity conference of the Afro-Asian countries is the most important and the most representative conference ever held in the history of these continents."[11] This enthusiasm was matched by the Egyptian press, and to a slightly lesser extent, by the press of the other Arab countries. The Egyptian *al-Ahrām* wrote: "The Afro-Asian conference is the conference of the peoples seeking peace, prosperity and well-being for all humanity."[12]

Thus the stage was set. The Egyptians outdid themselves to make a favourable impression on the hundreds of delegates, observers and journalists who streamed into Cairo in the last week of 1957. Large crowds cheered each 'plane-load of new arrivals, welcoming arches inscribed in Arabic, Russian, Chinese, French and English had been erected along the route from the airport to the city, while enormous placards proclaiming the need for Afro-Asian solidarity were hung from rooftops. Cairo was setting the tone; its example was later to be copied throughout the length and breadth of the Afro-Asian world as the number of conferences grew with each year that passed.

The Cairo conference opened on December 26, 1957, with an inaugural speech by Anwar as-Sadat, chairman of the Egyptian Solidarity Committee, and by then one of the leading figures in the Egyptian regime. Delegates from forty-four countries and territories[13] crowded into the Cairo University auditorium where the ceremony took place. More than one hundred journalists and some three thousand guests were present for the occasion[14]; so were a large array of observers from the World Peace Organization, from the World Federation of Trade Unions, and from most other Communist "front" organizations based on East Europe. It was, said Soviet delegate Sharaf Rashidov, the most representative assembly of Afro-Asian peoples ever held, the delegates being "not only of the peoples who had gained liberty from colonialist slavery but also of the peoples still bearing the colonialist yoke." The conference was, without doubt, the largest Afro-Asian assembly ever to have been held—in numbers it far surpassed the Bandung conference—but whether it was the most representative, as Rashidov and others claimed, is open to question. For the delegates at Cairo were not official delegates representing their countries, as the Bandung delegates had been. They had not been chosen by their governments; in many instances the contrary was true, for some of the delegates had been outlawed by their governments. The Afro-Asian Solidarity Conference was a peoples' conference. The delegates represented, or were supposed to represent, the peoples of Africa and Asia. In the eyes of the conference organizers many of the governments of African and Asian countries were not the true representatives of their people; rather, they had been installed with the help of the "imperialists," and were repressing the true representatives, namely the "progressive forces." Some of these "progressive forces" were bona fide opposition parties; others had been forced to go underground or were in exile. Some had split among themselves, and, in addition to being in opposition to their governments, were also at loggerheads with each other. Thus the question of who was representative of the peoples of Afro-Asian countries, and who was not, was not a simple one; in effect this was decided by the Cairo preparatory committee[15] whose members acted as judges of all the movements who applied for membership from countries in which Solidarity Committees had not yet been established. Thus, countries considered "progressive" were represented by delegates who had been chosen by their governments— these included the Soviet Union, Communist China, North Vietnam, North Korea, Mongolia, Egypt, Ghana, the Sudan, Syria, and Indonesia.[16] Other countries were represented by their Solidarity Committees, which included Communists and extreme left-wing politicians in addition to more representative intellectuals, members of Parliament, etc.[17] Typical of the latter was the delegation from India, whose head was Mrs. Rameshwari Nehru, a left-leaning distant relative of the Indian premier. But the real powers in the Indian delegation were the Indian representative in the Cairo Secretariat Dr. Malaviya, and Dr. Anup Singh, who was known as a Communist. Lastly there was the third category of delegates, mainly political exiles, who had been chosen by the Cairo committee to represent their countries but had no backing or jurisdiction to do so from any real political organization of size in their home countries. Typical of these were the Jordanian delegate Shafik Rashidat, lawyer and former cabinet minister who became a political exile in Damascus and later in Cairo,[18] Hassan Waris, an exile from Kenya, the Nigerian delegate Gidi Kwadri, and the delegate from Oman, Muhammad al-Harisi.

It was, therefore an extremely varied group of delegates which came together in Cairo.[19] But, as the delegates got down to the business of the nine-point agenda, one theme was repeatedly stressed by most of the speakers, namely that those present had a common past, a past dominated by their subjection to colonial rule. Anwar as-Sadat put it succinctly in his opening speech: "We have all witnessed one history of imperialism and exploitation and are partners in one struggle and one future."[20] The common colonial past was seen as the base on which the solidarity of Africa and Asia was founded, and, as an almost natural corollary, the common desire to participate in the struggle against colonialism and imperialism became the base on which the ideology of this Afro-Asian solidarity was founded. There was hardly a speaker who did not have something to say on this subject. Khaled Muhyi ad-Din,[21] who opened the debate on imperialism, spoke of the new forms of imperialism, with the US at their head, of the danger of receiving economic assistance and even more so of regional military pacts. In the Middle East, he said, there was a new phase of colonialism "depicted by the Eisenhower Doctrine which shows the trend of American imperialism to fill the vacuum created by the ousting of Britain and France."

India delegate Romesh Chandra later described the work of the conference in these terms:

> Cairo was not just a conference . . . it was a trumpet call to the world to rout out colonialism, old and new colonialism, in all its shapes and forms. . . . What did we plan? The funeral of imperialism and the funeral feast. And unlike certain other plans, there was no danger that this plan would have to be modified and scrapped. The confidence in the voice of hundreds of delegates from nearly fifty countries present at Cairo was the guarantee that the death-knell of imperialism which we sounded rang true.[22]

If the struggle against imperialism and colonialism became the dominant theme of the conference, there were a number of subordinate notes played no less persistently. One was the effort to project the Cairo conference as the natural continuation of Bandung. Thus, Anwar as-Sadat declared in his opening speech: "Today this peoples' conference meets to salute and continue the Bandung spirit, on the one hand, and to be another step forward on the other." His words were echoed in one form or another by most speakers.[23] Another theme equally frequently heard, was the need to take positive action to preserve peace and prevent war. Again Anwar as-Sadat set the tone:

> ... Our determination must not be passive. It must be turned into positive action for peace .... We, in Egypt, for instance, believe in neutralism and non-alignment. This principle has been adopted by many of our friends in Asia and Africa. We believe that by adopting this attitude we ward off the shadow of war, narrow the area facing conflicting blocs, and establish a wide area of peace which will impose its existence gradually on the whole world.[24]

The Russians pressed home a theme of their own. Speaking to the Economic Commission of the conference, Arzumanya A. Arzoumanian, chairman of the International Economic Institute at the Academy of Sciences in Moscow, announced his widely reported offer of aid-without-strings:

> We are ready to help you as brother helps brother .... Tell us what you need, and we will help you and send, to the best of our capabilities, money in the form of loans or aid .... We can build for you institutions for industry, education and hospitals. We can send economists to your country. Follow the route you consider best. We don't ask you to join any blocs or change governments or change your internal or foreign policies.

This offer, which was greeted enthusiastically by the delegates, was followed up a day later, on December 28, by a similar offer, this time made by the head of the Soviet delegation, Sharaf Rashidov, in a speech to the Political Commission:

> The Soviet Union renders disinterested help to the peoples of Asia and Africa in developing their economy and particularly their industries. It establishes mutually advantageous economic relations, the aim of which is raising the peoples' living standards. The liberated peoples accept this help with satisfaction, for we do not attach to it any strings, political, military, or others. We do

not interfere in the internal affairs of the countries that are getting our aid. We are guided by one feeling, one aspiration, one aim only, and that is peace and friendship between peoples.

Rashidov concluded his speech with the following words: "The end of slavery is near! The fresh wind of freedom and independence disperses the gloomy clouds of colonial slavery! The sun of freedom and independence is already shining over the road peoples have taken."

The inference was plain. The peoples of Asia and Africa were on the road towards freedom and independence, and were being helped along by the generous and altruistic aid of the Soviet Union. Rashidov's and Arzoumanian's speeches admirably sum up the public attitude taken by the Soviet Union at the Cairo conference and indeed at all forthcoming Afro-Asian conventions. This attitude was pragmatic, offering aid, decrying any attempt at overt influence and pressure, and, at the same time, attacking imperialism, colonialism and neo-colonialism, the enemies of the peoples of Asia and Africa struggling for full freedom and independence.

Despite the great diversity in the five-hundred-odd delegates present, there was surprisingly little dissent and argument concerning these themes. The conference was dominated from the start by a militant anti-Western line, and few delegates stood out against this common mood.[25]

Not surprisingly, the general declaration of the conference and the dozens of resolutions passed "by acclaim" reflected the militant anti-Western attitude. The Cairo declaration made very different reading from its Bandung predecessor, despite the claim to follow in its footsteps. Above all, the declaration linked the preservation of peace in the world with the liquidation of imperialism:

The Afro-Asian peoples believe that imperialistic domination, foreign exploitation and the other evils which result from the subjugation of peoples are a denial of the fundamental rights of man and a violation of the UN Charter, apart from the other harmful effects of both governments and governed, which impede the development of peace and international cooperation. The continued existence of imperialism is not compatible with the new era the world is now passing through.

Delegates from China addressing an Afro-Asian conference in Cairo in 1961.

One of the more important regional conferences held in the Third World was the so-called "Casablance conference" in 1961 of eight militant African states. This picture, taken after the first session of the conference, shows, from left to right, Mr. Fehrat Abbas (FLN), Mr. Nkrumah (Ghana), Mr. Sékou Touré (Guinea), Mr. Modibo Keita (Mali), the King of Morocco and his youngest son Prince Moulay Abdallah.

The political and economic resolutions were much more specific. The political resolutions condemned imperialism in the Cameroons, Kenya, Uganda, Chad, Togo, Madagascar, Yemen, the Arabian Gulf, Indonesia, Okinawa, Cyprus, Goa, Korea, Vietnam, Morocco, Somaliland, Algeria, "Palestine" and the Arab nation.[26] Other political resolutions called for support for the forthcoming conference against atom and hydrogen bombs,[27] and for the seating of China and Mongolia in the United Nations. The opening of the economic resolution was no less forthright: "The peoples of Asia and Africa who have achieved political independence are determined to continue their struggle against all forms of colonialism and imperialism and particularly to secure the complete economic independence of their countries."

However, perhaps the most important resolutions were those dealing with the organizational aspects of the Solidarity Movement. Here the departure from Bandung was complete. Whereas the participants at Bandung were purposefully vague regarding any institutionalization of Bandung-type Afro-Asian conferences, the organizers of the Cairo conference went to the opposite extreme. The resolution on organization stated specifically that "the Afro-Asian Peoples' Solidarity Conference, realizing the importance of continuing and developing the work for solidarity among the Afro-Asian peoples, resolves to establish a permanent organization to carry out the following tasks:

1. To implement and put into practice the resolutions and recommendations of the conference.
2. To promote and strengthen the Afro-Asian Solidarity movements in all countries of the two continents.
3. To act as a permanent liaison between the solidarity movements in the various countries."

Furthermore the conference decided that the permanent organization would be composed of an Afro-Asian Peoples' Solidarity Council on which each country would be represented by one delegate, and which would be convened at least once a year, and a Permanent Secretariat consisting of one secretary-general and ten secretaries. The headquarters of this Secretariat was to be at Cairo until the next conference meeting; the secretary-general was to be nominated by

Egypt, and the ten secretaries were to be nominated by the Cameroons, China, Ghana, India, Indonesia, Iraq, Japan, Sudan, Syria and the USSR.

These organizational decisions were put speedily into effect. The first meeting of the council was held in Cairo on January 3, 1958, two days after the ending of the conference; an Egyptian, Yūsuf as-Sibā'i, was elected president of the council, and representatives of the Soviet Union, Algeria, India, and the Sudan were elected vice-presidents. Soon afterwards the Egyptians nominated Yūsuf as-Sibā'i as sec-retary-general, and the Secretariat began functioning, aided by a large Egyptian technical staff.

In contrast to the previous half-hearted attempts to set up Asian and African organizations, this one was quick off the mark, acting with professional efficiency. The last delegates to the conference had not yet left Cairo when the Secretariat had already begun functioning in its handsome offices supplied by the Egyptian government. Previous meetings in Asia and Africa had produced no institutionalized follow-up, whereas the Cairo conference gave birth to a ramified organization of committees, institutions, and daughter organizations. As the Secre-tariat began functioning, it had before it the conference's proposals to establish seven subordinate organizations,[28] and to plan four new conferences.[29]

Thus, the Afro-Asian Movement received a new impetus. This new drive centered on Cairo was, however, very different in both form and context from the previous Afro-Asian activity revolving around the New Delhi and Jakarta axis. Even the transfer of the centre of ac-tivity from New Delhi to Cairo indicated the nature of this change. The Indians were now to play a much less decisive role in the Afro-Asian Movement, their place being increasingly taken by the more militant Egyptians. Of much greater significance was the emergence of the Soviet Union as one of the new leaders of the Afro-Asia reflected in the Solidarity Movement. It was the Soviet Union, together with Communist China and Egypt, which covered the expenses of the conference; these three countries were to cover virtually the entire budget of all subsequent activities of the Solidarity Movement. Again, the delegates of these three countries were the most active in formu-lating the conference resolutions, and in particular the key question of organization. For the Soviet Union in particular, the political advantages of this new movement were plain: it had made possible the Soviet Union's entry into the Afro-Asian bloc, from which she had been kept out at Bandung; it mobilized the only organized Afro-Asian body into a militantly anti-Western direction; and it provided the Soviet Union with an admirable channel through which the Russians could approach, influence and win over the delegates from Asia and Africa, of whom many, particularly among the latter, were leading nationalists in their own countries and for whom the Solidarity Movement provided their first contact with Soviet officials. Above all, the Soviet Union succeeded in equating the aspirations of the Afro-Asian Movement as expressed at Cairo — namely, to liberate these countries from all vestiges of colonialism and imperialism— with those of the Socialist camp. This was one of the points most stressed before and after the conference by Communist propaganda.[30] The Russians had every reason to be pleased with the success of the Cairo conference. Soviet Premier Bulganin wrote to Abdel Nasser immediately after the conference:

> I should like to express to you the Soviet government's sincere satisfaction with the results of the recent Cairo Conference of Afro-Asian Solidarity. We fully share the conference's appraisal of the international situation, particularly in Africa and Asia, and we are in warm sympathy with those measures for the solution of urgent international problems for which the conference expressed its support.[31]

This success, from the Soviet point of view, would not have been possible without the active cooperation of the Egyptians.[32] For although the first initiative for the establishment of the Solidarity Movement had come from the Communist-controlled WPC, the Communists on no account wished the movement to be considered Communist. From the Communist point of view the greater the appeal of the Solidarity Movement to the genuine African and Asian nationalists, the more advantageous it would be to them. Such an appeal would manifestly not be great if the movement had its headquarters in a Communist country and if the Communists openly directed and manipulated it. They therefore needed a non-Communist ally, who would make the cause of the Solidarity Movement his own aims, without caring whether these coincided with Communist objectives or not. India was out of the question, for Nehru had studiously avoided taking on the mantle of Afro-Asian leadership. President Nasser proved to be the ideal answer. The Egyptians had their own reasons for throwing their weight behind the Solidarity Movement. By the end of 1957 they were embarking on an increasingly activist foreign policy, one of the basic tenets of which was to extend and deepen Egyptian influence in Afro-Asia and in particular in the Arab world and Africa. By 1957 the Egyptians were becoming increasingly conscious of the African continent, and the role they would be able to play there in view of their advanced position compared with that of any other country on the continent excepting South Africa.[33] Whereas Nehru had stepped back, conscious of India's great size and of the fears entertained by India's smaller neighbours—Ceylon, Burma, and Nepal as well as the countries of South-East Asia—for any signs of Indian attempts to assume the role of a big power, Abdel Nasser had no such qualms. His foreign policy was militantly nationalistic. He wished to put Egypt on the world map as a force to be reckoned with. Thus the offer to transform Cairo into the centre of the Afro-Asian Movement was tempting in the extreme. The underlying Communist connotations to the offer were evidently not sufficient to deter him, while the militantly anti-Western tendency of the Solidarity Movement fitted well into Egyptian attitudes in 1957, one year after the Suez affair.

For all these reasons, the Egyptians agreed to become one of the principal organizers and moving powers in the Afro-Asian Peoples' Solidarity Organization. Their reward was the choice of Cairo as the home for the Permanent Secretariat, and the nomination of an Egyptian to the post of secretary-general. The importance which the Egyptians attached to this reward is underlined by the fact that as-Sibā'i has remained secretary-general, and Cairo the home of the Secretariat, despite all the storms which have buffeted AAPSO since its establishment and the opprobrium with which it has been regarded by much of the world.

NOTES

1 Chairman of the Soviet Peace Organization and a prominent Soviet writer. The choice of Tikhonov as head of the Soviet delegation would indicate that the Russians, at that time, still viewed the New Delhi conference as an Asian projection of the World Peace Organization.

2 According to the diplomatic correspondent of *The Times,* London, 24.12.1957. According to Homer A. Jack, who made special studies of the Bandung and Cairo conferences, a national committee was organized in India and Japan in October 1955, in China in February 1956, in Russia and North Korea in May 1956 and in North Vietnam in October 1956. See his *Cairo: The Afro-Asian Peoples' Solidarity Conference,* p. 9.

3 See, *The Afro-Asian Solidarity Committee,* Saigon, 1958, p. 16; see also Guy Wint, in *Burma Star,* Rangoon, 30.11.57: "ostensibly the committees have a comprehensive membership. They aim at enlisting members of Parliament, writers, university professors and intellectuals. The Communists keep in the background. But in many of the countries they succeed in harmonizing the pronouncements of the Solidarity Committees with the tactics of the Communist Party."

4 According to Egyptian sources, these decisions were taken at a meeting of the General Committee for Asian Solidarity at New Delhi on 29.12.56, which was attended by representatives from Burma, the Soviet Union, Pakistan, Vietnam, Mongolia, Japan, Korea, Nepal, Egypt and India. See *Scribe,* Winter, 1957–58, p. 17; also *Le Progres Egyptienne,* Numéro Spécial, January 1958, p. 9.

5 According to an article by Mursi Sa'd ed-Din, technical director of the AAPSO permanent Secretariat, in *Ghana Evening News,* 30.4.1965.

6 *The Times, loc. cit.* According to *Afro-Asian Solidarity Committee, op. cit.,* p. 73: "President Nasser accepted this suggestion with the illusion that he would be the leader of the Afro-Asian bloc."

7 *The Times, loc. cit.* A similar argument was made by *Washington Daily News,* 3.1.1958: "Though the Reds are in nominal minority on the control board, Russia and Red Chinese members will control. It will be vastly

more effective for Mr. Krushchev's purpose than any cominform because this one is disguised as a Nationalist independence movement . . . ."

[8] *Nation*, Rangoon, 25.11.57.

[9] See, for example, *Tokio Aschi Evening News*, 10.12.1957; *Mainichi Tokio*, 25.1.58; *Japan Times*, Tokyo, 12.1.1958; *Hindustan Standard*, Calcutta, 28.12.57; *Indian Express*, Bombay, 31.12.1957; *Manila Times*, 27.12.57.

[10] The Polish trade union paper *Glos Pracy Izvestia*, 26.12.1957, quoted in *Polish Facts and Figures*, 11.1.58, describes the Cairo conference as the second meeting of representatives of Asia and Africa after Bandung.

[11] *Jen min Jih Pao*, 26.12.1957, quoted in *La Documentation Francaise: Articles et Documents*, Paris, No. 0.599, 31.12.1957.

[12] *Al-Ahrām*, 26.12.57.

[13] These included several delegations whose countries were never again represented at an Afro-Asian Solidarity Conference: Afghanistan, Bahrain, Burma, Ethiopia, Madagascar and Togo. According to H. A. Jack, *ibid.*, p. 9, invitations had been sent to fifty-three countries.

[14] According to Sharaf Rashidov, head of the Soviet delegation, later Soviet representative on the Permanent Secretariat of AAPSO and one of the movement's most active members—*Afro-Asian People's Solidarity Conference, Cairo, 26.1 2.57–1.1.58*, Moscow, 1958. At the time of the conference Rashidov was president of the Uzbek SSR and vice-president of the Presidium of the Supreme Soviet of the USSR. The fact that the Russians chose an Asian Muslim to head their delegation has significance.

[15] In conferences held after the Cairo meeting, the Permanent Secretariat of AAPSO would decide who should be invited.

[16] Some of these countries were represented by government officials. Thus, Sudan's delegation was headed by that country's minister of interior, and minister for foreign affairs, the Syrian delegation was headed by the chairman of the Foreign Affairs Committee of the Syrian National Assembly, while the Egyptian head of delegation served as the vice-president of the Egyptian National Assembly.

[17] Exceptions to this rule appear to have been Japan, whose delegation was led by five members of the government Liberal Democratic Party, and Ethiopia, whose delegation received permission from the emperor before leaving for Cairo. Both of these delegations were moderate in tone throughout the conference, but in later AAPSO conferences the Japanese delegation completely changed in composition and became one of the most militantly pro-Communist of them all, while the Ethiopians withdrew from the organization altogether.

[18] He represented Jordan at every single AAPSO assembly since Cairo, although still living in exile.

[19] For a full list of delegations at the AAPSO conference held in February 1967, see Appendix 2.

[20] *Afro-Asian Peoples' Solidarity Conference, op. cit.*, p. 48. Also printed in *Scribe*, Winter 1957–58, p. 18, and several other newspapers.

[21] Deputy leader of the Egyptian delegation. A member of the National Assembly, and one of the original group of officers who organized the revolution against King Farouk.

[22] Romesh Chandra in the Indian Communist weekly, *New Age*, 26.1.1958.

[23] Thus Romesh Chandra's article (*op. cit.*) was significantly entitled: "Cairo gives Flesh and Blood to Bandung Spirit." Dr. Anup Singh, of the Indian delegation, declared "Let the Cairo conference be the peoples' Bandung." The phrase "Peoples' Bandung" was coined by a number of speakers and journalists. The spirit and principles of Bandung were mentioned in the messages of greeting sent to the Cairo conference by Mao Tse-tung, by Ho Chi Minh, by Professor Frédéric Joliot-Curie, chairman of the WPC, and by the National Assembly of Egypt.

[24] *Afro-Asian Peoples' Solidarity Conference, op. cit.*, pp. 48–49.

[25] The delegations which followed a moderate line at the conference were from Burma, Ethiopia, Ghana and Tunisia. The following are some examples of delegates who refused to accept the militant policies of the majority:

> The Tunisians protested at the presence of exiles and refugees as delegates, but waived their protest when they saw that no one supported them;
>
> two Lebanese delegates protested against the participation of Soviet delegates in the disarmament committee on the grounds that the Soviet Union was manufacturing nuclear weapons and was a part of the cold war. Their protest passed unheeded and they left the conference in disgust;
>
> the Ghanaian delegate declared in a press conference that in his opinion the Soviet intervention in Hungary was a form of imperialism to no less an extent than French activities in Africa;
>
> the Burmese delegation protested the presence of a Palestinian delegation on the ground that the Palestinians were not representatives of any country. Later, the Burmese protested against the anti-Israel resolution, but without effect; A paragraph accusing the US of atrocities in Korea was removed from one of the resolutions after several delegates objected to it.

These dissensions found no place in the final resolutions which were accepted "by acclaim." This has proved to be the system followed by all future AAPSO conferences—the chairman would read out the resolution and the delegates would register their approval by clapping. As no votes have been taken, there is no way of knowing if all the delegates approved of resolutions, and how large the number of objectors has been.

26 The resolution on the Arab nation condemned the 1955 Baghdad Pact and the Eisenhower doctrine and called for unity, freedom and independence from foreign influence.

27 The fourth such conference was to be held in August 1958 in Tokyo, organized by the World Peace Council (WPC).

28 These were:

An Afro-Asian Economic Committee, to collect and publish statistics and information about Asian and African countries, and to promote economic relations among them.

An Economic Committee for Dependent Countries, to study the economic problems of the dependent countries.

An Afro-Asian Trade Union Federation, proposed by the Labour and Cooperatives subcommittee of the Economic Committee of the conference. It was also suggested that a permanent council to propagate trade unions in Afro-Asian countries should be set up in Cairo.

An Afro-Asian Cooperative Union, proposed by the same subcommittee.

An Afro-Asian Federation for Women.

An Afro-Asian Youth Union. An "interim bureau for youth welfare" affiliated to the Secretariat was proposed until the Union of Afro-Asian Youth was set up.

An Afro-Asian Medical Committee. The Secretariat was instructed to set up a "permanent body for medical pharmaceutical and social services for the Afro-Asian countries."

29 These were:

An Afro-Asian youth conference, to be held in 1958 in Egypt, India or Indonesia.

Afro-Asian youth festivals, at regular intervals.

Conference of Afro-Asian Chambers of Commerce, to be held in Cairo at the end of 1958.

The first conference of Afro-Asian writers, to be held in Tashkent in the autumn of 1958.

30 For example the organ of the Indian Communist Party, *New Age*, 29.12. 1957, declared: "The artificial wall that imperialism has all along striven so hard to build between the underdeveloped countries of Asia and Africa on the one hand and the countries of the Socialist camp on the other, has been powerfully breached, thanks to sincere efforts from both sides, efforts that have been guided by a solid community of interests." See also a speech by Kuo Mo-jo, president of the Chinese Afro-Asian

Solidarity Committee, on 14.12.1957: "The solidarity of the peoples in the Socialist countries, the former colonial and now independent nations and the peace-loving people of the whole world now predominates over the forces of imperialism"— *New Age, ibid.*

[31] Bulganin's letter to Nasser was published in Moscow on 15.1.1958.

[32] Thus, the *New York Times*, on 3.1.1958 wrote: "President Gamal Abdel Nasser of Egypt has in effect granted the Soviet bloc a base in Egypt from which Communists may direct and finance anti-Western movements and rebellions throughout Africa. . . . The proposed headquarters could not be established without President Nasser's approval . . . what has occurred, therefore, is tantamount to a deal between President Nasser and the Soviet bloc to allow Cairo to become the nerve center for a vast campaign of subversion and rebellion against all Western interests in the area." Jack called the Cairo conference "a marriage of convenience between President Nasser of Egypt and Asian Communism" — Jack, *Cairo,* p. 1.

[33] This consciousness can be seen in numerous articles and speeches by Egyptian leaders as well as in the now famous passages on Egypt's role in Africa in Abdel Nasser's *Philosophy of the Revolution*, Cairo (n.d.).

8 THE SOLIDARITY MOVEMENT TAKES ROOT

As if the sluice gates had suddenly been opened, the Cairo conference of December 1957 marked the beginnings of a tremendous thrust forward of renewed Afro-Asian activity. But now this activity was centred on Cairo and the Solidarity Movement. Official Afro-Asian governmental cooperation was relegated to second place, and New Delhi and Jakarta became provincial backwaters in the Afro-Asian world. Its new capital was Cairo, with Conakry and Algiers becoming increasingly important as the new Solidarity Movement took root. The Communist capitals remained discreetly in the background.

The Permanent Secretariat of AAPSO, now housed in its headquarters in the Maniel quarter of Cairo, organized and directed the new Afro-Asian activity. The Solidarity Movement gradually broadened to include a wide number of activities on different levels. First was the conference of Afro-Asian writers, which opened in Tashkent in October 1958; it was followed in December by the conference of Afro-Asian Chambers of Commerce, in Cairo. Two months later, in February 1959, Cairo played midwife to the birth of the Afro-Asian Youth Movement, and in the same month the Council of AAPSO convened in the Egyptian capital. In the months and years to follow new organizations, committees, seminars and conferences on a mass of subjects were planned and implemented, mainly by the Cairo AAPSO Secretariat. The first conference of Afro-Asian women was held in Cairo in January 1961, a conference of youth was held in Cairo in February 1959, and there was a journalists' conference in April 1963 at Jakarta. The first lawyers' conference was held in Damascus before the Cairo conference, and the following, organized by the Secretariat, took place in Conakry, Guinea, on October 15–20, 1962. A doctors' conference was held in Cairo on October 24, 1964. Conferences were held on housing (Cairo, Decem-

144

ber 7, 1963), rural development (New Delhi, April 17, 1963), railways (Cairo, October 10, 1962), and insurance (Cairo, September 3, 1964). There were economic seminars—one not organized by the Secretariat, was held in Pyongyang, North Korea, in June 1964; a second, under Secretariat auspices, was held in Algiers in February 1965. The Solidarity Fund held its first meeting in Conakry in February 1961, and had a number of subsequent sessions in the Guinean capital. (See also Appendix 1.) Emergency meetings on the situation in Congo and special committees for aid to Algeria also convened. From the Cairo Solidarity Conference in December 1957 to the end of 1962 a total of twenty-three Afro-Asian conferences, seminars and special committees had been convened, and of these twelve, or more than half, took place in Cairo. Only one—the second Afro-Asian Conference for Economic Cooperation—was held in New Delhi.

The two conferences held in 1958 were of special interest. The writers' conference, which opened in the Navoi Theatre in Tashkent on October 7, 1958, was the only major Afro-Asian event to take place in the Soviet Union, and reflected the Soviet anxiety in the early days of the Solidarity Movement to underline its presence as a bona fide Asian member of the movement. According to *Pravda*[1] more than two hundred delegates from thirty-nine Afro-Asian states attended the meeting. Whether all were writers is open to question. Certainly most of the speeches were highly political, ranging widely beyond the main subject of discussion, which was "the development of literature and culture in the various countries of the two continents and their role in the struggle for the progress of mankind, for national independence, against colonialism, and, for freedom and peace throughout the whole world"[2]—a wide enough subject. The Soviet hosts, however, were very circumspect not to transform the conference into open Communist propaganda; indeed, the word "Communism" was hardly once heard throughout the week-long deliberations, the term "Socialism" being preferred. But the Russians laid great stress on Tashkent as a natural continuation of Bandung. Typical was the *Pravda* headline: "Bandung—Delhi—Cairo—Tashkent."[3] Once more, however, there was a departure from the Bandung precedent by laying particular stress on organizational questions; the relevant resolution called for the establishment of a permanent office of Afro-Asian writers in Colombo.[4] An Egyptian offer to play host to a second conference of Afro-Asian writers in Cairo in 1960 was accepted.

The Russians had much less cause to feel satisfied with the second conference held in 1958, that of the Afro-Asian Chambers of Commerce, which opened in Cairo on December 8. The conference had been the brainchild of the 1957 meeting of Arab Chambers of Commerce in Beirut, but had been adopted by the AAPSO Cairo conference and incorporated in its resolutions. However, in contrast to the help it gave other activities of the Solidarity Movement, the Permanent Secretariat in Cairo did not take an active role in preparing the conference, preferring to leave the arrangements entirely in the hands of the Egyptian and other Arab chambers of commerce.

The conference was viewed with foreboding by much of the Western press. It was feared that the Soviet Union would exploit the holding of this first purely Afro-Asian economic conference to launch a large-scale bid for economic preponderance in the countries of Asia and Africa. Thus, *The Times,* in London, commented ten days before the beginning of the conference:

> The AAPSO, which was established in Cairo almost exactly a year ago, is about to reach a climax in its work for the year. There are unconfirmed reports in some Arab newspapers that Mr. Khrushchev will attend the meeting of the Afro-Asian Economic conference which is being organized for December 8th. This seems improbable, but reflects the extent of Communist interest. . . . The Afro-Asian Economic conference will have before it an Egyptian proposal to set up a permanent economic secretariat in Cairo, and there is every likelihood that the Soviet Government, which sent a large delegation last year, will this year announce further and substantial economic support for the the Afro-Asian movement. Future Communist economic aid might well be channelled to African countries through the proposed economic secretariat. [5]

Returning to the subject of the proposed economic secretariat a few days later, *The Times* commented: "No doubt Colonel Nasser suffers this cuckoo in his nest as a means to his own African ambitions." [6]

In the event, *The Times,* and those whose views coincided with those of *The Times,* need not have worried so much. Delegates from thirty-nine countries attended the opening of the conference, including representatives from the Soviet Union, Communist China, North Korea, North Vietnam and Mongolia. But at the beginning of the opening session it became clear that the conference was not going to proceed according to plan; members of chambers of commerce are not ideal promoters of revolutionary ideas, and the absence of the professional guiding hand of the AAPSO Secretariat in the preparations soon became apparent in the organizational chaos that followed. The two main items on the agenda were the European Common Market and its effect on the economies of the Afro-Asian countries, and the possibility of setting up an Afro-Asian common market. However, politics soon intruded into what many delegates had expected would be a serious, professional discussion on the economic aspects of the two items on the agenda. "Unless politics are excluded, many nations will not come back to another meeting like this," declared the delegate from the Philippines, at a press conference. He revealed that no rules or procedures had been drawn up at the conference and that the eight-nation preparatory committee had appointed itself as steering committee as well, without reference to the plenary session. "A picture of confusion behind the scenes at the Afro-Asian economic conference emerged here tonight," commented *The Times*.[7] Neither the Russians nor the Egyptians could gain any satisfaction from the opening of what should have been one of the major events in the Afro-Asian Movement. A Russian proposal that "Anglo-American aggression" in the Near East should be condemned was rejected by the majority of those present. The Russian presence was strongly attacked by a number of delegates, especially by the Indonesian Muhammad Soebehan, who demanded that only those who had attended the Bandung conference, or who had become independent since then, should be allowed to attend. This met with the approval of the businessmen of Asia and Africa, who, at a later meeting, excluded the Russians altogether from their organization.

The Egyptians fared better. But their bid to create a permanent economic secretariat, parallel to the AAPSO Secretariat in Cairo, was only partially successful. The Indians, obviously annoyed at this concentration of power in Cairo, objected. The resolution had to be amended to provide for the secretariat to remain in Cairo only "until

The large trading shed at the back of the headquarters of the Parti Démocratique de Guinée in Conakry which was converted into a conference hall to hold the Second Assembly of the Afro-Asian Peoples' Solidarity Organization in April 1961.

such time as [the organization's] charter is finally confirmed." The Indians had their own interests in this body: when the second conference of Afro-Asian Chambers of Commerce met in New Delhi on December 11, 1961, Prime Minister Nehru himself opened the conference; moreover, of the two hundred delegates attending, the Indians sent, in addition to their eleven-man official delegation, twenty-four representatives of the Export Developing Council, fourteen representatives of Indian government ministries and sixty-six observers![8]

Despite the inauspicious beginning of this Afro-Asian economic get-together, a permanent organization was set up, which became known as the Afro-Asian Organization for Economic Cooperation (AFRASEC). An Egyptian, Muhammad Rif'at, was elected secretary-general. The aim of the organization was defined as to bring about an increase in the economic collaboration between national federations of chambers of commerce in member countries. Resolutions on the need for the exchange of technical and financial aid, for greater trade cooperation, and for the need to industrialize in the face of the threat from the European Common Market, were passed. *The Times* was no longer worried: "There is little prospect of this organization doing more than coordinate some studies of the real problems which underline all the other resolutions adopted by the conference, none of which has had any real discussion,"[9] adding that the conference "had little to show for its four days of discussion."[10]

The first real test of the Afro-Asian Solidarity Movement, however, was not to come until its second plenary assembly, which was held in Conakry from April 11–15, 1960. The Parti Démocratique de Guinée had agreed to act as hosts, and an advance party of the Cairo Secretariat visited the Guinean capital in October 1959 to coordinate preparations. Invitations were sent out to organizations in sixty-seven countries. In addition three international organizations were invited to send delegations and a delegation was invited from Gaza.

Delegations from forty-nine countries and territories (an additional delegation comprised Palestine refugees) attended the opening of the conference in the large "Trading-factory" at the back of the party headquarters, which had been converted into a conference hall.[11] Some five hundred people—delegates, observers, journalists and guests—crowded into the large store shed to hear President

Sékou Touré deliver the opening speech. Huge banners welcoming the delegates and proclaiming Afro-Asian solidarity were strung across the shed; others proclaimed the motto of the conference: *"Peuples d'Afrique et d'Asie Unissez-Vous pour la Liberté, L'Égalité et la Paix."* Outside the flags of the participating countries hung limp in the April heat of the West African coast, while hundreds of women members of the Parti Démocratique de Guinée, dressed in gaily coloured clothes, swayed and danced to the sound of xylophones and drums. A gay festive atmosphere pervaded the entire proceedings. This was the first time an international conference of such size, bringing so many people from outside the African continent, was held in an African country south of the Sahara, and the African delegates as well as the Guinean onlookers were proudly conscious of the fact. This was indeed the first time that the Africans began to assert themselves within the Afro-Asian Movement. Until the Conakry conference they had played the role of junior partner, with the Asians and Arabs taking the initiative and calling the tune. Now, for the first time, the African voice began to be heard: Guinea, Mali, Ghana, Congo, the delegates from the non-independent territories under Portuguese and British colonial rule and other African delegations began to take an increasingly active interest.

Despite this shift of emphasis, however, the proceedings at Conakry were still largely directed by the Cairo Secretariat: by the Communist members on one hand, and the Egyptians on the other. The conference agenda,[12] as well as the key draft resolutions was prepared beforehand by the Secretariat, mainly by the Indian delegate, H. D. Malaviya, a Communist, who was generally considered to be the most gifted in formulating resolutions and speeches. Yet the Communists, from the beginning of the conference, went out of their way to be pliable and avoid annoying non-Communists. Typical of this attitude was their behaviour in the key subcommittee for peaceful coexistence and disarmament set up within the framework of the conference's political committee. The subcommittee had been presented with a "draft resolution for discussion" which had been prepared by Malaviya. It contained a strong attack on CENTO and on SEATO, as well as on the "powerful US base" in Taiwan. On the other hand the draft proposed that "this conference expresses its appreciation of the initiative taken by the USSR in the lessening of international tensions," and called for a conference within four months of "Afro-Asian peoples and all other peace forces." The proposal had the blessing of the Cairo Secretariat; both the Communists and the Egyptian secretary-general had approved it. In the subcommittee the proposal met with considerable opposition. The Pakistani delegate objected strongly to any mention of CENTO and SEATO. The Iranian concurred, declaring that the resolution should be a general one, without mentioning specific treaties. Whereupon, without further discussion, the Chinese chairman of the committee agreed to the changes, and the resolution was completely rewritten, leaving out any mention of specific treaties, bases, etc.

Similarly, the opening sentence of the Secretariat's draft resolution for the economic committee read: "This conference declares that the new type of relationship which is fast growing between the countries of Africa and Asia and the states with centrally planned national economics, especially the Soviet Union, is a source of strength and confidence to us." After some discussion this was changed to: "The conference declares that the new type of relationship which is growing between the countries of Africa and Asia and the friendly and anti-imperialist countries is a source of strength and confidence to us." The Communists, all smiles, offered no objection to the change.

There was only one committee in which the Communists proved to be less accommodating, and this was in the key committee on organization and statute. As in the other committees, the Secretariat had prepared a draft proposal. This one, heavily weighed to favour Egypt, called for the continuation of the Secretariat in Cairo, for the cooption of Guinea and Rhodesia to its members, and for the re-election of Yūsuf as-Sibā'i as secretary-general. However, the Chinese delegate objected.[13] He claimed it was necessary to widen the basis of the Solidarity Movement. A more democratic and more efficient organization was needed. He proposed the following reorganization:

The General Assembly should meet once every two years as before;
a Council of heads of delegations should meet every year;
an Executive Committee of twenty-seven members, to be elected by the Council, should meet every six months, and it should supervise and direct the work of the Secretariat;

Mrs. Rameshwari Nehru, head of the Indian delegation at the Conakry AAPSO Assembly, seated next to Mr. Ismail Touré, of Guinea, who chaired the sessions.

The Conakry AAPSO Assembly: At the far right is Mr. Joshua M. Nkomo, the Zimbabwe leader. At the extreme left is Mr. M. Sipalo, who, at the time of the Assembly, was national secretary of the United National Independence Party of N. Rhodesia.

a Permanent Secretariat of twelve members should be elected by the Executive Committee and be answerable to it.

In the opinion of the Chinese delegate it would be good for the Solidarity Movement as a whole if the Secretariat was not permanently located in the same country and if the post of secretary-general was rotated every two years.

The Chinese declaration brought the atmosphere of euphoria which had existed at the conference until then to an abrupt end. At least in the opinion of the Egyptian delegates, the mailed fist was appearing beneath the velvet glove. They were dismayed at the prospect of the Secretariat being transferred from Cairo, and, largely with the help of their Uganda ally, John Kale, made frantic efforts to organize opposition to the Chinese proposal. The impasse appeared complete. Eventually, however, an agreement was reached according to which an Executive Committee "to direct the Secretariat" was to be established, while the Secretariat itself was to remain in Cairo with Yūsuf as-Sibā'i as secretary-general.[14] The Egyptians maintained their predominating influence in the Solidarity Movement, with Cairo its unchallenged centre. The Communists had strengthened their hold on the Egyptians by establishing the supervising Executive Committee, and at the same time they maintained the unity of the movement as a whole behind a respectable, non-Communist "front," namely, the Egyptians. The compromise was made possible because both the Communists and the Egyptians were, each for their own reasons, keenly interested in the success of the conference and of the Solidarity Movement as a whole.

The Conakry conference thus served to consolidate the Solidarity Movement and to widen its base. The speeches and resolutions served to underline the anti-imperialistic, and thus anti-Western, nature of the movement, to which both Communists and non-Communist nationalists subscribed. The Ugandan John Kale, speaking at Conakry, summed up this strengthened unity of the movement: "A firm ideological conviction of an organization is the main cohesive force that keeps it together . . . this movement should be built on our unifying common denominator of anti-imperialism as its foundation-stone." From the Communist point of view the success of the movement and the strengthening of its organizational structure were of

considerably greater importance than the wording of the political
and economic resolutions. Many delegates, particularly those from
Africa, left the conference convinced that the Communists were in a
a small minority and had had no great influence on the conference
proceedings. These delegates pointed to their "victories" in modifying
extremist passages in some of the resolutions as proof of their conten-
tion.

Indeed, it appeared immediately after the Conakry conference
as if the Communists were having second thoughts concerning an
Afro-Asian Movement centred on a non-Communist country.
The Soviet and Chinese members of the Secretariat did not return
to Cairo. The pro-Communist Indian member returned home.
No financial contributions were received. For six months the continued life of the organization hung in the balance until in November
the Communists returned with renewed force for the first meeting
of the Executive Committee. Here they demonstrated once more
that they were the directing force behind the Solidarity Movement.

The AAPSO Executive Committee met for the first time on
November 9, 1960, in Beirut, under the chairmanship of the Lebanese
minister of education, Kamāl Jumblāṭ. This time the tone of the
meeting was much sharper, the proposals more extremely anti-
Western, than at Conakry. Whereas at Conakry the British and the
French, as classic colonialist powers, had been singled out for attack,
the main target now became the US, which was accused of creating
a new colonialism and of retarding the progress of the liberation
movements. The Congo was a central subject, and the Egyptians
in particular strongly attacked the UN for its stand on that issue.[15]
One of the decisions called for the creation of a special committee
for financial assistance to Afro-Asian national liberation movements.
Another saluted the Cuban struggle against the US, and, for the first
time within the Solidarity Movement, a call was made to contact
the popular movements in Latin America to form a united front
against imperialism. Again the main clashes during the meeting were
reserved for organizational matters. This time the cudgel against
the Egyptians was taken up by the Tunisian delegate, who demanded
a reduction in the authority of the secretary-general, and that the
the Secretariat be moved every one or two years to a different country.
He was supported by the Guinean and Indonesian delegates. In the

The Assembly of the Afro-Asian Peoples' Solidarity Organization convenes at Conakry, Guinea, in April 1961: the UAR delegation is headed by Mr. Anwar as-Sadāt. Next to him is the late Mr. Fuād Galal, the adviser on African Affairs at the Egyptian presidency.

The Soviet delegation at the Second Assembly of AAPSO, Conakry, Guinea, April 1961. Seated in the first row to the right is Mr. Tursun-Zade. The pipe-smoking delegate is Prof. Potekhin, the late leading Soviet Africanist.

heated discussion which followed the Egyptian stand was, significantly enough, saved largely by the support of the Soviet delegate. By now it was amply clear to the Egyptians that their favoured position in the Afro-Asian Movement depended very largely on the acquiescence of the Soviets. From the Beirut meeting onwards, the Egyptians were to cooperate to an ever increasing extent with the Soviet delegates in the movement.

The tendency to increased militancy evident at Beirut became heightened at the AAPSO council meeting which convened in Bandung on April 10, 1961.[16] The days when the presence of a Soviet delegate was questioned were past. Even in comparison with the Conakry conference the change was enormous. The Communists were now asserting themselves to a much greater extent. At Conakry there were still many delegates who believed that AAPSO had nothing to do with Communism; at Bandung there could have been only a few delegates who did not realize that the Communists were largely running the show.

The AAPSO Council meeting was held in the modern Merdeka hall where Afro-Asian history had been made exactly six years earlier. A life-size statue of Patrice Lumumba gazed out at the delegates from one corner of the platform, while outside the hall heavily armed units of the Indonesian army kept guard against possible terrorist attacks by the outlawed Dar-u-Islām. Delegates from fifty-three countries had been invited[17]; of these, delegates from forty-four countries as well as a Palestine delegation attended the conference.[18] In addition some twenty organizations received "observer" status, including the World Peace Council, the Asian Pacific Peace Liaison Committee, the International Association of Democratic Lawyers, and, as a newcomer to an Afro-Asian Solidarity conference, the Instituto Cubano de Amistad a los Pueblos (Cuban Institute for Friendship between Peoples).[19]

The meeting opened with a fiery speech by President Sukarno. He called on all representatives to lobby their governments to call for a second heads of Afro-Asian states conference, a favourite hobby-horse of the Indonesian president to which he often returned in future speeches. But his central theme was his warning that imperialism was appearing in a new form, namely that of neo-colonialism. This proved to be the main theme of nearly all the speakers. The doctrine of neo-colonialism emerged to full light at the Bandung Council meeting, and was, henceforth, to become the main target of attack of all subsequent Afro-Asian Solidarity conferences.[20] Typical of this hardening line at Bandung was the speech of the Egyptian secretary-general of AAPSO, Yūsuf as-Sibāʿi, who lashed out against the United States, the United Nations and the West in general: "In its vicious attempts to dominate the Afro-Asian world," he declared, "the neo-colonialists of the US are using the United Nations Organization by means of the mechanical majority it possesses." As-Sibāʿis' Secretariat had, by now, taken on a distinctive Communist colouring. Of the eleven members, five were open Communists; these were the delegates of the Soviet Union, China, Japan, the Cameroons and Indonesia.[21] Of the other six the new Indian member, M. Kalimullah, had once been a Communist Party member, and sided on almost every issue with the Communists, the Uganda member had studied for several years at the Karl Marx University in Leipzig, the Congolese had recently been appointed ambassador of the Congolese Rebel Government of Stanleyville to Poland, and the Algerian, Ahmed Zimerline, had lived for several years in Moscow.

Had the Communists remained united, they would have swept the board at the AAPSO Bandung meeting. But the meeting was, above all, significant as the first Afro-Asian meeting in which the subterranean rumblings of Sino-Soviet differences erupted into the open; the astonished delegates from Asia and Africa became, for the first time, witnesses to the unsavoury spectacle of rival Communist delegates shouting each other down. In the years to follow these delegates were to become tried and tired spectators of the Sino-Soviet struggle, one of whose principal outlets was the Afro-Asian Peoples' Solidarity Organization.

The trouble between the two first broke at the Bandung Council over the question of peaceful coexistence, which the Russians had raised as one of the key subjects for the political resolution. The Chinese strongly objected. Peaceful coexistence, they said, was a contradiction of terms. There could be no peaceful coexistence between the socialist camp and the imperialist and colonialist countries. The dominated cannot exist peacefully side by side with the dominators. Peaceful coexistence, they said, could only come about after colonialism in all its forms had been liquidated. This was to be one of the major subjects of the clash between the two Communist giants. But at Bandung in those spring days of 1961, there was not yet any tightening of lines across the Afro-Asian world. There was still no crystallization into two opposing and hostile camps; the Indonesians, for example, who later were to become the closest allies of the Chinese in the Solidarity Movement, sided this time with the Russians, while the Egyptians, who in the course of time were to throw their weight solidly behind the Soviet Union, here made herculean efforts to mediate between the Chinese and the Russians and thus preserve the solidarity of the Afro-Asian Movement. In this they were largely successful, due to no small extent to the skilful approach of the head of the Egyptian delegation, Fuad Galal.[22] However, that the idea of peaceful coexistence, which had been so strongly advanced by Chou En-lai and the Chinese delegates at Bandung in April 1955, should now be so strongly attacked by the Chinese delegation in that same Merdeka hall six years later indicates the measure of change which had transformed the Afro-Asian Movement from those early days of the official Bandung conference to the very different gathering at Bandung in 1961.

This conference, though, however different from the original Bandung gathering, set the tone for the future activities of the Afro-Asian Peoples' Solidarity Organization. From then until the convening of the first tri-continental conference in Havana in 1966, there was to be no more open friction between the Communists and the non-Communists on such matters as the seat of the Secretariat and organization. There were no longer discernible differences in attitudes among the members concerning issues like condemnation of the the West or support for the liberation movements. The quarrelling became introspective; differences of opinion centred on the Sino-Soviet fissure, and the Sino-Indian border dispute.

Just how far the movement went in identifying itself with Communist anti-Western propaganda can be gauged from the following words of the movement's secretary-general, the Egyptian Yūsuf as-Sibā'i, at the meeting of the Executive Committee at Gaza on December 7, 1961. The movement's duty, he said, was to reveal the collusion between imperialism and reactionary forces, such as the governments of Jordan, Turkey, Guatemala, and the "ultra-reactionary Brazzaville group." He continued:

President Sékou Touré, of Guinea, with Yusuf as-Sibāʻi, secretary-general of AAPSO, at the Conakry Assembly, April 1961.

President Ahmad Sukarno together with Yusuf as-Sibāʻi, secretary-general of AAPSO, at the Bandung Council meeting, April 1961.

... US imperialists, in particular, have been able to impose on some of our countries the so-called volunteers of the Peace Corps. Fortunately the peoples of these countries have come to know that those alleged 'volunteers of peace' are in fact espionage agents working for perpetuating the cold war and maintaining the imperialistic grip on the colonies and semi-colonies. On these grounds, public opinion demands the expulsion of these peculiar volunteers of peace.

Or again as-Sibā'i commented on the failure of the summit conference between the US and Soviet leaders due to have been held in Paris in May 1960, in the following terms:

The Permanent Secretariat for AAPSO deeply regrets the failure of the summit conference. This failure is due to the aggressive attitude taken by American militarists who are actively engaged in preparing for a new world war. . . .[23]

Despite this unison in feelings against the West, the harmony of the movement deteriorated sharply from the 1961 Bandung meeting onwards, and the history of the Solidarity Movement from that time became ever more turbulent. Rarely had a movement been named so ineptly!

The first major clash after the Bandung conference occurred within the "mother-movement" of AAPSO, the World Peace Council, during a meeting of the WPC in Stockholm from December 16–20, 1961.

At Bandung that year several speakers had spoken of the need to broaden the Solidarity Movement to include Latin America; the delegate from Ceylon had even made a formal proposal on this subject. The subject was brought up again at the Gaza meeting of the Executive Committee and it was decided to consult the World Peace Council on the matter. Subsequently, a delegation of twelve members of the Permanent Secretariat left for Stockholm in order, in their own words, to have a preliminary exchange of views on the idea of ALAAPSO with the Latin American delegates there. Shortly after arrival they met delegates from Cuba, Colombia, Ecuador, Peru, Brazil and Argentina in what was to be the first direct contact of the Afro-Asian Peoples' Solidarity Organization with the Latin

Americans to discuss the possibility of holding a tri-continental conference. The WPC leaders, however, thought that the role of the the WPC should be a much more active one in these preparations, and they organized a special plenary session devoted to discussing the proposed conference. The AAPSO delegation felt that this was going too far. It was beyond the brief they had been given in Gaza. The African members of the Secretariat objected to the way these "outsiders" were taking over the direction of a vital subject affecting the future of the movement. The Chinese, supported by the Japanese and the Guinean members of the Secretariat, formally opposed the participation of the WPC in organizing ALAAPSO. In the end, all the secretaries with the exception of the Russian and Indian delegates[24] left the session, and returned to Cairo.

This rift with the WPC represented a severe setback for the Russians, and a victory for the Chinese.[25] It explained why the entire question of broadening the Solidarity Movement was, in effect, shelved; the first tri-continental conference took place only four years later.

The Chinese were quick to take up the advantage they had gained at Stockholm. They returned to the attack against the Russians with renewed vigour in the next large Afro-Asian gathering to be held. This time it was the second conference of Afro-Asian writers, which was opened in Cairo on February 12, 1962, by Sarwat Okasha, the Egyptian minister of culture. According to the Egyptians, three hundred delegates from forty-five countries attended the conference,[26] whose main subjects on the agenda were "the role of writers in the anti-imperialistic struggle and for peace and the consolidation of the spirit of Afro-Asian solidarity." The conference opened on a tone which appeared favourable to the Russians. Okasha spoke of the conference as another landmark in the struggle for "economic, political and cultural liberty, for peace and peaceful coexistence, for general and complete disarmament"; a message from Nikita Khrushchev was read amid applause; a report was read of the work of the Colombo Bureau of Afro-Asian Writers, which stressed the need for writers to take a more active role in creating a new world, progressive and free from imperialistic domination. All this was as could be expected. But then the Chinese took over. In the words of Colin Legum: "In a discussion on war and peace they accused the

Russians of having got their priorities mixed up. They forcefully put the needling question: 'are you for peace or for African independence?' They accused the Russians of putting higher priority on disarmament and peaceful coexistence than on the colonial liberation struggle."[27] This was a heady and telling argument for the African nationalists. On the crucial question of disarmament versus the anti-imperialistic struggle, the line of the Chinese was adopted in the resolutions of the conference.[28] The Soviet disarmament proposal did not get past the committee stage.[29] Commenting on the conference, the *Times of India* reached the conclusion that there was no real "meeting of the minds" at Cairo, as the writer-delegates had been caught in "the currents and cross-currents of the Sino-Soviet cold war."[30]

Throughout 1962 the Chinese increased their pressure against the Russians within the Solidarity Movement. It was particularly felt at the conference of Afro-Asian lawyers, which convened in Conakry from October 15–20, 1962, and at the meeting of the preparatory committee for a conference of Afro-Asian journalists, which met in Jakarta from February 10–15, 1963. Both of these "daughter-organizations" of the Solidarity Movement were to become strongholds for China and her supporters. For the former, a Permanent Secretariat of Afro-Asian Lawyers was eventually established in Conakry which included a Chinese delegate, but did not include one from the Soviet Union,[31] while the latter, after hard discussion, decided that the Soviet Union should send representatives at the forthcoming journalists' conference in the guise of observers only, and not as fully fledged delegates.[32]

The climax of the Chinese offensive, however, or at least of the success of that offensive, came at the third plenary assembly of AAPSO held this time in the picturesque holiday resort of Moshi in northern Tanganyika, from February 4–10, 1963.[33] Moshi was to be the high watermark of Chinese influence in the Solidarity Movement; never again were they able to score such a victory over their Russian and Indian opponents as they succeeded in doing at that conference.

The Sino-Indian conflict had already cast its shadow across official Afro-Asian relations. It had undermined the faith of Indians, and of many others, in the formula of *Panch Sheel* and Bandung. Now it was to crack the solidarity façade of AAPSO as well. From

African delegations at an Afro-Asian conference. Above: Kenyan delegation, headed by Oginga Odinga (second from left).

Below: Cameroon delegation. On the right is Dr. Felix Moumié who was later assassinated by the French "La Main Rouge" organization. To the left is M. Ernest Onandie, who was one of the most active members of the AAPSO Secretariat in Cairo.

the beginning of the conference the conflict loomed large. The Indians were in an uncharacteristically pugnacious mood, and were determined to force the issue. To lend weight to their efforts they had sent two Congress members of parliament to head their delegation. They lost no time in submitting their draft resolution which called upon the conference to approve of the "Colombo proposals"[34] for settling the conflict "without reservation." They let it be known that India would, if necessary, quit the organization altogether if this resolution was not passed. But the Chinese objected strongly. The issue was now the subject of friendly negotiations, they argued. Any statement of the conference would serve no useful purpose. This was all very reasonable, and most Africans present agreed heartily with the Chinese stand. Why bring up family quarrels when there was the much more important business of chasing the imperialists out of Africa at hand?[35] When the political committee ruled against the Indian proposal, the Indians walked out in disgust. The Chinese carried the day and the final resolutions did not include the Indian proposal.[36] The Chinese appeared in a most attractive light at Moshi. The speech of Liu Ning-yi, head of their delegation, was very well received. He put forward a six-point proposal for unity and anti-imperialism which could not fail to impress his listeners. Included in the proposal were the following points: support for the just struggle for national independence by the people who had not yet attained independence; all countries, large or small, are equal and their independence, sovereignty and territorial integrity are sacred and inviolable; the five principles of peaceful coexistence and the principles of Bandung should be the base for cooperation and mutual assistance among the Afro-Asian countries.[37] This was the echo of Chou En-lai at Bandung, and if the words of Liu Ning-yi sounded hollow to some, in view of the Chinese border dispute with India, they expressed the feelings and sentiments of a great many of the delegates present, especially among the Africans. In comparison, the Russian emphasis on disarmament and peaceful coexistence made less impact.[38] A typical African reaction was that of Camara Mamady, of Guinea, who declared: "We are willing to have disarmament, but it cannot condition our struggle for national independence. In fact we believe that our struggles for liberty are components of peace, because in reality there can be no peace without freedom."[39]

The Africans were increasingly asserting themselves. The opening speech of President Nyerere of Tanganyika departed from the usual style and tone of AAPSO pronouncements. The president sought, instead, to restore the atmosphere of true non-alignment. "Much too often the weaker amongst us are regarded as no more than pawns in the cold war conflict," he declared. The world was witnessing a second "scramble for Africa," "not only between the capitalist powers." He underlined his point by adding that they were facing a coming international class struggle between rich and poor countries, "with capitalist and socialist countries on both sides of the conflict. This is the coming division of the world—a class, not an ideological, division."[40] The only other person who spoke in the same vein was, significantly enough, Jomo Kenyatta, given a hero's welcome when he arrived for the closing session. Kenyatta, as Nyerere before him, ignored the prevailing mood of the conference; instead, he warned the delegates "against the automatic use of slogans, of being too concerned with a fixation about imperialism, without positively defining tasks and facing the challenge of nation-building in unity." But in the heady militantly anti-imperialistic atmosphere at Moshi, this advice could hardly have much effect.[41]

Yet the Africans had hoped to be able to influence the conference, and thus the Solidarity Movement as a whole, to a much greater extent than they eventually did. The PAFMECA delegates, for example, tried to form a bloc at the initiative of Koinange, the organization's general-secretary. But the Kenya delegation was hardly existent, each member working mainly for himself; the Ugandans were weak and passive; the Northern and Southern Rhodesians were caught up in the conference in-fighting as both Russians and Chinese sought to woo them to their side, while the Tanganyikans, as hosts, were too busy and too much at the centre of things to form part of a bloc. Thus the PAFMECA block hardly got off the ground. The Tanganyikans did not hide that they were none too happy at the concentration of power in the hands of the Communists and Egyptians. "We intend to change the course of the organization," one of the delegation told a journalist. The Tanganyikans were indeed left in the all-important drafting committee, where they were represented by the able Oscar Kambona, but there is no indication that they succeeded in altering the basic aims of the movement. The

French-speaking Africans of West Africa, on the other hand, were conspicuous by their absence.

As in previous conferences, it was again in the organizational committee that the sharpest differences emerged. And again, it was the degree of cooperation with the World Peace Council on the question of Latin America which set the sparks flying. The Soviet Union, supported by India and South Africa, insisted that the WPC be given a hearing and a say on which organizations to invite from Latin America. They wished at least to give a hearing to the four Latin American members of the WPC delegation at Moshi in the the capacity of observers. The Chinese, backed by Ceylon, Indonesia, Tanganyika and Camara Mamady of Guinea, were equally insistent in their opposition to the WPC. They objected also to allowing the Latin American WPC members to be "unofficially consulted" by the organizational committee. In the event the Chinese line was adopted. An eighteen-member preparatory committee[42] was entrusted with the task of preparing a tri-continental conference.

This was a severe defeat to Soviet prestige. They had been caught napping at Moshi.[43] At the next AAPSO conference, at Nicosia, they were to come much better prepared. The Egyptians, on the other hand, had every reason to feel satisfied with the outcome of the conference. They had arrived at Moshi armed with a warmly worded message of greeting from President Nasser. As in previous conferences, they played a leading role, especially behind the scenes over such questions as the Sino-Indian conflict, of Malaya,[44] etc. This time the Egyptians sided with the Chinese more frequently than usual, probably because of the impressive manner in which the Chinese conducted their political offensive. Above all the Egyptians were pleased that at this conference no one had suggested that the Secretariat be moved from Cairo, and that the post of secretary-general be given someone else. Moreover, they had succeeded in pushing through an anti-Israel resolution although the conference was being held in a country known to be friendly to Israel.[45] This satisfaction was, however, somewhat offset by the statement made immediately after the conference by Kambona, when he commented on the resolution: "We are friends of all and have said right from the beginning that we are not going to accept the enemies chosen for us by others."[46]

The delegates dispersed after having approved by acclaim the usual resolutions condemning imperialism, supporting the national liberation movements, and calling for Afro-Asian solidarity in an even greater number of fields.[47] The Indians left disgruntled and angry. For them Moshi had been an exercise in Afro-Asian cynicism. The Russians, as borne out in the comments in the Soviet press,[48] were saddened and disillusioned by their week-long stay in the shadow of Kilimanjaro. The Africans left with mixed feelings. There were those who would agree with the spokesman of the leading political party in eastern Nigeria, the NCNC, who commented: "The unfortunate impression has been given that the purpose of the Afro-Asian conference is to provide platforms for minority elements to engage in vile propaganda against their home governments."[49] The last word in cynicism undoubtedly went to the *Sunday Nation* of Nairobi, which commented: "If the conference at Moshi has achieved anything apart from the usual resolutions, it is in revealing that even brothers can cut each others' throats."[50]

NOTES

[1] *Pravda*, 23.10.1958.

[2] See von Stackelberg, "The Spirit of Tashkent: a Review of the Conference of Afro-Asian Writers," *Bulletin of the Institute for Study of the USSR,* Vol. V, No. 12, December 1958.

[3] *Pravda*, 10.10.1958. Many delegates called the conference "a literary Bandung"—*New Age, loc. cit.*

[4] *Ibid.* Those elected to the bureau were Ghana, Indonesia, Cameroons, China, UAR, the Soviet Union, Sudan, Ceylon and Japan.

[5] *The Times*, 28.11.1958.

[6] *Ibid.*, 3.12.1958.

[7] *Ibid.*

[8] *Bangkok Post*, 13.12.1961.

[9] *The Times*, 12.12.1958.

[10] *Ibid.*, 15.12.1958.

[11] Among countries to which invitations were sent and from which no delegations arrived were Afghanistan, Baḥrayn, Burma, Cambodia, Dahomey, Ḥaḍramawt, Kuwait, Laos, Malaya, Nepal, Nigeria, Philippines, Saudi Arabia, Thailand, Togo and Upper Volta.

[12] The agenda included four subjects:
complete liquidation of imperialism and colonialism in Africa and Asia, and the study of problems concerning independence, unity, coexistence and disarmament;
problems of economic development in Africa and Asia;
problems of cultural and social development in Africa and Asia;
promotion of the Afro-Asian Solidarity Movement.
See *Le Monde*, Paris, 12.4.1960.

[13] The Chinese were considerably more active than the Russians at Conakry. At the time, it was assumed that their respective stands were fully coordinated. Now, with the advantage of hindsight, this appears not so certain.

[14] Delegates from the following countries were elected to the Executive Committee: Algeria, China, Cameroons, Congo, Ghana, Guinea, India, Indonesia, Iraq, Iran, Japan, Kenya, Lebanon, Liberia, Morocco, Mongolia, North Korea, Pakistan, Somalia, USSR, Tunisia, UAR, Uganda, Vietnam, Yemen.

The composition of the Secretariat was changed at Conakry to the following: Algeria, Cameroons, Congo (Kinshasa), China, Guinea, India, Iraq, Indonesia, Japan, USSR, UAR, Uganda.

[15] The militant line taken by AAPSO was reflected in a resolution adopted in the course of a meeting in Cairo held a month later on the occasion of "Africa Day," which denounced "the crimes committed in the Congo by the imperialist powers under the cloak of the United Nations" and expressed gratitude to the UAR, Ghana, Guinea, Mali, the Soviet Union, India, Indonesia and China for their attitude "hostile to the Belgian-American imperialist manoeuvres in the Congo"—AFP, Cairo, 10.12.1960.

[16] Yūsuf as-Sibā'i, the secretary-general, called for maximum participation at the Bandung Council meeting in an appeal issued by him on 2.3.1961 to "the national committees and popular movements." To a large extent, the extreme militant tone taken at Bandung was set by as-Sibā'i's appeal.

[17] According to AFP, Bandung, 10.5.1961.

[18] According to the official documents of the Council meeting, there were 121 delegates.

[19] Represented by S. Giraido Mazola, who arrived at the end of the Council meeting, and subsequently made what was probably the longest speech ever delivered at an Afro-Asian meeting, when he addressed the Executive Committee which met immediately after the Council.

[20] Neo-colonialism is not, in itself, a Marxist term, but it has become a vital rallying-cry to which the Communists fully subscribe. Neo-colonialists and the industrial countries have become practically synonymous. The term has been used above all to describe the relations between rich and poor countries, and is thus particularly attractive to the countries of Africa and Asia. See Ardant, "Le Néo-Colonialisme, Thème, Mythe et Realité," in *Revue Française de Science Politique,* October 1965, p. 837. He maintains inter alia that whereas the struggle against colonialism was the slogan which engendered a certain dynamism in the internal situation of the colonies, the term neo-colonialism was needed after independence to maintain that internal dynamism. Neo-colonialism, he adds, enables the maintenance of unity at international Afro-Asian gatherings, for who would oppose any resolution attacking neo-colonialism? On the other hand, Kudryavtsev, "Fighting Africa's Daily Round,"

International Affairs, October 1962, p. 51, gives the following description of the emergence of the issue of neo-colonialism: "Without waiting for the national liberation war to reach its peak they [the imperialists] granted national independence to many African countries 'of their own will.' This manoeuvre, the starting-point of neo-colonialism, was designed to weaken the national liberation struggle and make political capital which would help to retain actual control in the former colonies."

[21] The Indonesian delegate, Ibrahim Issa, while not officially a member of the Communist Party, was secretary of the "Peace Movement" in Indonesia. After the Sino-Soviet differences came out into the open, he consistently followed a pro-Chinese line. He became an exile after the abortive September 1964 coup in Indonesia, but continued for some time to represent Indonesia in the AAPSO Secretariat.

[22] Fuad Galal was special adviser to President Nasser on African affairs. He died in 1962 and his place was taken by Muḥammad Fāʿiq, who maintained that position until he was appointed minister of information in 1966. Although Fāʿiq never appeared as head of the Egyptian delegation at an AAPSO conference, as did his predecessor, he was active in the movement behind the scenes. At the first tri-continental conference at Havana in January 1966, for example, Muḥammad Fāʿiq arrived at the Cuban capital at the time of the conference, although officially he was not part of the Egyptian delegation.

[23] Statement by Yūsuf as-Sibāʿi, *Documentation of the Permanent Secretariat for Afro-Asian Solidarity,* Cairo, 23.5.1960. See also, for a similar statement, *idem,* "Afro-Asian Solidarity Marches On," *Monthly Bulletin of the Permanent Secretariat for Afro-Asian Peoples' Solidarity,* Cairo, Nos. 11–12, Sept.–Oct. 1960.

[24] Yūsuf as-Sibāʿi, the Egyptian member in the Secretariat, was not among the members of the delegation to Stockholm.

[25] However, the Chinese were outvoted by 166 votes to 25 at the first open vote taken at the WPC on a Russian versus pro-Chinese resolution. The issue voted on was the subject of peaceful coexistence versus national liberation—see Richard Lowenthal, "The Sino-Soviet Split and Its Repercussions in Africa," in Hamrell (ed.), *Soviet Bloc, China and Africa,* p. 134 ff.

[26] *Arab Observer,* Cairo, 19.2.1962. According to Colin Legum, there were some two hundred delegates from forty countries—*Observer,* London, 11.3.1962. As official lists of delegates were not usually handed out during most Afro-Asian conferences, it was often difficult to know exactly how many delegates attended. For a composite list of the representation generally attending AAPSO functions, see Appendix 2.

[27] Legum, *Observer*, London, *loc. cit*. According to *Neue Zuercher Zeitung*, 16.2.1962, the argument between the Chinese and the Russians began after the Turkish delegate, Nazim Hikmet, had spoken of the need for general disarmament.

[28] Legum, *Observer, loc. cit*.

[29] Richard Lowenthal, *op. cit*.

[30] *Times of India*, 19.2.1962. A much less condescending viewpoint of the Writers' Conference was given by a leading newspaper in the Malagasy Republic: "Il ne peut y avoir de littérature Afro-Asiatique, cela saute aux yeux," the paper averred. "Ce qui est écrit en Indonésie ou en Chine est totalement différent de ce qui peut se lire en Egypte ou en Afrique Noire . . . la Conférence des Ecrivains Afro-Asiatique, tenue sous son égide (de l'Egypte) se resume-t-elle, une fois de plus a une grande parlotte axée sur la politique et une seule politique, soit celle qu'oriente le Président Nasser"— *France-Madagascar*, Tananarive, 9.3.1962.

[31] This was decided by the executive committee of the Afro-Asian Lawyers' Association which met in Conakry on 22–23.11.1963. The members elected to the Secretariat were Algeria, China, Guinea, Indonesia, Japan and Nigeria—*Zanzibar News Service (Zanews)*, 2.12.1963.

[32] Thirteen countries participated in the preparatory committee. The Egyptians proposed that the Russians be invited; the Chinese and the Indonesians opposed—AFP, Jakarta, 23.2.1963. The conference was eventually held, without the Russians, on April 26–30, 1963, in Jakarta, and forty-two countries took part (according to *Ghanaian Times*, 27.4.1963). A new Organization of Afro-Asian Journalists was set up, in which the Chinese and Indonesians played the dominant roles.

[33] Sixty-four delegates were invited (Tanganyika Information Service, pp. 3 and 7, 30.1.1963). Among those invited who did not appear were Hastings Banda of Nyasaland and Kenneth Kaunda of Northern Rhodesia.

[34] See Chapter 5, p. 99, for mention of the Colombo proposals.

[35] In the words of the commentator of Brazzaville Radio, 7.2.1963 quoted by BBC Monitoring, ME/1171/E/1): "Many of the African countries believe that the foremost task of the conference is to put the emphasis on the struggle against imperialism and avoid straining the fragile plant of Afro-Asian solidarity by bringing up topics such as Israel, Indian-Pakistan relations, the Sino-Indian conflict, Brunei, etc." M'biju Koinange, secretary of PAFMECA, put it even more plainly when he said: "Africans do not wish controversial internal problems to be raised. Priority must be given to the struggle against imperialism and colonialism and to the freeing of the rest of Africa"—*L'Essor*, Bamako, 8.2.1963.

[36] The Indians later claimed they had been tricked. They had been assured by the Egyptians that the Chinese had agreed to a slightly watered-down resolution. On the basis of this compromise the Indian delegation continued to take part in the conference without further demands.

[37] Quoted by New China News Agency (*NCNA*), 5.2.1963, and brought in BBC Monitoring, *loc. cit.*

[38] See Mircos Tursun-Zade's speech, *Tass,* 6.2.63, brought by the BBC, *loc. cit.*: "It is possible to achieve full victory in the national liberation movement without sacrificing hundreds of millions of human lives. There is need to intensify the struggle for disarmament, and for the banning of nuclear arms."

[39] BBC, *ibid.* The General Declaration of the conference, while supporting "general and controlled disarmament" preluded this support with the following statement: "The struggle for national liberation and national sovereignty is a mighty force for the realization of peace and disarmament," a statement which, according to the Russian way of thinking, was putting the cart before the horse.

[40] Press release issued by the Tanganyikan Information Service, 4.2.1963.

[41] One of the few speakers who made at least a passing reference to President Nyerere's "scramble for Africa" was the Moroccan delegate, Mehdi Ben Barka, in a particularly thoughtful speech—see conference document No. 154/111.

[42] Six members from each continent. The six Latin American representatives were to be chosen by Fidel Castro of Cuba and General Cardenas of Mexico. For the decision to set up the preparatory committee and for a letter of the four Latin American members of the WPC expressing their dissatisfaction at not having been allowed to appear before the organizational committee—see conference document No. 220/111, fifth.

[43] The greater efforts of the Chinese as opposed to the Russians is borne out by the fact that Peking Radio broadcasts on the conference gave it five times more coverage than those from Moscow, and the *NCNA* coverage was fifteen times as much as that of *Tass*—according to the *Economist Intelligence Report*, London, July 1965.

[44] The Malays had sent a strong governmental delegation to Moshi to seek admission to AAPSO and to prevent any Indonesian attempt to condemn Malaya as an imperialist entity. The Egyptians and Indians promised them that they would raise their issue. But at the end of the conference the Malays were dismayed to learn that not a word had been spoken in their favour and that the resolution condemning Malaya had been passed without a word of protest.

[45] The head of the Egyptian delegation, Dr. Mahdi Allam, devoted a large

part of his speech to attacking Israel, as, indeed, did most of the Arab speakers. For Allam's speech, see conference document No. 109/111, n.d. . . .

[46] *East African Standard,* Nairobi, 11.2.1963.

[47] The most urgent needs, as outlined by the General Declaration of the conference, were:

(a) intensification of the struggle against colonialism;

(b) maximum contribution towards the speedy liberation of the non-liberated areas of Africa and Asia;

(c) formation of a united national front in any one country not yet liberated and coordination of action among the different national fronts to make their struggle more effective.

Again, these "urgent needs" reflect the Chinese way of thinking more than that of the Russians. The Russians would have placed emphasis on the ties between the national liberation movement and the socialist camp.

[48] Thus V. Kudryavtsev, who had been present at Moshi, commented in *Mezhdunarodnya Zhizn* (No. 5, 1963, pp. 51–6): "There have been changes in the atmosphere of these conferences since the first one held in Cairo in 1957, and what is more not all these changes have been for the better. . . ." He continued: "In general, there is a danger of giving the solidarity movement a kind of nationalistic slant, and this danger was evident at the Moshi conference." (Kudryavtsev's article appeared in English in *International Affairs,* Moscow, May 1963, under the title "Problems of Afro-Asian Solidarity: Thoughts at the Foot of Mt. Kilimanjaro." It is also quoted in *Mizan Newsletter,* London, Vol. 5, No. 6, June 1963. p.1.)

[49] *Daily Times,* Lagos, 9.2.1963.

[50] *Sunday Nation,* Nairobi, 17.2.1963.

9 THE SINO-SOVIET SPLIT AND THE SOLIDARITY MOVEMENT

The outcome of the Moshi conference highlighted a fact which had been becoming increasingly evident in the last months of 1962, namely, that the Sino-Soviet rift was severely damaging the relations between the Soviet Union and the progressive movements in the Afro-Asian world. The apogee of these relations was the Solidarity Movement, and it was there that the estrangement between orthodox Communist thinking as expressed in the Soviet Union and between the militantly left-wing movements of Afro-Asia was most felt. There were a number of ideological points in the dispute between the Soviet Union and China which had a direct bearing on Soviet relations with Afro-Asia. Principal among these points were the questions of peaceful coexistence and disarmament as opposed to the notion of armed struggle, the importance of the non-Communist and nationalist elements in the national liberation movement as opposed to the Communist Party as the vanguard of the anti-colonial revolution, the place of the world Communist movement in the revolutionary struggle of the peoples of Asia and Africa, and the Soviet attitude to the policies of non-alignment and positive neutralism.

After Moshi it became evident that the Russians would, at the very least, have to make a reappraisal of their policy regarding these points if they wished to prevent a recurrence of the victory which the Chinese gained there at Russian expense.

A new Soviet attitude gradually crystallized in 1963, which is best reflected in the words of their own theoreticians, as they appeared in *Pravda, Izvestiia* and a host of other papers and periodicals. The questions of peaceful coexistence and disarmament were, from the beginning, treated as basic ideological principles about which there could be little compromise. While the Moshi conference was still in progress, the Soviet press was already stressing the support of the delegates for these ideas. Thus, *Pravda,* on February 13, 1963, commented: "At the Moshi conference there was broad support for the idea of the organic link between the national liberation movement and the struggle against imperialistic plans for unleashing thermo-nuclear war." The paper continued: "Peaceful coexistence creates all the conditions for the victorious development of the national liberation movement." But, and here came the rub, "the USSR and other socialist states with all their forces support liberation wars and armed struggle against the colonialists."[1] It was a question of priorities: from the Soviet point of view, peaceful coexistence created "the conditions" in which the national liberation movement could best succeed. Therefore peaceful coexistence should be a primary objective for all those fighting imperialism. This dogma had, however, been increasingly attacked by the Chinese as a betrayal of the fighting liberation movements. The Russians, therefore, added their corollary which, they insisted, was not incompatible with their demand for peaceful coexistence, namely, that they supported with all their forces "liberation wars and armed struggle against the colonialists."

This became the formula for all subsequent Solidarity conferences. The idea of peaceful coexistence was supported, while the call was made for armed struggle. Again, it was a matter of emphasis and priorities. There were those who saw the main idea in peaceful coexistence; there were others who put the emphasis on the call for armed struggle. The Russians, for purely national interests, were keen to discourage the spread of local liberation wars, which could so easily be elevated into something much larger. As a nuclear power they had no wish to set off the sparks which would lead to a nuclear confrontation. Hence their insistence on peaceful coexistence and their stringent efforts to bring about a nuclear test-ban treaty, efforts which were crowned with success in the summer of 1963.[2]

Moreover, in their eyes, the question of peaceful coexistence versus armed struggle was inextricably bound up with the role of the national liberation organizations in the anti-imperialistic movement.

According to the Chinese, the national liberation movements, and not the Communist countries, had become the focal point of world revolution. Their struggle, in Asia, Africa and Latin America would be the decisive issue which would bring the downfall of capitalism and the end of imperialism and colonialism. The Russians did not see it that way. While agreeing that the national liberation movements played an important role in the struggle against imperialism, they insisted that the peoples of Africa, Asia and Latin America could not put an end to the world system of capitalism on their own without the aid of the Soviet Union and of the world proletarian movement. They accused the Chinese of deliberately trying to isolate the liberation movements of the three continents from the progressive forces in Europe by preaching a solidarity of the oppressed and coloured peoples. Thus, commenting on the Moshi conference, V. Kudryavtsev wrote: "Some of the more chauvinistically inclined leaders would like to direct the solidarity movement not against imperialism, colonialism and its agents, but against all white people. They are ready to sacrifice the truth, as they did, so far cautiously, in Moshi, and to shrug their shoulders at the participation (even though only partial) of international organs such as the WPC, international women's and youth organizations, etc."[3] Similarly, the periodical *Kommunist* described the Chinese theory that there exists a special community of interests between the peoples of Asia, Africa and Latin America as "diametrically counter to Marxism-Leninism" and as one which "isolates the peoples of these continents from the socialist states."[4]

The Russians believed in working in accordance to Lenin's precept: "The revolutionary movements of the peoples of the East can develop successfully, reach consummation, only if directly linked with the revolutionary struggle of our Soviet Republic against international imperialism."[5] The most clear and concise description of the Russian point of view was given by G. Mirskii in *Izvestiia*, and he deserves to be fully quoted. The Chinese concept, he wrote, "in which the national liberation movement rather than the international working class and the world socialist system . . . is made central in the modern epoch, is erroneous and non-Marxist." He continued:

It is precisely from this concept that there arises the pernicious and harmful theory of the so-called 'separate solidarity' of three continents which are allegedly 'the only real revolutionary anti-imperialistic force of modern times.' These views are linked specifically with the attempt of the Chinese leaders to counterpose in practice the Afro-Asian Solidarity Movement to the other progressive anti-imperialistic movements of our times. The Afro-Asian Solidarity Movement, linked with the name of Bandung, is an integral part and a further development of the struggle of the oppressed peoples against imperialism. Just as the national liberation movement is a part of the total world revolutionary stream, the Afro-Asian Solidarity Movement is only a part of the total solidarity movement of all the oppressed and exploited masses of the globe and the victorious proletariat in the struggle against imperialism, against the exploiting world bourgeoisie.

Mirskii went on to stress that the national liberation movement, however much it helped the cause of world socialist revolution, was not a class movement. "Marxists cannot substitute for the solidarity of all anti-imperialistic forces of the world, and above all the proletariat masses and the socialist parties, the solidarity of one category of oppressed peoples, i.e., the peoples of the former colonies and semi-colonies." He then gave the following view of the efficacy of the movement's struggle: "The Afro-Asian Solidarity Movement," he wrote, "supplemented by the movement for solidarity with Latin America, is a serious anti-imperialist force, but it is not powerful enough to bring about a victorious outcome in the struggle against imperialism without an alliance with the forces of world socialism and the international proletariat." There was no ground for treating the three continents as a unified social entity, Mirskii continued, and he concluded: "The concept of 'isolated solidarity' merges . . . with the views of the bourgeois nationalists in Asia and Africa who . . . preach their own brand of racism in reverse."[6]

Mirskii and Kudryavtsev all but expressed the Russian fear that the Afro-Asian Solidarity Movement was getting out of hand. For an independent solidarity movement, free from ties with the world Communist movement and claiming to be the vanguard of the revolutionary movement of Asia and Africa would, in Soviet eyes, be much worse than no solidarity movement at all. It would be playing straight into Chinese hands. Soviet efforts, as expressed in solidarity movement conferences, were directed primarily at strengthening the links between "the socialist camp" and the solidarity movement. For the same reason Soviet theory, while set firmly on the course described by Mirskii, was made as pliable and thus as palatable as possible to the non-Communists of the Afro-Asian world. Thus the Russians stressed that economic and social progress was no less important than armed struggle, and that they could provide the aid and know-how needed for such progress. Similarly, with their eyes on the neutralist governments of Asia and Africa, they decried the Chinese call for armed struggle "against national progressive governments." Typical of this line of thought was an article in *Pravda* by K. Brutents, who wrote:

> The application of the call to armed struggle to countries with national progressive governments is tantamount to an order for the violent overthrow of these governments which have the respect of the masses and which adhere to an anti-imperialistic line. This would be political adventurism, very profitable to the imperialists, and fatal to the prospects of *progressive development* in those countries. . . . *Social progress coincides with the progress of national liberation.*[7]

Similarly, M. A. Suslov declared in a speech to the central committee of the Soviet Communist Party that if the Communist parties were going to put all their hopes on armed struggle alone, to the exclusion of all else, regardless whether the masses of the people were ready to support such a struggle, this would "inevitably lead only to bitter defeat." He continued:

> Now that the winning of economic independence and forward movement on the path of social progress have become the chief direction of the anti-imperialist struggle of the liberated countries, particular importance attaches to the expansion of economic cooperation between them and the socialist states and the extension of economic assistance to them.[8]

The Soviet Union and "the truly democratic forces," he said, would help the countries of Asia and Africa towards full social and economic independence; this was far more important than the "stereoscopic demand" of the Chinese for armed struggle. Suslov, too, warned against the idea "that Afro-Asia could manage without the Soviet Union."

These warnings against the "separate solidarity" of the Afro-Asian Solidarity Movement did not mean that the Russians were negating the right of existence of an Afro-Asian movement. Such a movement had legitimate common interests, which, however, coincided to a large degree with the interests of the "socialist camp." This point of view was clearly expressed by Lev Stepanov, in an article in *New Times*:

> Afro-Asia is not just a sum of two geographical units. It is a political concept whose substance is the community of the Afro-Asian peoples' fundamental national interests. Anti-imperialism and anti-colonialism, the need for a world at peace, the vital interest in preserving independence and territorial integrity—these are the major factors in Afro-Asian unity. . . . It is no mere coincidence that Afro-Asia's biggest achievements and the growth of its international standing have invariably gone hand in hand with common policy positions with the socialist states. That is an expression of a natural process of our time—the growing practical unity and mutual support between all the anti-imperialist forces: world socialism, the international revolutionary working class and the national liberation movement. There are some who no longer regard the Afro-Asian Movement as an instrument of collective struggle against imperialism but as a tool for achieving their narrow national ends.[9]

These attitudes of the Soviet Union on questions vital to the future of the Afro-Asian Solidarity Movement were fully expressed in an exchange of letters between the Communist Party of the Soviet Union and China which began in March 1963 and continued through the summer of that year. The Russians, opening the exchange, pointed to the necessity of collaborating with various non-Communist "Third World" leaders in order to gain a victory over imperialism and the West.[10] The Russians admitted that some of these leaders might set up reactionary regimes and persecute Communists. Such regimes would, however, be "shortlived"[11] and would be replaced by more progressive ones. The Chinese, replying in June, declared that the liberation movement included "not only workers, peasants, intellectuals and petty bourgeoisie but also patriotic national bourgeoisie and even certain patriotic-minded kings, princes and aristocrats."[12] The Chinese were willing to cooperate with these elements, but the "proletarian party" must maintain "its ideological, political and organizational independence and insist on the leadership of the revolution. The proletarian party and the revolutionary people must learn to master all forms of struggle, including armed struggle." The need for armed struggle was justified by the fact that in the newly independent countries the "big bourgeoisie" increasingly tended to identify itself with the imperialists. "If the proletariat becomes the tail of the landlords and bourgeoisie in the revolution, no real and thorough victory in the national democratic revolution is possible, and even if victory of a kind is gained, it will be impossible to consolidate it."[13]

The inference that only through armed struggle would the final revolution be attained is categorically rejected in the Russian reply.[14] "The central place among all the tasks that confront the anti-imperialist forces in the modern epoch is occupied by the struggle for averting a thermonuclear war," the Russian reply stressed. As for the national liberation struggle, "the task of the working class and the Communist parties is to take maximum advantage of the presently existing opportunities for a peaceful path to a socialist revolution, not connected with civil war, and at the same time to be prepared for non-peaceful paths, for the armed suppression of the resistance of the bourgeoisie . . . the struggle for peace, democracy, national independence and socialism—this, in brief, is the essence of this general line."[15]

This ideological dialogue between the Russians and the Chinese forms an essential backdrop to further events in the Afro-Asian Peoples' Solidarity Movement. Without understanding this background much of what happened in the Solidarity Movement after the Moshi assembly would be meaningless. For it was in this movement that the Sino-Soviet ideological dispute was mainly fought out, and the decisions and actions of the African and Asian members of the movement were governed largely by this dispute.

The first test for the Soviet Union after Moshi came in September, 1963, with the opening of the conference of the AAPSO Executive Committee in Nicosia, Cyprus. Just as at Moshi seven months earlier, the Sino-Soviet quarrel and the Sino-Indian dispute dominated the meeting. But this time the Soviets had come prepared. The chief Soviet delegate, Mircos Tursun-Zade, forcefully made the point that the only alternative to peaceful coexistence was world catastrophe.[16] He denied that they were calling for peaceful coexistence between the imperialists and the oppressed exploited peoples. At the same time the Soviet delegates distributed a long statement of the Soviet Afro-Asian Solidarity Committee entitled "For the Future of the Afro-Asian Solidarity Movement" which elaborated Soviet views on peaceful coexistence, disarmament, the need for collaboration between the Afro-Asian Movement and the "socialist camp" and on nationalist-racialist views of separate solidarity.[17] "The invincible ideas of socialism are spreading ever more extensively in the world," the statement ran. It went on:

This sets the Afro-Asian Solidarity Movement new important tasks for uniting in their ranks truly anti-imperialist forces fighting for the eradication of everything reactionary. . . . We are of the opinion that the Afro-Asian Solidarity Movement does not constitute a boxed-in movement . . . any attempt to tear the Afro-Asian Solidarity Movement away from the other revolutionary forces of our times . . . would only be to the advantage of imperialism and to the disadvantage of the movement itself. . . . We cannot reconcile ourselves to appeals for the unification of Asia and Africa on a racial basis.[18]

On peaceful coexistence the statement rejected the allegation that the Soviet Union believed in reconciliation between the oppressed and the oppressor. The Russians were evidently out to appear their best in the eyes of the Afro-Asians, for the statement continued: "The whole world knows that the Soviet Union has indeed supported liberation wars, considering them to be the sacred right of the peoples to win social and national liberation." The statement then makes a rare Soviet reference to one of the basic policies of many of the Afro-Asian countries: "Only in conditions of peace and the further lessening of international tension can the policy of active neutralism opposing aggressive forces, of non-alignment and non-participation in war blocs proclaimed by many young states find complete development."[19]

Thus the Soviet statement at one and the same time allayed Afro-Asian fears regarding the Soviet attitude to liberation wars and voiced tacit consent to the policy of non-alignment. This placatory attitude paid off all the more in the face of the headlong attack which the Chinese launched against the Russians over the signing of the Moscow Nuclear Test-Ban Treaty. The Chinese bloc adamantly refused to allow a resolution supporting the Moscow treaty,[20] while the Chinese delegate declared that the Soviets had "betrayed the world" by signing the treaty. In the fierce debate which developed over this issue the final compromise favoured the Russians: it was to express "appreciation" of the Moscow treaty instead of downright support.[21] The meeting went in favour of the Russians on other issues too. The General Political Resolution calls for "the consolidation of our relations with world anti-imperialist progressive movements" and "reaffirms its adherence to the principles of peaceful coexistence among independent states with different social political systems, to the struggle for peace, for total and complete disarmament and for the prohibition of nuclear tests. . . ." This was the most unequivocal statement yet made on that subject by the Solidarity Movement.

One of the reasons for the Soviet success at Nicosia was that most of the African delegates, many of whom had supported the Chinese stand at Moshi, now moved over to the Soviet camp. They could not understand the Chinese attack on the Test-Ban Treaty, which they heartily approved, nor were they willing to accept blindly the fury of the Chinese onslaught, which, they felt, was endangering the unity and solidarity of the Afro-Asian Movement. This fear was expressed in a private message from President Kwame Nkrumah of Ghana delivered to the Nicosia participants by the Ghanaian delegate, Nathaniel Welbeck. Nkrumah called for the reinforcement of Afro-Asian solidarity by forging firm links with Latin America:

> This will destroy any manifestation of racialism that can upset our anti-colonialist and anti-imperialist struggle. Our goal should be to seek the unity of the socialist countries, for it is only through this unity that they can support us in our struggle against imperialism and colonialism. It should be our concern that this conference appeal to China and the Soviet Union most

strongly to eliminate their differences and to come together again without delay. Afro-Asian solidarity should also not lose its anti-colonialist and anti-imperialist force. Afro-Asians should avoid all forms of racialism and discrimination in this struggle. We are fighting not against race, creed or colour. We are fighting against an economic system, which is designed to exploit us and to keep us in a state of perpetual subjection.[22]

Nkrumah's message had a great effect on the African delegates at Nicosia. By accident or by design it helped to swing them into the pro-Soviet camp, and encouraged them to assert themselves, which they did, strongly. Speaking of the Nicosia meeting, Welbeck declared: "For the first time in the history of the Afro-Asian Solidarity Movement, I felt very proud that Africans spoke in frank terms and without inhibition or commitment to any group."[23]

The African impact on the Nicosia conference is described in the following terms by the correspondent of the *Indian Express*:

The outcome of the executive meeting of the AAPSO in Cyprus last week has driven home an important moral to India—the importance of African opinion in Afro-Asian conclaves. The discomfiture and isolation of China at this meeting was mainly because of the hesitant African opinion crystallizing into a solid bloc behind India and the Soviet Union. . . . Impatient African leaders shouted down the Chinese leaders for too much speech-making and also accused the Chinese of introducing racialism in the Afro-Asian Movement when the latter asked for the inclusion of an 'Asian' into the three-member drafting committee composed only of Africans. The Tanganyikan delegate pointed out that the Chinese demand was an expression of lack of confidence in the Africans.[24]

The conference was, indeed, much more favourable to India than the assembly at Moshi had been. The chairman, Dr. Vassos Lyssarides of Cyprus, called for the endorsement of the Colombo proposals on the Indian-Chinese dispute, and generally took a pronounced pro-India stand. This, however, did not prevent the leader of the Indian delegation, Mrs. Aruna Asag Ali, from declaring that so long as the

Sino-Indian differences were not resolved, Afro-Asian solidarity would remain seriously weakened and incomplete.[25]

No reference at all was made to the Sino-Indian dispute in the resolutions of the conference, which followed the general militantly anti-imperialistic pattern of previous Afro-Asian Solidarity conferences. Eleven out of nineteen political resolutions singled out "US imperialists" for specific condemnation.[26] The only real novelties in these resolutions were a strong attack on the Moroccan regime, support for the Greek Cypriot demand for self-determination, and, for the first time in the annals of the Solidarity Movement, the absence of any condemnation of Israel.[27]

One of the effects of the Chinese defeat at Nicosia was an increased tendency on the part of the Chinese and their allies to sponsor Afro-Asian activity outside the scope of the Afro-Asian Peoples' Solidarity Organization and its Cairo-based permanent Secretariat. This tendency, which had begun in 1963, was eventually to lead to the virtual splitting of the Afro-Asian Solidarity Movement. The first phenomena of this Chinese move were the establishment of the Afro-Asian Journalists' Association in Jakarta in April 1963 and the takeover of the Afro-Asian Lawyers' Association in Conakry in October 1963 (see preceding chapter).[28] This activity was now considerably extended. The Afro-Asian Journalists' Association, which was described by its deputy secretary-general as "a legitimate child of the Bandung spirit,"[29] established in late 1963 an Afro-Asian Film Festival, and called for a conference of journalists from Asia, Africa and Latin America. At the same time, the Chinese organized a meeting of Afro-Asian writers in Bali, and completely ignoring the Permanent Writers' Secretariat based on Colombo, Ceylon, called for a third conference of writers to take place in Indonesia in June 1964. Another Chinese initiative was a planned conference of Asian, African and Latin American students, to take place in Indonesia in April 1964,[30] and an Afro-Asian Trade Unions Conference whose preparatory meeting was held in Jakarta on October 27, 1963.[31] In addition there was the Chinese-Indonesian initiative in creating GAMEFO, the Sports Organization of "Emergent Forces," and the Afro-Asian Economic Seminar held in Pyongyang.

The Pyongyang Economic Seminar was a particularly blatant example of independent activity on the part of the Chinese. Delegates and guests from thirty-four countries attended the seminar, which opened in the North Korean capital on June 16, 1964. Neither the Soviet Union nor the UAR had been invited to send representatives, nor was the Permanent Secretariat of AAPSO informed beforehand of the seminar. In the week-long deliberation, a strong Chinese line was adopted, with the accent on self-reliance, and condemnation of "economic cooperation," "economic aid," and all forms of great-power chauvinism and national egoism. This was the Chinese answer to the Soviet efforts to stress the importance of the economic progress of newly liberated countries and the manner in which the Soviet Union could help this progress. Hardly surprisingly, the Soviet representative at the AAPSO Permanent Secretariat in Cairo roundly condemned the seminar for not having been organized by means of the Secretariat.

Coupled with this increased Chinese activity through the good offices of Indonesia came a more direct Chinese thrust, in the form of Chou En-lai's tour of a number of African countries at the end of 1963.[32] The Chinese premier was obviously out to disarm his African hosts. He appeared on his best behaviour, exuding charm and good-will in a manner which recalled his performance at Bandung nearly nine years earlier. At Rabat and Cairo he resuscitated the badly frayed five principles, the *Panch Sheel,* averring that countries with different social systems could coexist peacefully on the basis of these five points. "The Chinese Government," he declared, "has persistently pursued a policy of peace. . . ."[33] In Algiers Chou En-lai was even more placatory. He declared that the Chinese government "supports the governments of the African countries in their pursuance of a policy of peace, neutrality and non-alliance. . . ."[34]

It was with this Chinese activity as a background that the Council of the Afro-Asian Peoples' Solidarity Organization met in Algiers on March 23, 1964, for the most stormy head-on clash that the Solidarity Movement had yet experienced. Neither the Russians nor the Chinese pulled any punches. "The Sino-Soviet quarrel surpassed anything seen previously," wrote *Le Monde.*[35] It quoted a Kenyan delegate as saying in one of the commissions:

We are not Marxist-Leninists, and most of us haven't read a line of 'The Capital.' So what interest can we have in your doctrinaire quarrels? I have had enough of this situation where whenever I eat my sandwich I am accosted by someone who wants to know my opinion on the Soviet stand, and when I drink my coffee, by someone who asks me about the Chinese arguments. I want to be able to eat in peace!

The Chinese delegation at the conference, headed by Mrs. Kuo Chien, led the attack:

A certain outside force . . . propagates the view that the main task now confronting the Afro-Asian peoples in their struggle is 'peaceful coexistence' with imperialism and old and new colonialism, and general and complete disarmament. This erroneous line in fact meant that the oppressed nations must for ever suffer imperialist plunder and enslavement.

Mme Kuo was no less outspoken on the question of disarmament: "To tell oppressed people to expect the imperialists to lay down their arms, to have mercy on them and to present them with milk and honey on silver plate, this is not only daydreaming but pure opium to drug the people." The Moscow Test-Ban Treaty was, in Mme Kuo's words, "a great fraud, engineered by the US, Britain and the Soviet Union by exploiting the aspirations for peace of the peoples of the world." The Chinese head delegate was particularly virulent over the proposal made by Nikita Khrushchev at the beginning of January 1964 concerning the solution of territorial disputes by peaceful means:

If some people should ask the Afro-Asian peoples to capitulate unconditionally to the aggression of imperialists and old and new colonialism under the deceitful slogan that no use of force is allowed to settle the territorial dispute, the Chinese people will reply categorically 'No, a thousand times no' and we will tell these people: Your expansionism and national egoism have since long made it difficult to draw a line between you and the imperialists and the colonialists, old and new. As birds of the same feather flock together, it is not at all strange that you should stand on the side of the imperialists and the colonialists.

When the Mongolian delegate suggested that the Council approve Khrushchev's proposal, the Chinese tabled the following draft resolution:

. . . the proposal runs counter to the interests of the people of the world, as it has confused the struggle waged by the people of the world against imperialist policies of aggression and war with territorial disputes and boundary questions, and urged the people to renounce the use of force to settle the question of their territories forcibly occupied by the imperialists. The proposal made by N. Khrushchev is absurd and reactionary and should be condemned and opposed by Afro-Asian peoples. The Afro-Asian peoples declare that in the struggle of the oppressed peoples to overthrow the imperialist rule and for national liberation . . . these people have the right to choose the most suitable ways of struggle, including armed struggle. Only in this way can we truly contribute to world peace.

In the final resolutions Khrushchev's proposal was not mentioned: this, undoubtedly, was a feather in the Chinese cap. Nor was the Chinese draft accepted, however.

The Soviets went over to the counter-attack after the Chinese accused them of being morally responsible for the assassination of Patrice Lumumba. The Soviet delegate, Bobodjan Gafurov, added at the end of his set speech, which had already been distributed, the following statement:

Many African and Asian delegates paid us a visit yesterday to beg us to reply to the Chinese. We adhere to this request insofar as these delegates told us they understood very well that in the slanders uttered at this conference the Chinese delegation has fallen too low. They told us they perfectly understood that the Soviet people, when speaking of disarmament, mean imperialist disarmament, not the disarmament of the Afro-Asian movements. They perfectly understood the fact that peaceful coexistence is the only thing which has prevented thermonuclear war, and this does not mean coexistence between oppressed and oppressors.

The statement caused an uproar. A number of delegates hotly objected to the Soviets generalizing in this manner and quoting anonymously other delegations. Many of the African delegates, in particular, voiced their disgust at the bickering of the two Communist giants.

A growing impatience and frustration of the delegates from the smaller countries became increasingly evident. In the words of the Algerian chairman of the Council, Muḥammad Yazid: "If the small nations need the large ones, these are also in need of the small ones."

The resolutions condemning US imperialism and calling for support for those struggling for freedom and independence just enabled the Council to maintain some semblance of unity.[36] Two organizational questions remained unsettled, no solution having been found possible in the heated atmosphere engendered by the Sino-Soviet quarrel: one was the forthcoming Afro-Asian Women's Conference, and the other was a proposed Afro-Asian Economic Seminar. The Chinese had succeeded in preventing the election of the Soviet Union to the preparatory committee for the women's conference, and were obviously making efforts to take over that organization in a manner similar to the fate of the Journalists' and Lawyers' Associations. The Egyptians, Indians and Russians fought tooth and nail against this attempt, and the matter was eventually left in abeyance for the Permanent Secretariat in Cairo to handle. As for the economic seminar, the Chinese objected strongly to a decision to hold it in Moscow, proposing Ceylon instead as its venue, but the Russians refused to agree to this change. This question, too, was referred to Cairo.

Thus the charged atmosphere of Algiers was brought back to Cairo, where, with the energetic help of Muḥammad Yazid, the Secretariat sought to grapple with the unfinished business of the Council session. The African members of the Secretariat did not hide their bitterness at the fiasco in Algiers. Yazid openly condemned "those who wished to introduce ideological debates in the organization,"[37] and stated that Algeria would reconsider its participation in the committee set up by the Secretariat to deal with the outstanding problems if the Chinese and the Soviets continued their 'dissension.' Yazid and his committee submitted a draft resolution to the Secretariat requesting China and the Soviet Union to refrain from "stirring up their ideological dispute in the forthcoming meetings of the organization in order to preserve unity and solidarity within the framework of the organization."

But the crisis within the movement had gone too deep for it to be so easily overcome. Both sides refused to budge. In desperation, the Secretariat charged Yazid with a mission of conciliation to the major Afro-Asian capitals in order to "preserve the cohesion of the movement."[38] That that cohesion was greatly endangered could be seen from the following dispatch of the *AFP* correspondent in Cairo:

> A la demande des Africains et notamment des Algériens, les débats qui se sont deroulés au Caire ont parté moins sur l'ordre du jour, que sur le fond du problème: empêcher l'effritement de l'organisation.[39]

The immediate issues—the women's conference[40] and the economic seminar—faded before the stark fact that the Chinese and Russian delegates were at complete loggerheads and refused to agree together on virtually any subject. At the end the work of the Secretariat ground to a halt when Yūsuf as-Sibā'i, the Egyptian secretary-general, walked out of the meeting on June 28 in which the Chinese delegate was particularly vituperative. The work of the Secretariat was postponed indefinitely. *The Times* in London commentated:

> The ideological quarrel between Russia and China has been reflected for some time in the AAPSO. Recently it has brought the very existence of the body into doubt. A protracted meeting of the AAPSO Secretariat ended in Cairo last month in failure to agree to almost any detail.[41]

The Secretariat did not stay moribund for long. Neither the Russians nor the Chinese, and certainly not the Egyptians, were prepared to witness the break-up of the Solidarity Movement. Within a month the Russians had agreed to back down and transfer the proposed economic seminar from Moscow to Algiers. The Secretariat once more resumed its activity. At the beginning of September 1964 an Afro-Asian conference on insurance was opened in Cairo; in October a Medical Conference was held in the Egyptian capital which was attended by representatives from thirty-six countries from Africa and Asia.[42] A Secretariat spokesman announced that four "professional" Afro-Asia conferences were planned for Cairo in 1965, dealing with shipping, banking, tourism and administration.[43] There appeared to be no limit to the range of activities to be organized in an Afro-Asian framework.

Hardly surprisingly, however, the work of the Secretariat was taken up much less by these specialized conferences than with the outstanding political problems, centred around the Sino-Soviet conflict. There was not to be much respite. The economic seminar at Algiers was scheduled for February 1965 and another full-scale AAPSO assembly meeting was planned for the summer of that year (according to the movement's constitution, the assembly was to convene every two years). It is to these two events that we must turn for the further developments in the Afro-Asian Solidarity Movement.

The Afro-Asian Economic Seminar, which opened in Algiers on February 22, 1965, in the presence of Algerian President Ben-Bella, was remarkable for the absence of Sino-Soviet in-fighting. Both the Russians and the Chinese appeared restrained. The much awaited— and feared—Chinese speech contained not a single attack on the Soviet Union. In these circumstances, it was all the more significant that the outcome of the seminar was much closer to the Chinese way of thinking than that of the Soviets. It showed that without pressure and without histrionics a large number of the African and Asian delegates voiced opinions which were much closer to the militant Chinese line than to the more gradualist Soviet one. This is not to say that those delegates were pro-Chinese and anti-Soviet. Far from it. Politically many were pro-Soviet; but ideologically they supported the Chinese. This dualism, which emerged clearly at the Algiers economic seminar, was to become one of the dominant features of the Solidarity Movement, and was particularly apparent at the first Solidarity Conference of the Peoples of Asia, Africa and Latin America which was held in Havana in January 1966. Among the resolutions of the Algiers Seminar which gave the Chinese particular satisfaction was the condemnation of "the control and manipulation of the United Nations Organization by the imperialists of the US," the call for assistance to liberation movements through the offer of arms, money and military training, and the stress on self-reliance in building up independent national economies.[44]

A week after the economic seminar came to an end there occurred an off-beat Afro-Asian event which cast light on the attitudes of some of the more conservative elements in Africa and Asia to the political initiative of the Afro-Asian militants. The Indonesians, with the usual Chinese encouragement, had for some time been trying to organize an Afro-Asian Islamic congress. The traditionalists of the Muslim world, in particular those of Saudi Arabia and other Arab countries, agreed to participate in the preparations for the conference, without great enthusiasm. But political questions were soon bedevilling efforts to reach Islamic solidarity. The Indonesian refusal to invite Muslim Malaysia aroused the ire of the Saudis who retired from the preparations in a huff. The reluctance of the hosts to invite a delegation from the Soviet Union strengthened the feeling of many that this would be one more conference to further Chinese aims.

The conference finally convened in Bandung on March 6, 1965. Delegations from twenty-one Muslim countries took their seats in the historic Merdeka Hall. The Soviets were there, despite Chinese objections. But the Malaysians were not, nor were the Saudis, the Iranians and the Turks. The object of the conference was to seek ways to reach full "unity of the Islamic peoples and cooperation among them," but from the opening speech of President Sukarno, in which he called on the Afro-Asian peoples to fight against and destroy colonialism "which is contrary to Islam," [45] the conference was deeply divided between the militant politicos and those who wished to stress the religious, Islamic, content of the conference. But to the chagrin of the Indonesians and their friends, it was the latter who had the upper hand. In the final resolutions the Indonesians succeeded neither in gaining recognition for the North Kalimantan exile government nor in obtaining the condemnation of Malaysia; the Chinese failed in obtaining the condemnation of the US, and the Pakistanis of India over the Kashmir question. There were, however, resolutions supporting the national liberation movements of Angola, Mozambique, Oman, the Maldives and South Arabia, a resolution condemning Britain for its aggressive activities against Indonesia in South-East Asia and one stating that it was the duty of every Muslim to combat colonialism. The conservative delegations from the Middle East and North Africa expressed their disappointment "at the political turn of the conference." [46] Finally, it was agreed to set up a special Afro-Asian Islamic Organization with headquarters in Jakarta, having Indonesia, Egypt, Pakistan and Nigeria as members of the Secretariat—one more Afro-Asian body within the Chinese orbit.

The Winneba conference was the last of the large Afro-Asian Solidarity conferences to be held before the birth of the Tri-Continental Solidarity Organization in Havana in January 1966. It was held from 10–16 May 1965 at the Ideological Institute of the Convention People's Party, the government party of Ghana, at Winneba, some thirty miles from Accra. This was the first time the Ghanaians were playing host to a solidarity meeting, and they intended to make the most of the opportunity. Their aim was similar to that of the Tanganyikans at Moshi, namely, to make the African voice heard and to transform the movement to serve exclusively the interests of those still suffering under colonialism instead of those of the Soviets, the Chinese, and the Egyptians. "Our mission is to speak less and to elaborate on an efficient, militant organization which will eliminate imperialism, colonialism and neo-colonialism," commented Kwaku Boateng, the Ghanaian minister of education. But the Ghanaians fared no better than the Tanganyikans had done, for yet once more the Sino-Soviet conflict burst over the heads of the Africans and Asians, shattering their hopes and aspirations for a unified front. Thus the hopes of those Africans and Asians non-aligned in the Sino-Soviet struggle to inject new life into the Solidarity Organization was once more frustrated. Their leadership of the "alternatives" proved to be too weak to prevent the delegates from dividing into pro-Soviet and pro-Chinese groups.

Both the Soviets and the Chinese scored successes at Winneba, though neither could claim a clear-cut victory. But the Chinese won on points; once more the attitude of the independents proved to be closer to that of the Chinese. Nkrumah's accent on aid to the national liberation movements fighting the remnants of colonialism in Africa suited the Chinese admirably. In most of the disputes the delegates of Mali, Tanzania, the two Congos, Bechuanaland, and South-West Africa, as well as of Japan, Indonesia, North Korea, North and South Vietnam, North Kalimantan, and Thailand could be expected to support China while many others, including the Ghanaians, sided with China on issues dealing with colonialism and imperialism. The atmosphere at Winneba was distinctly anti-Russian. The indefatigable Chinese spared no efforts to besmirch their erstwhile Communist allies. Rumours of racial discrimination in Moscow mysteriously made the rounds; African and Arab delegates were offered "presents" —dollar bills in closed envelopes—by the Chinese. Many were invited to Peking to see for themselves the country of hope for Afro-Asia.

This attitude was reflected in the Winneba resolutions. They were more specifically anti-US than ever before. They endorsed the need for "revolutionary violence." They issued a clarion call for armed struggle, mentioning specifically Congo Brazzaville, Malaysia, Morocco, Niger, South Vietnam, Thailand, Venezuela and the traditional colonial areas as countries ripe for internal revolution and armed struggle. They rejected the idea of peaceful coexistence as meaningless unless the imperialists ceased their intervention in developing areas. All these questions directly affected the independent delegations, the Africans in particular. They could support such resolutions without feeling that they were taking sides in the Sino-Soviet conflict. But in questions in which they had no direct interest they sided heavily with the Russians. Thus only some five delegations apparently supported the Chinese bid to condemn the UN, or the the Chinese efforts to bar observers from socialist countries. This was not directly connected with the drive against imperialism and colonialism, and there was thus no interest in supporting the Chinese efforts. On the other hand, the Indonesians, with Chinese support, succeeded in convincing the other delegations that the eight-member Malaysian delegation which sought to join the Solidarity Movement at Winneba was in the service of imperialism and colonialism, and the Malaysian request was rejected.[47] This brought the comment from Tunku Abdul Rahman, prime minister of Malaysia: AAPSO is "a Communist set-up, established in Cairo for their own ends. It is being financed by Russia and Communist China and I am quite sure about this. They had never admitted us into the conference and I had no hope of it at all."[48]

Perhaps more important for the Chinese than all the favourable resolutions was the decision to hold the following assembly of the movement two years later in Peking. The decision was taken despite the strongest Soviet opposition: on home territory the Chinese could go to any lengths to discomfit the Russians. But the Peking conference never took place. Another organizational resolution at Winneba was destined to change the character of the Solidarity Movement and to hasten the split into Chinese-oriented and pro-Soviet groupings: for at Winneba, succeeding three years of desultory discussions, the date and venue were finally fixed for the first Tri-Continental Solidarity Conference—at Havana, on January 3, 1966.

NOTES

[1] Quoted by *Mizan Newsletter*, London, Vol. 5, No. 3, March 1963, p. 8.

[2] For an excellent analysis of Soviet and Chinese attitudes to war and peace, see Lowenthal's "Sino-Soviet Split and its Repercussions," in Hamrell (ed.): *Soviet Bloc, China and Africa*, pp. 131 ff.

[3] Kudryavtsev, *op. cit.*

[4] *Kommunist*, Moscow, No. 15, November 1963.

[5] V. I. Lenin Report at the Second All-Russian Congress of Communist Organizations of the Peoples of the East, ("Works," Vol. XXX, p. 130).

[6] *Izvestiia*, 16.7.1963, reproduced in *Current Digest of the Soviet Press*, Vol. 15, No. 29 (14.8.1963), p. 11.

[7] K. Brutents in *Pravda*, 17.9.1963, quoted in *Mizan Newsletter*, London, Vol. 5, No. 9, October 1963. A few months later, Brutents had this to say: "The thing that radically distinguishes the national liberation movement of our day from the anti-colonial movement of the past is that it is an integral part of the world revolutionary process"—*International Affairs*, Moscow, No. 2, February 1964.

[8] Report by M. A. Suslov on 14.2.1964 at the Plenary Session of the CPSU Central Committee—*Pravda*, 3.4.1964, pp. 1–8; also in *Current Digest of the Soviet Press*, Vol. 16, No. 13, 22.4.1964.

[9] Lev Stepanov, "The Future of Afro-Asia," *New Times*, Moscow, No. 51, 21.12.1965.

[10] For analysis of the exchange of letters, see U. Ra'anan, "Moscow and the 'Third World,'" *Problems of Communism*, Vol. 14, No. 1, Jan. Feb. 1965, p. 24.

[11] *Pravda*, 3.4.1963: CPSU Central Committee letter to CCP Central Committee, quoted by Ra'anan, *op. cit.*

[12] *Pravda*, 14.7.1963, pp. 5–7: The Letters from the Chinese Communist Party to the Central Committee of the CPSU, June 14, 1963, reproduced in *Current Digest of the Soviet Press*, Vol. 15, No. 28, 7.8.1963, pp. 3–5.

[13] *Ibid.*, p. 6.

[14] *Pravda*, 14.7.1963, pp. 1–4: The Soviet Reply to the Chinese Letter,

from the Central Committee of the CPSU to all Communists of the Soviet Union. Reproduced in *Current Digest of the Soviet Press*, pp. 16–30.

[15] *Ibid.*, p. 27.

[16] *Pravda*, 14.9.1963.

[17] The statement is reproduced in full in a brochure entitled *Unity Won: Nicosia September 10–12, 1963*, Peoples' Agency, Nicosia, Cyprus, n.d., pp. 33–40. It is also reprinted in *Pravda*, 14.9.1963.

[18] *Ibid.*, pp. 34–36.

[19] *Ibid.*, p. 37.

[20] *UPI*, Nicosia, 11.9.1963. The *Associated Press* report of the same day stresses the moderate attitude of the Soviet delegation.

[21] The Chinese expressed their anger at the compromise by leaving, in company with the North Koreans, before the final session. In the twelve-member committee which drafted the resolution expressing appreciation of the treaty, the Indonesian and Japanese delegations supported China, while those of Angola, Guinea, and South Vietnam abstained.

[22] Nkrumah's message was obtained by the author from one of the participants at the conference.

[23] *Ghanaian Times*, Accra, 17.9.1963.

[24] *Indian Express*, 24.9.1963. It was, perhaps, because of this increased Indian awareness of the African voice after Nicosia that twenty-two chiefs of Indian diplomatic missions in Africa and the Middle East met in New Delhi in December 1963 to discuss ways and means of promoting increased Indian activity in Africa. According to *Jeune Afrique*, Tunis, 15.12.1963, the conference was convened because of a falling off of Indian influence in Africa.

[25] *Times of India*, 11.9.1963.

[26] There were, all told, twenty-two such political resolutions, but not all of them dealt with subjects related to specific countries. There was a resolution supporting GANEFO, one on the Afro-Asian Trade Unions' Conference, and one expressing appreciation of the Nuclear Test-Ban Treaty. For full text of the resolutions, see *Unity Won . . ., op. cit.*

[27] The Egyptians tried their utmost to insert the usual anti-Israel resolution, but the Cypriots categorically refused to agree, on the express orders of Archbishop Makarios—see *Haaretz*, Tel Aviv, 16.9.1963.

[28] The purely African Lawyers' Association, which convened in Lagos in in August 1963, did not invite any representatives of the Afro-Asian Association to their meeting, nor did they wish to be affiliated to any outside organization.

[29] Joesoef, in an article in *Afro-Asian Journalist*, Jakarta, No. 3, May-June 1964.

[30] The initiative for the students' conference was taken by the Indonesian Students' Organization P.P.MI. in April 1963.

[31] The conference was originally planned for May 1963 but was postponed several times, mainly because of the strong opposition to it by the WFTU. In order to prevent the conference taking place solely under Chinese-Indonesian sponsorship, the AAPSO Executive Committee at Nicosia decided to convene it "under the sponsorship of the Permanent Secretariat and with the collaboration of Indonesia, so that preparatory work undertaken by Indonesia to commence this conference may be completed"—see *Unity Won . . ., op. cit.,* resolution No. 21, p. 25.

[32] In the period 14.2.1963–5.2.1964 Chou En-lai visited the following ten African countries: UAR, Algeria, Morocco, Tunisia, Ghana, Mali,
[33] Guinea, Sudan, Ethiopia, and Somalia.
Le Monde, 1.1.1964. The joint communiqué at the end of Chou En-lai's visit to Cairo stated, inter alia: "Afro-Asian countries should settle all their disputes in accordance with the five principles of peaceful coexistence and the ten principles of the Bandung conference through peaceful negotiations and amicable consultation without resorting to force."

[34] *Ibid.,* 29/30.12.1963. For an analysis of Chou's visit to Africa, see M. Dhin'an, "The Results of Chou En-lai's Visit to Africa," *Bulletin of the Institute of Study of the USSR,* Vol. XI, July 1964, No. 7, p. 43 ff., and *Mizan Newsletter,* Vol. 6, No. 5, May 1964, p. 45 ff.

[35] *Le Monde,* 28.3.1964.

[36] The General Declaration appealed to Afro-Asian peoples to:
1. exert all necessary efforts to facilitate the formation of a joint front . . . and to actively help the freedom strugglers both materially and morally;
2. to intensify the struggle against colonialism and neo-colonialism as well as against imperialism and racial discrimination. . . .
Radio Algiers, 27.3.1964, quoted by USIS Broadcasts 31.3.1964. Also quoted in *Zanews,* 31.3.1964.

[37] *AFP,* Cairo, 7.4.1964.

[38] *Le Monde,* 11.4.1964.

[39] *AFP,* Cairo, 10.4.1964.

[40] According to *Times of India,* 13.4.64, this problem was solved when a twenty-member preparatory committee was convened by the Secretariat. The Chinese were defeated in their attempt to take over the Women's Organization, the paper noted.

[41] *The Times,* London, 30.7.1964.

[42] *Egyptian Gazette,* Cairo, 25.10.1964.

[43] *Al-Akhbār,* Cairo, 13.10.1964.

[44] "Reliance essentially on one's own strength, on the enthusiasm, dynamism, and initiative of the peoples' masses." Algiers Radio, 1300 GMT, 28.2.1965, in BBC ME/1799/EZ/1.

[45] *Haaretz*, Tel Aviv, 7.3.1965.

[46] *New York Times*, 15.3.1965.

[47] *Daily Graphic*, Accra, 17.5.1965.

[48] *Straits Times*, Kuala Lumpur, 20.5.65. The Tunku's reaction was fairly typical of a number of the more moderate Afro-Asian countries. Abidjan Radio, for example, commented: "The Afro-Asian Solidarity Conference came to an end in Accra yesterday. What did it achieve? The customary verbiage of international Communist dialectics which masks its active imperialism. . . ." Abidjan Domestic Radio Service, 18.5.65, 1245 GMT, in BBC (ME/1861/E/8).

10 HAVANA—BROADENING THE SOLIDARITY MOVEMENT

On the face of it the Havana Solidarity Conference of the Peoples of Asia, Africa and Latin America falls outside the scope of this book. It was not an Afro-Asian conference. It was not held on the soil of either Asia or Africa. Neither its president nor secretary-general was an Asian or African. Yet the Havana conference forms an integral part of the history of the Afro-Asian Peoples' Solidarity Movement. It was the Afro-Asian Movement which gave birth to the Havana conference. Both its preparation and its implementation were carried out largely by members of AAPSO. And, most important of all, the Havana conference had a profound effect on the future of the Afro-Asian Solidarity Movement. Havana caused it to alter course, to enter new, uncharted waters. For these reasons the Havana conference, despite its non-Afro-Asian character, became one of the crucial turning-points in the route which the Afro-Asian Solidarity Movement took. It must, therefore, be fully surveyed.

It will be recalled that the decision to examine the possibility of widening the framework of AAPSO to include Latin America was first taken at its council meeting in Bandung in April 1961. (See Chapter 8, p. 160.) That nearly five years should have elapsed before the decision was implemented is, in itself, indicative of the doubts and hesitations which existed within AAPSO concerning the ways to bring the broadened movement into being. As could be expected, these doubts were polarized into sharp differences of opinion between the Soviet and Chinese camps in AAPSO, and were centred on two basic points: which Latin American organizations should represent countries at the proposed conference?, and what form of organization should be set up after the conference?

The Soviets, as we have already seen, wanted the Latin American representatives of the World Peace Organization to decide on Latin

198

President Suharto of Indonesia.

American representation. The Chinese opposed this, demanding on their part that the sub-continent should be represented by the militant liberation movements which were operating, albeit on a small scale, in most of the countries of Latin America. This point was finally settled during a meeting of the Preparatory Committee[1] which was held in Cairo on September 1, 1965. It was agreed to let the six Latin American members of the committee decide, after consultation with the committee chairman, Mehdi Ben Barka, and the secretary-general, about the invitations to Latin American participants at the Havana conference. This decision was taken despite the objection of the Chinese and their friends, who wished the entire eighteen-member committee to approve nominations.[2]

The second question was not easily settled. It was known that the Soviet Union, confident that the majority of the Latin American delegations would prove to be pro-Soviet, were in favour of the creation of a single tri-continental organization which would, in effect, supersede and absorb the existing Afro-Asian Peoples' Solidarity Organization. The Chinese, on the other hand, were adamantly opposed to any change in the existing structure of AAPSO. They envisaged the creation of a Latin American Solidarity Organization which would work parallel to, and in coordination with, the Afro-Asian Movement, but not as an integral part of it. The interest of both the Russians and the Chinese in this question was increased, for opposite reasons, after the decision was taken at Winneba to hold the next AAPSO Assembly in Peking. The creation of a new tri-continental movement in place of AAPSO would automatically cancel this decision, which was something the Russians were very anxious to achieve and the Chinese were determined to prevent.

Thus from the outset of the Havana conference the organizational question overshadowed all else. On this issue the crucial battle was to be fought.

These storm-clouds were hardly noticeable to the unseasoned onlooker at Havana as the conference opened on January 3, 1966. There was a festive atmosphere unsurpassed at any previous Solidarity conference. Havana outdid itself to make the occasion a memorable one. The city was festooned with giant banners and posters. Thousands of red flags adorned the streets adding their bright colour to the colourful hues of the Cuban capital. Public buildings and main thoroughfares were lit up at night and enormous slogans, emblazoned in neon, proclaimed the solidarity of the fighting peoples of Asia, Africa and Latin America.

The conference was opened in the presence of the president of Cuba, Dr. Osvaldo Dorticos Torrado, the prime minister, Fidel Castro, and other leading members of the Cuban government. Some eight hundred delegates, observers, guests and journalists crowded into the Salle des Embajadores of the Hotel Havana Libre, formerly the Havana Hilton, to attend the opening ceremony. It was the largest Solidarity conference yet held, the greatest gathering of fellow revolutionaries the world had seen. Of those present 512 were delegates, coming from 82 countries: 197 from 27 Asian countries; 150 from 28 African countries and 165 delegates from 27 countries in Latin America. The Asians and Africans present were the by-now familiar figures attending the Afro-Asian conferences; the Latin Americans included many leading personalities from the various guerilla armies and liberation organizations, such as Pedro Medino Silva of Venezuela, Diego Montana Cuellar of Colombia, and Luis Turcios Lima, the young commander of the guerillas of Guatemala. But by and large, most Latin American delegations were headed by members of the respective Communist parties.[3]

As at most such conferences the proceedings were divided into the initial plenary meetings, at which delegate heads were each given an allotted time to make their statements, and the closed working committees, at which the real work of the conference was dealt with. Four such committees were set up at Havana: the Political, Economic, Social and Cultural, and Organizational committees.

As could be expected, the speeches at the plenary sessions followed a certain stereotype: praise of Cuba, and attacks on "Yankee imperialism," followed by a recital of the particular problems troubling the speaker—whether on the internal situation in Congo, Cyprus, or elsewhere—speeches accepted at Solidarity conferences as part of the necessary litany. At Havana everybody awaited the Chinese address with great expectation. Would the Chinese openly jeopardize the atmosphere of unity by an open assault on the Soviet Union? After some five minutes of US-baiting, Wu Hsueh-tsien, the head of the Chinese delegation, began the expected attack, without mentioning the Soviet Union by name:

There are some people who maintain that they stand for 'united action' to wage 'a common struggle against the enemy,' but their actual deeds cannot but oblige us to raise the following questions: with whom do they really take united action? and unity against whom? why do they regard US imperialism, the mortal enemy of the people of the three continents, as their principal ally, proclaiming that their policy of all-round co-operation with the United States will never change? why do they sabotage peoples' wars and why do they preach here and there that 'a tiny spark can cause a world conflagration'?[4]

The ball was now in the Soviet side of the court. But those who expected the Soviet delegate to reply to this attack were disappointed.[5] Sharaf Rashidov, the chief Soviet delegate, made no mention of the Chinese allusions, concentrating instead on the concrete methods by which his country could help in the struggle of the liberation movements. Rashidov revealed an important Soviet shift to increased militancy, at least for the sake of the record; he affirmed Russian support for armed struggle, declaring that "sacred is the right of the people to fight for the complete destruction of colonialism and neo-colonialism using all means at their disposal. The Soviet people has always supported peoples' war, the armed struggle of the oppressed peoples, and has been rendering them every possible support and assistance." This attitude, however, did not mean that the Soviet Union had weakened its support for the principles of coexistence. "Following the behests of Lenin, the Soviet Union is consistently working for world peace and the security of the people. We believe that relations between sovereign states with different social structures should be based on peaceful coexistence." However, he added: "It is quite clear that there is no peaceful coexistence, nor can there be peaceful coexistence between the oppressed peoples and their oppressors—the colonialists and the imperialists, between the imperialist aggressors and their victims."

Increased militancy on the part of the Russians accurately reflected the mood of the vast majority of those present. Any appeal to moderation on the question of the right to armed struggle would have put the Russians right out of step with the other delegates. As could be expected, the Cubans were in the forefront of this militancy. "Thus far not a single liberated people have won their liberation in any other way than by revolution," declared Osmany Cienfuegos, the head of the Cuban delegation. "This conference should benefit by the experience of these triumphant peoples, of those people who have won their victory, of those who, as in Vietnam today, are showing that no one can oppose with lasting success the heroic action and unshakable determination to obtain independence and liberation. Not a single example can be cited to the contrary."

Militancy, then, became the keynote of the conference, the need for armed struggle its clarion call. On this point, at least, the large majority of delegates, African, Asian and Latin American, displayed an enthusiastic show of unity. This militant temper of the conference was reflected in the resolutions and in the General Declaration, which, inter alia, proclaims "the right of peoples to counter imperialist violence with revolutionary violence" and "the inalienable rights of all peoples . . . to resort to all forms of struggle including armed struggle." It also affirmed "the right and the duty of the peoples of Asia, Africa and Latin America and of the progressive states and governments of the world to give material and moral support to peoples fighting for their liberation or suffering direct or indirect aggression from the imperialist powers." The General Political Resolutions declared that the peoples "should have recourse to the most effective forms of struggle, among which armed struggle is one of the highest forms, in order to achieve final victory." The right to embark on armed struggle was epitomized by the special attention given to the Vietnam war throughout the conference. A special resolution on Vietnam created the "Tri-Continental Committee for the support of the Vietnamese people in its struggle against the aggression of Yankee imperialism."

Vietnam was a central issue throughout the conference. A description of the conference in the *World Marxist Review* put it this way: "The struggle of the people of Vietnam and the effective solidarity with the struggle [can be considered] to be the central issue and the decisive link of progressive mankind's struggle in our day. Its [Vietnam's] fight, and solidarity with this fight are essential for the victory of the liberation movement over US imperialism." [6]

That solidarity was loudly proclaimed at Havana. But what of peaceful coexistence? The passage of a proposed resolution on this subject put forward in the Political Committee by the Indian delegate is indicative of how the various delegations felt on this fundamental and controversial question. The Indian proposal was sharply opposed by the Chinese. They objected to any mention of coexistence. They flatly refused to agree to the final conference declaration if it contained that term. The discussion over this point became increasingly heated with the delegates of Basutoland, Indonesia, Japan, Malaya, Nepal, North Kalimantan, South West Africa and Thailand backing the Chinese to the hilt. The Indians, on their part, received support mostly from Chile, Cyprus, Mauritius, Mongolia, the Soviet Union, the UAR, Uruguay and most of the Arab delegations.[7] Significantly, most of the other Asian and Latin American delegates kept quiet in the debate. The impasse appeared complete, but, as had happened already on a number of occasions, the Cubans, who more than any others were anxious to assure the success of the conference, sought a way out by means of compromise. They proposed that the Indian resolution should be amended, and that instead of becoming part of the General Declaration, as the Indians had wanted, it should be accepted as a separate resolution.[8] The Chinese opposed this proposal, but when put up to a vote it was accepted by thirty-one votes to nine, with the rest, including most of the Asians and many of the Latin Americans, abstaining.[9] Although this was a defeat for the Chinese, they appeared to be satisfied enough, for their main aim, to prevent the clause on coexistence from appearing in the main General Declaration of the conference, had been fully attained.[10]

There was no need for discussion regarding the clause in the Political Resolution which labelled US imperialism as the main force of international reaction, with West German imperialism as its principal ally. The extreme anti-US tone dominated the proceedings throughout the conference, and acted as the most cogent unifier whenever quarrels threatened to break the conference apart.

These quarrels centred mainly in the Organizational Committee. There the main battle was fought out between the Chinese and the Soviets which was to determine the future of the Solidarity Movement. It was because of the impasse reached on organizational issues that the conference was prolonged by nearly a week. The main question, put to the members of the Organizational Committee by its chairman, Abdoulai Diallo of Guinea, was whether the Afro-Asian Solidarity

Movement should be expanded to include Latin American Solidarity Committees or not. Whether a tri-continental organization should be established, what should be the locale of its secretariat, and whether AAPSO should be disbanded in favour of the wider organization were the three questions which occupied the delegates for more than a week and almost brought the conference to complete breakdown. They brought to the surface not only the cross-current of conflicting interests of the Chinese and Russians but also the regional interests of the Africans, the Latin Americans, and the Arabs. The Asians, it should be noted, unlike the Africans and the Latin Americans, never put regional calculations before wider ideological and political interests; in this respect, they were the least unified in the three continents.

In the days that followed Abdoulai Diallo's opening questions, the standpoints of most of the delegations crystallized in the heated discussions and intense activity which marked the work of the Organizational Committee. The Soviets, backed mainly by India and the UAR, were determined to establish a single Latin American-Afro-Asian solidarity organization with headquarters in Cairo. The Chinese agreed to the establishment of a new organization provided it would not supersede AAPSO and would act merely as a liaison between the Afro-Asian Solidarity Organization and a Latin American solidarity movement. The majority of the Africans were, on this vital point, fully in agreement with the Chinese. They were no less anxious than the Chinese were to prevent the framework of AAPSO from being expanded to include Latin America. They had come to Havana fearful of being relegated to a junior role in the conference proceedings, partly because of the war in Vietnam, which was mainly an Asian affair, and partly because the predominant emphasis was being placed on the Latin Americans, and in particular on Cuba. As they saw it, they would be swamped if the movement was expanded, and therefore they, like the Chinese, were keen to preserve AAPSO within its existing limits.

The Arabs, with the wavering exception of Oman, backed the Soviet Union for reasons of their own which were not identical with those of the Soviets. Half of the fourteen Arab delegations present in Havana were composed of exiles living in Cairo; these were entirely controlled by the Egyptians. Egyptian influence was, therefore, predominant in the Arab bloc and it was the Egyptians who set the tone. The Egyptians had one overriding objective at the conference, and that was to see to it that the headquarters of any new organization that might be created would be in Cairo, with an Egyptian acting as secretary-general. Whether or not AAPSO should be absorbed into the new movement was an entirely secondary question for them. Their task was narrowly and clearly defined: Cairo was, at all costs, to remain the world capital of the Solidarity Movement. According to delegates at Havana, the Egyptians openly admitted that they had made a deal with the Russians on this score: the Russians and their allies would support the nomination of Cairo as headquarters, and the Egyptians and the Arab delegations would, on their part, back the Russian demand for the absorption of AAPSO into the one all-embracing Solidarity Organization. It is indicative of the importance that the Egyptians placed on this point that they were willing to jeopardize their good relations with many of the Latin American governments by their intense activity at the Havana conference.

At the beginning of the conference it appeared as if the Soviet-Arab axis would win hands down. At the opening night of the conference a cable had been read out from President Nasser inviting the delegates to hold their second conference in Cairo in 1968. In the plenary session the UAR delegate had proposed that the Secretariat be situated in Cairo, and this proposal was specifically taken up in the speech of the Mongolian delegate, who was generally considered to be the mouthpiece of the Soviet Union. But much more significant was the speech of the Cuban delegate, Osmany Cienfuegos, for he clearly indicated that the Cubans would support the Soviet-Egyptian proposal:

> Some opinions have been advanced regarding the maintenance of the Afro-Asian Solidarity Organization and the parallel creation of a tri-continental organization with seat—at the suggestion of some of the delegations—in Havana. The selection of Cuba as the seat would undoubtedly be an honour to us, but our position is not conditioned by any aspirations of a nationalist nature that might create obstacles. If the conference should decide to create one sole organization to unify the anti-imperialist efforts of Asia, Africa and Latin America with Cairo as a seat, Cuba would back that decision . . . .

   This was as clear a hint as possible that the Cubans were willing to throw their considerable weight behind the proposal to set up one organization with Cairo as its headquarters. It was not stretching the imagination too much to conclude that the Russians and the Cubans had reached some form of collusion on this vital subject prior to the conference, in much the same manner as the Russians had with the Egyptians. Yet during the discussions in the Organizational Committee the Cubans made a surprising *volte face*. They agreed to a single organization, but insisted obdurately that its headquarters should be in Havana, and not in Cairo. The Latin American delegations solidly backed up this demand.

   The battle lines were thus drawn and none of the contestants would budge. The Soviets insisted on a single organization; the Chinese threatened to walk out of the conference and set up their own separate AAPSO if a single organization was agreed to; the Chinese were also against choosing Cairo for any new, additional organization and supported the Cuban demand for Havana; the Africans were against the single organization concept but were willing to agree to Cairo as the site for an additional organization; the Egyptians campaigned ceaselessly for Cairo and the Cubans just as determinedly for Havana.

   This then was the predicament. The impasse was solid, the deadlock complete. The discussions, heated and acrimonious, continued for five days with no visible progress. At this juncture Fidel Castro himself moved into the Havana Libre Hotel in order to reinforce the campaigning of the Cuban delegates. They poured scorn on the Soviets for supporting the "bourgeois military regime" of the UAR against the socialist Cuba. The Russians were put into an increasingly invidious position, for their stand threatened to estrange them from all the Latin American delegations. Finally, on January 12, the Russians broke. They switched sides declaring that they would vote with the majority, and since the majority appeared to favour Havana, they would support the Cuban capital as the site for the new organization. Now the Egyptians were left in a difficult position. As long as they were assured of support from the Soviet bloc, they had been certain that their bid for the Cairo site would be successful. Now they were left out on a limb. For two more days they fought on, earning the opprobrium of the Cubans and most of the weary delegates, until they finally agreed to withdraw, and Havana was adopted as the temporary seat of the organization until the convening of the second tri-continental conference in Cairo in 1968, when a permanent site would be decided upon.

This unexpected change also brought to nought the Soviet efforts to abolish AAPSO in favour of the enlarged organization. The Egyptians and the Arab bloc, once their prize had been snatched from them, were no more willing to fulfill their side of the bargain, for at least as far as AAPSO was concerned Cairo remained the site of its headquarters. The Africans rallied adamantly to the pro-AAPSO cause, and even the Cubans, who would have preferred a single organization, were chary of pressing the point for fear that the Chinese would carry out their threat and walk out of the conference. AAPSO, therefore, was left intact, and the new Tri-Continental Organization was set up alongside of it, and not instead of it.

The key to this Soviet-Egyptian setback was the sudden and unexpected about turn of Cuba. At the outset of the conference the Cubans had undoubtedly showed a strong pro-Soviet orientation. But the Cubans had aims of their own, independent from those of the Soviets. For one thing, they wanted the conference to succeed at all costs; they could not afford a failure. This need of theirs superseded, from their point of view, the need to nullify Chinese influence, which was the primary aim of the Soviets. They were thus ready to make tactical concessions to the Chinese to ensure this success, even if these concessions ran counter to the wishes of the Soviets. The Cubans also wanted to gain something tangible from the conference, not just a Soviet victory.

It was this second point which caused the Cuban switch. The more nationalist elements in the Cuban establishment wished to see Havana an important centre. They failed to understand why the Egyptians should gain all the prestige of having the Secretariat in Cairo after they, the Cubans, had devoted so much time, energy and expense to preparing the conference. This attitude on the part of some of the Cubans coincided with a growing feeling among the Latin American delegations, and especially among the members of the liberation movements, that the centre of the new organization should be in the American sub-continent. The members of Communist parties in the Latin American delegations still tended to support the Soviet-UAR line, but when sharply criticized by Fidel Castro for not thinking in terms of their regional needs the Latin American bloc came down solidly in favour of Havana. For the Cubans had also decided to adopt the more nationalist line, despite the damage that this would cause the Soviet Union.

Thus the die was cast. The Afro-Asian Solidarity Movement was given a new lease on life, and beside it was formed the new, cumbersome Afro-Asian-Latin American Peoples' Solidarity Organization.

What did the major delegations gain or lose at the Havana conference? The Soviet aims have already been enumerated. Above all they wished to nullify Chinese influence in the organization, to prevent Chinese advances into Latin America, and to consolidate their own position in that sub-continent. Soviet tactics at the conference, aimed at achieving these ends, were to avoid head-on confrontations with the Chinese. From the beginning they displayed a moderate and elastic mode of approach which won the approval of the delegates. If the Chinese attacked them they did not bother to reply; if the Chinese challenged them on a particular subject, they rarely took up the challenge. Their attitude was described by a number of delegates as being "constructive," "pragmatic," and "friendly."

These tactics, however, enabled the Chinese to win a number of important rounds on points. They exploited the Soviet reluctance to clash with them to the full. The Chinese extremist demands did not encounter an inflexible wall of opposition, and for this reason they often had their way. The tactics of the Chinese were, indeed, controlled by three factors: (a) the pro-Chinese group was in a small minority, except within the Asian caucus meetings, so they did everything to prevent voting on issues, preferring to agree to compromise solutions than to fight to the end; (b) the Cubans wished to avoid a crisis at all costs, thus by taking an extremist, intransigent line, the Chinese could hope to wring concessions from them, and (c) the tactics of the Soviets. Thus by a mixture of bluff, bluster, threats and intransigence the Chinese gained much more from the conference than they could have hoped for, but they also gained the opprobrium of many of the delegates, particularly those from Africa. Above all, the Chinese succeeded in preventing the disbanding of AAPSO, and the establishment of the Tri-Continental Organization in Cairo. This was no mean victory for them, but they achieved it, not because they enjoyed the support of the majority of the delegates, but because their stand coincided with that of those Africans and Latin Americans who felt that their own particular interests would be furthered by taking a similar stand to that of the Chinese.

The Cubans without doubt made the biggest gains at the conference. Castro's position as a leader of the "Third World" was enhanced, his capital was chosen as focal point for tri-continental activity for at least two years, and the US and the world were shown that the blockade of Cuba was ineffective.

The Africans openly expressed their dissatisfaction at the course the Solidarity Movement was taking. From the beginning they held African caucus meetings, and African solidarity, as opposed to the wider Afro-Asian solidarity, became, for the first time, a strong factor in the Solidarity Movement. Regional interests were strengthened at the expense of the wider ideological interests of the movement. In this development the Algerians played a prominent role. Their particular aim at the conference was to reach some sort of rapprochement with the Africans and restore the good relations which had existed during the rule of ex-President Ben Bella. Thus in the African caucus meetings the Algerians diligently sought to attain an all-African line. They constantly appealed for African unity, and on occasion even sided with the Africans against the UAR. The Egyptians, on the other hand, were accused by the Africans of following a pro-Soviet line without taking into account the wishes and interests of the African continent.

The Asian delegations were divided among themselves. Most of them, and in particular the Japanese, Indonesian, Malayan, Nepalese, Thai and North Kalimantan delegates, supported the Chinese. So did the Pakistanis and Iranians, though less enthusiastically. The Indians, for their part, were the most devoted supporters of the Soviet Union and the UAR. Their aim was to avoid controversies, but at the same time to counter Chinese influence.

The Havana conference was a success. This in itself was a remarkable feat. As Castro himself said in his speech in the final plenary session, "contrary to all the auguries of imperialism, contrary to all its forecasts which revealed the great hope that this conference would not result in anything; that this conference involving the problems of the International Communist Movement was bound to be divided; that it was bound to be a great failure—what has happened is something that they least, or perhaps never, expected: that the conference has been a success!" The apparatus of a new organization was established. But at the same time the conference demonstrated the vast divergences existing between the three continents and the differences in the mode of struggle employed by them. It highlighted the gulf separating the liberation movements and the delegations composed of Communist Party representatives. For all that the conference marked a new phase in the Solidarity Movement, not only because it brought Latin America into its orbit for the first time, but because this was the first time that such a conference openly called on its members to embark on the course of armed struggle and openly preached revolution to those operating in independent countries which, in the opinion of the conference, were not yet sufficiently independent.

NOTES

1 The Preparatory Committee consisted of eighteen members—six from each of three continents. Mehdi Ben Barka was its chairman. The countries represented on the committee were China, India, Indonesia, Japan, South Vietnam and the Soviet Union; Algeria, Ghana, Guinea, South Africa, Tanzania and the UAR; Chile, Cuba, Guatemala, Mexico, Uruguay and Venezuela.

2 This and a number of other facts related in this chapter were told to the author by participants at the conference. He regretfully cannot reveal their names.

3 For a lengthy description of the delegations at the conference see Lentin, *La Lutte Tricontinentale*, pp. 51–54.

4 This and other citations of speeches at the Havana conference and its resolutions are taken from the official documents issued by the conference Secretariat.

5 This particular Chinese-Soviet confrontation was continued with much greater intensity in the Political Committee. The Chinese delegate turned to the Russian and asked him why he had not yet answered the questions he had put to him in the plenary session. In a blistering attack on the Soviet Union, the Chinese then accused the Soviets of collaborating with the US in the United Nations, and of manufacturing rumours that China was slowing up the passage of arms to Vietnam. Throughout this attack the Soviet delegates sat in silence, and they refused to answer the Chinese speech or refer to it. The Chinese later again attacked the Russians in this committee after the Pakistanis attempted, without success, to introduce a resolution on the Kashmir issue.

6 Lionel Soto, "First Conference of the Peoples of Three Continents," *World Marxist Review*, vol. 9, No. 4. (April 1966), p. 6.

7 Except the delegate of Oman, who systematically sided with the pro-Chinese delegations.

8 The wording of the resolution was interesting. Peaceful coexistence, it stated, "is related exclusively to the sphere of relations between states

with different social and political systems. It cannot refer to coexistence among the exploited social classes and their exploiters within a country; it can neither refer to the struggle of the peoples victimized by imperialism against their aggressors." The resolution also proclaims the right of the peoples to carry out social revolution and demands respect for the principles of self-determination of nations.

[9] Among those abstaining were, significantly, the two Vietnamese delegations.

[10] It should be noted in this context that whenever a vote was taken in one of the committees the Chinese bloc generally numbered between seven and nine—those countries mentioned above—while those voting against the Chinese line ranged usually between twenty-one and thirty-one votes. The remaining delegations always abstained. Many of the Asian delegations—Korea, Laos, Cambodia, the two Vietnams, Pakistan, and Iran— were generally considered to be more pro-Chinese than pro-Soviet, and in the discussions usually took the Chinese line. But when it came to downright voting most of them usually abstained. Only Cyprus, India, Mongolia and most of the Arab delegations of Asia sided solidly with the Soviet Union.

11 THE CASE OF INDIA

The early ties between Indian leaders and the nationalists of Asia
and Africa have been noted at some length in the first chapter. So
have Nehru's early activities in the field of foreign relations—such as
his role in the Brussels conference of the Association of Oppressed
Peoples in 1927—and the increasing attention paid by the Indian
National Congress to the plight of nationalist movements in Asia
and Africa. The historical setting will thus not be repeated here.
This chapter examines the ideological basis of India's foreign policy
as propounded by Nehru and the execution of that policy in practice,
Nehru's views on the Afro-Asian Movement and India's place in that
movement through the years.

Foreign policy, as Nehru himself never tired of pointing out,
concerns itself primarily with the national interests of the country
applying it.[1] Thus, despite the strong ideological overtones which
Nehru gave to his foreign policy orientations, they were actually never
in any way divorced from what he considered to be the national needs
of India. These ideological overtones recur in his speeches and
writings. Basic among them was Nehru's fear of another world war,
and his desire to contribute towards the maintenance of world peace.
This aspiration forms one of the fundamental planks of Indian
foreign policy, on which an entire series of ideological principles and
practical actions rest. Nehru's fear of war was very real and he
constantly harped on it. Thus he said in a broadcast in 1948: "Tortured
humanity hungers for real peace, but some evil fate pursues it and
pushes it further and further away from what it desires most,"[2] and
again, in a broadcast from London in 1951: "today, these hundreds
of millions all over the world live under some kind of suspended
sentence of death and from day to day an atmosphere is created in
peoples' minds of the inevitability of war."[3] Fear for the destiny of

humanity was, however, combined with a very shrewd appreciation of the importance of world peace for India's vast economic programmes. Nehru himself made this point when he declared that "apart from our desire for peace is our feeling that peace is absolutely essential for our progress and our growth."[4] The outbreak of war would wreck the ambitious economic plans, which, the Indian leaders hoped, would transform their country in much the same way that the Soviet Union had been transformed within twenty years. War, therefore, had to be prevented at all costs; Brecher goes so far as to say that all other factors which have shaped India's world view were subordinate to this consideration.[5]

Thus, in her crusade for world peace, India was at one and the same time fulfilling her international obligations and also defending her national interests. India as a champion of world peace was projected into the forefront of world diplomacy. For the active championship of world peace entailed a number of concrete foreign policy attitudes: it meant first and foremost that India was willing to be a peacemaker. This role of world mediation could, in turn, only be fulfilled if India herself was not partner to the conflict. India, therefore, in order to play this role, could not be committed to one or other of the two sides in the cold war, and must follow a policy of non-alignment. Moreover, the active championship of peace necessitated, in the view of the Indian leaders, continuous efforts to reduce tensions between the two world blocs; this could best be achieved by non-adherence to either of the blocs, and by enlarging what the Indians called the "area of peace." The final aim should be the abolition of the cold war and the fulfillment of the notion of One World in a world federation of nations.

Here, then, a gamut of principles emerges from the underlying policy of preserving world peace. The idea of One World was popular in the early years of Indian independence; later the Indian leaders were to become disillusioned. The following passage, taken from the first important policy speech of Nehru after he became Prime Minister in 1946, typifies his beliefs on that subject:

The world, in spite of its rivalries and hatreds and inner conflicts, moves inevitably towards closer cooperation and the building up of a world commonwealth. It is for this One World that free

India will work, a world in which there is the free cooperation of free peoples, and no class or group exploits another.[6]

This rather utopian outlook was gradually combined with a belief already strong, namely, in one Asia, and eventually in Afro-Asia. From speaking of One World, Nehru passed increasingly frequently to the destinies of "free Asia," "resurgent Asia," etc. Thus, "Free Asia is determined to shape its destiny without outside interference,"[7] or "unless the basic problems of Asia are solved, there can be no world peace"[8]; eventually he was wont to include Africa in such references. Nehru summed up these views in the following passage:

> We cannot remain unaffected by the highest single fact of contemporary history—that is, the resurgence of Asia and Africa. We are affected by this tremendous event because we are part of it, part of the movement and the revolution as well as part of the geography, at the very heart of these two continents, placed as we are in the centre of the Indian Ocean. And now that we are free and more and more countries are breaking out of colonialism, naturally we come together and re-establish old relationships with other countries in Western, Eastern and South-East Asia, and, of course, Africa also.[9]

Thus the basic interconnection which existed in Indian eyes between the various facets of Indian foreign policy becomes apparent. Desire for world peace led naturally to the role of mediator and this, in turn, necessitated the approach of non-alignment, the call for a lessening of world tensions through the enlargement of the "area of peace" and the abolition of the cold war through the creation of the concept of One World. From here the step was short to a revival of the theme of One Asia, and its modification to the solidarity of the peoples of Afro-Asia. At the bottom of it all lies the peculiarly Indian legitimatization for this approach: the basic Hindu concept of *himsa*, one of the main founts of the philosophy of non-violence developed so effectively by Mahatma Gandhi,[10] in conjunction with, as observed by Brecher, the notion of tolerance in Hinduism and Buddhism, which rejects all claims to the totality of truth, justice and good in the world.[11]

Strongly connected with the concept of One Asia and the solidarity of the Afro-Asian peoples was Nehru's attitude to the former colonial powers, and to the Western world in general. This attitude, moulded by the years of struggle in the vanguard of the nationalist movements in the colonized territories, can best be summed up in Nehru's own words: "For too long have we in Asia been petitioners in Western courts and chancelleries. That story must now belong to the past. We propose to stand on our own legs. . . ."[12] Nehru objected strongly to any form of subservience on the part of the former colonized territories to their erstwhile metropolitan centres. He fought against the implied attitude of superiority so common in the dealings between Europeans and the peoples of Asia and Africa. The peoples of Asia and Africa had now to take their destiny in their own hands, and the part they had to play, in Nehru's view, was to safeguard world peace.

Yet this desire for world peace was only one strand from which Indian foreign policy attitudes emanated. There were others. The passages quoted above point to Nehru's deep-seated belief that India's historical and moral heritage, as well as her geographical position, made it imperative for her to follow a certain course in world affairs. Professor S. L. Poplai, one of the principal Indian historians at the Indian Council of World Affairs, believes that the clue to the meaningfulness of Indian policy "is to be found in 'the sense of history,' in the habit of looking at contemporary international conflicts through the glass of history."[13]

Relying on the historical greatness of India, Nehru selected a policy that a potentially great and powerful country might adopt. Poplai continues: "Lacking military power, India can only use its influence in the game of diplomacy. And in a world divided . . . the pre-condition for the diplomatic use of this influence is that India must be unaligned, unallied and uncommitted."[14]

Nehru himself made numerous statements which underlined the importance with which he viewed India's historical heritage and geographical position. Perhaps one of the most revealing was a speech he made in the Constituent Assembly in 1949:

Look at the map. If you have to consider any question affecting the Middle East, India inevitably comes into the picture. If you have to consider any question concerning South-East Asia, you cannot do it without India. So also with the Far East . . .

whatever regions you may have in mind, the importance of India cannot be ignored. . . . *India is growing into a great giant again.*[15]

Two weeks later, in a speech at the Indian Council for World Affairs,[16] Nehru elaborated this approach: ". . . a certain responsibility is cast on India. India realizes it, and other countries realize it too. The responsibility is not necessarily for leadership, but for taking the initiative sometimes and helping others to cooperate."

In other words, India had a mission in the world, and this assumption, too, found a particularistic *Indian* legitimatization in the theories of such philosophers as Swami Vivekananda who spoke of the need for the spiritual conquest of the world by India in order to save humanity. The teachings of Mahatma Gandhi helped to strengthen this belief in the mission of India, a mission to establish peace and friendship among all nations. This, once more, led naturally to a policy of non-alignment and the causes and effects described earlier as emanating from the desire for peace.

For Nehru India's unique position had practical connotations. Thus, "India's championship for freedom and racial equality *in Asia as well as in Africa* is a natural urge of the facts of geography and history. India desires no leadership or dominion or authority over any country. But *we are compelled by circumstances* to play our part . . . ."[17]

Here then, was another reason for Nehru's Afro-Asian activity. He believed that India was destined to play a leading role within the Afro-Asian context. If he rejected the idea of a military "third force" which had been propounded by some,[18] he nevertheless believed in the need for India to display a moral leadership, at least of the Afro-Asian peoples, and this belief was one of the causes which made India pass from purely negative non-engagement in world affairs to a more active form of neutralism or non-alignment.[19]

Non-alignment was, as we have seen, an essential corollary to the basic needs of India's foreign policy. But, to Nehru's mind, non-alignment in itself was also a natural development of India's historical heritage. He made this point with great effect in a speech at the National Defence College at New Delhi on April 28, 1960:

We have tried to develop a certain attitude to the world, called non-alignment or whatever you may call it. I should like you to remember that this policy has not suddenly come out of a hat. It had developed years before independence. It was a natural inevitable thing, both because of our thinking and because of our geography . . . it is a basic way of thinking which I think lessens dangers in the practical sense and promotes an atmosphere which is better than the atmosphere of cold war.[20]

Non-alignment was not a passive concept. S. C. Jha, one of the most active of the Indians dealing with Afro-Asian questions, defined it as a dynamic concept of ideology whose exponents work *actively* for peace. The doctrine of non-violence was reflected in non-alignment, though not applying to every case (Gandhi himself believed in defending Kashmir by force). Whereas, according to Jha, other states had adopted non-alignment as a convenient state policy which kept them out of the two world blocs, India's conception of non-alignment "had a metaphysical and psychological background."[21]

The leading role which Nehru believed that India must play in the Afro-Asian context was, first and foremost, the widening of the "area of peace," or, to put it in another way, the spread of the stand on non-alignment. For this reason, Nehru fought tooth and nail against the policy of military defence pacts, such as the Manila treaty, espoused particularly by the US in the early 1950s.[22] In this context must also be seen Nehru's wooing of China, culminating in the Tibet pact of 1954 with the famous *Panch Sheel* principles, and India's efforts to have China accepted at the Bandung Asian-African conference in 1955. After Nehru's meeting with Chou En-lai in 1954 he wrote in a letter to Indian National Congress leaders that no one could guarantee peace for a given number of years, but even a few years gained were well worth striving for. If the great powers declared their adherence to the policy of non-intervention (as set out in the *Panch Sheel*) there would be an immediate change for the better. Nehru added: "Even if such declarations are not sincerely meant the result will be to create a force in favour of peace and non-interference." The onus, he concluded, was now on China.[23]

The passage is significant because it goes a long way to explain Nehru's determination in pushing the principles of the *Panch Sheel*.

This, and his desire to spread the doctrine of non-alignment, formed as seen in Chapter 4 (p. 59 f.), the main reason for his advocacy of the Asian-African conference at Bandung. In the years following Bandung Nehru deliberately closed his eyes to the steady deterioration in relations with China, until the open clashes along the border became a fact for the entire world to see.[24] As champion of the ideas of world peace, coexistence, non-interference and non-alignment, and of the solidarity of the Afro-Asian peoples ranged behind these principles, Nehru had to be on good terms with China. No matter how different their economic and political systems, only an alliance between the two Asian giants would serve as a foundation for that Afro-Asian solidarity, synonymous with the "area of peace" for which Nehru was striving. Not for nothing was there such a great deal of talk in India in the early 1950s that China and India should jointly pledge themselves to respect the frontiers of the countries of South-East Asia, and that such a "guarantee" should then be made the basis for a demand for the withdrawal of American, British and French forces from the Asian mainland.[25] Peking's acceptance of the principles of peaceful coexistence, non-interference and the other points of the *Panch Sheel* appeared to be a vindication of Nehru's policy. In a very real sense, the signing of the *Panch Sheel* made the Bandung conference possible; without this, it is highly doubtful whether Nehru would have added his weight to the call for an Asian-African conference.

After the *Panch Sheel* the Chinese themselves began putting pressure on India for collective action in Asia. The Chinese in 1954 were in the throes of a peace offensive; in an effort to achieve recognition they had launched a "good neighbour" policy which reached its culmination at Bandung. It was the Chinese who now urged Asian countries to "consult among themselves with a view to seeking common measures to safeguard peace and security in Asia"[26]; it was they who suggested to the Indians the establishment of an Asian Consultative Committee to seek ways to extend the "area of of peace."[27] The Chinese were in favour of collective security; they wished to see some kind of Asian organization which could stand against the South-East Asian defence organization. They wanted the countries that subscribed to the theory of the "area of peace," and above all India, to face collective responsibility, at least in the political if not in the military sense, in meeting external threats to disturb peace. These demands were put to Nehru during his visit to Peking in October 1954. However, this was going too far for the Indian leader, whose anathema for anything akin to a "third force" has already been noted. He refused to commit himself, relying instead solely on the *Panch Sheel*. The Sino-Indian friendship was not to last long—until barely after Bandung. The two were soon to part ways, and the increasing rift between India and China—which eventually erupted into war—undermined the entire edifice of foreign policy conceptions which Nehru had so laboriously built. Nehru had evidently failed to grasp the almost inherent conflict existing in the different political outlooks of China and India. For China, India was a "capitalist country," led by a "reactionary bourgeoisie"[28]; as such China could not allow Nehru to be a rival leader of a neutralist grouping of nations. Friendship towards India, which had had its uses to China during the "good neighbour" policy of 1954, was soon discarded after Bandung, and from then on India's policy was doomed to failure. With tension between India and China steadily mounting, the entire advocacy of an "area of peace" in the Afro-Asian world, and with it the solidarity of the Afro-Asian peoples, became unreal.

Thus on this one point, on which Nehru had placed so much emphasis in his speeches and writings, the Indians were blatantly unsuccessful. What of the other foreign policy aims of India, and what were these aims? Nehru himself described India's foreign policy objectives in a speech at Columbia University in October 1949 in the following highly idealistic terms:

The pursuit of peace, not through alignment with any major power or group of powers, but through an independent approach to each controversial or disputed issue; the liberation of subject peoples; the maintenance of freedom, both national and individual; the elimination of racial discrimination; and the elimination of want, disease and ignorance which afflict the greater part of the world's population.[29]

Put more pragmatically, India's foreign policy objectives can be divided into two groups. First were the universalist, idealist aims propounded so often by Nehru, including anti-colonialism, anti-racialism, non-alignment, the pursuit of peace and mediation with a view to relaxing international tensions; second were the more particularistic aims specific to Indian requirements, such as maintenance of Indian independence, the development of Indian economy —thus keeping open all channels of international aid—the winning of international support over the Kashmir issue, the integration of the Portuguese settlements on the Indian sub-continent, and the recognition of Afro-Asia as a new vital force in the world, which, under Indian guidance, would reduce the possibility of a third world war.

The specifically Indian issues, such as Kashmir, the Portuguese settlements, the development of Indian economy, and even the maintenance of India's independence, fall outside the context of this study. More relevant are the more general aims, and in particular the role of India in fostering the image of Afro-Asia as a new and vital force in the world. India had played a major, almost preponderant role in the first steps leading to an Afro-Asian togetherness. In this her foreign policy actions fitted her foreign policy objectives. After Bandung, however, there was a waning of influence, a gradual decline in the role of leadership on the part of India which becomes more noticeable as the years pass. The first and foremost cause for this decline has already been described, namely, the Sino-Indian conflict. There were, however, two additional causes. One of them is to be found in the divergence in attitude between Nehru and other Afro-Asian leaders, in particular Abdel Nasser (see Chapter 5). The other emanates from the change in quality of the leadership of India after the death of Nehru.

A study of Indian participation in the Afro-Asian Movement shows that this went through three distinct stages. The first one led up to Bandung, in which India played a preponderant role in creating, in particular, an atmosphere of Asian solidarity (see Chapter 3). Africa hardly came into the picture in these early years in the 1950s; lip-service was occasionally employed to include the peoples of Africa, but, as the Bandung conference itself demonstrated, African participation then was minimal. The second stage came in the post-Bandung period. Nehru continued his policy of seeking to widen the "area of peace," of opposing military pacts and of encouraging other countries to adopt a stand of non-alignment.

President Nasser with Mrs. Gandhi and Marshal Tito during a Three-Power conference between India, Yugoslavia and Egypt in New Delhi in 1966.

An Afro-Asian meeting: Ghana President Dr. Kwame Nkrumah pictured with Mrs. Indira Gandhi in New Delhi in 1966—when he was on his way to Peking. It was while he was in Peking that he was deposed by a military coup.

Yet as more countries adopted these policies, India found herself losing the position of *primus inter pares* which had characterized her attitude vis-à-vis the other countries of Asia and Africa in the earlier period. The other adherents to non-alignment were not inclined to see India as their leader; for them Afro-Asian solidarity was not a means to enlarge the "area of peace" but an instrument in the struggle against the colonial powers and a means to obtain a better deal for the newly independent countries. The decline in the stature of India, and the difference in attitude between that adopted by India and by some of the more militant leaders of the Afro-Asian Movement, was shown most dramatically at the Belgrade conference of non-aligned nations in September 1961. Nehru had not been among the original sponsors of the conference; he had, in fact, displayed little enthusiasm for it from the start. His reasons for eventually joining the sponsors were mundane and far from the idealistic motives which Nehru usually attributed to such events. India agreed to the conference mainly because the exclusion of China and Pakistan (neither of which was considered non-aligned) gave her a better chance to bring forward her own point of view to the detriment of her two adversaries. But at the conference itself Nehru failed to create a consensus behind his opinions: for him the question of peace and coexistence was of top priority, while for others, such as presidents Sukarno and Nkrumah, the continuation of the anti-colonial struggle was far more important.

Thus already in this second phase of Indian activity within the Afro-Asian framework, there was a decline caused by India's own problems with China and by divergent attitudes among the Afro-Asian leaders. The Belgrade conference gave expression to this decline and marked the beginning of the third stage, of Indian withdrawal, alongside the decline of the Afro-Asian Movement itself. In the more militant expression of Afro-Asianism, namely the Afro-Asian Peoples' Solidarity Organization, the Indians ceased to play any significant role, their lead being taken over by the Egyptians; at the UN Afro-Asian group, the initiative passed increasingly into African hands, the Africans being far more united than the Asians and also more militant. On governmental level India continued to be active in the international arena, as evinced, for example, over Suez and in the Congo crisis. However, her influence on this level was fast waning:

the Sino-Indian conflict, India's action at Goa, which was contrary to Nehru's teachings, the continued tension with Pakistan over Kashmir, and Sukarno's bid for a "second Bandung" against the wishes of India all contributed to this decline. Moreover, Abdel Nasser had increasingly drawn away the Arab countries into his own orbit, while the African countries, and in particular the French African territories, had never come under Nehru's spell. Yet despite all these facts India continued to enjoy enormous prestige because of the stature of Nehru himself. When he died in 1964 this positive element was also lost. Neither Shastri nor Indira Gandhi, who became prime minister in 1966, was capable of restoring India to the central position she had filled in the early days; nor were the circumstances the same, for the Afro-Asian Movement had changed and declined to the same degree that India's influence in it had waned. For that there were additional reasons, which will be examined later.

NOTES

[1] For example:

"Ultimately, a foreign policy is the outcome of economic policy, and until India has properly evolved her economic policy, her foreign policy will be rather vague . . . "—Nehru, in speech in Constituent Assembly, 4.12.1947, quoted in Nehru, *India's Foreign Policy: Selected Speeches. Sept. 1946–April 1961.*

"Every country's foreign policy, first of all, is concerned with its own security and with protecting its own progress . . . a deliberate policy of friendship with other countries goes farther in gaining security than almost anything else"—Nehru, in reply to debate on foreign affairs in the Lok Sabha, 9.12.1958, quoted in *ibid.*, p. 79.

"Ideological urges obviously play some part . . . especially in a democracy because . . . no policy can go very far if it is quite divorced from the people's thinking. However, in the final analysis, all foreign policy concerns itself chiefly with the national interest of the country concerned" —Nehru to Brecher, in Brecher's *Nehru*, p. 217.

[2] Broadcast from New Delhi on 3.4.1948, quoted in Nehru, *India's Foreign Policy*, p. 182.

[3] Broadcast from London on 12.1.1951, quoted in *India's Foreign Policy*, *loc. cit.*

[4] Nehru to Brecher in *Nehru, a Political Biography*, p. 217.

[5] *Ibid.*, p. 213; See also M. S. Rajan who wrote that "*the primary goal* of India's foreign policy has been the maintenance and promotion of international peace and security"—*India in World Affairs—1954–1956*, p. 40.

[6] Nehru, *India's Foreign Policy*, p. 2.

[7] Nehru, at rally in honour of President Abdel Nasser and the deputy prime minister of Afghanistan—*Times of India*, 14.4.1955. This was no new attitude on the part of Nehru. On the contrary, his advocacy of an "Asian personality" went back to the 1930s. He made particularly eloquent pronouncements on this subject at the Indian National Congress in 1939.

[8] Nehru, in speech in the Canadian Parliament, Ottawa, on 24.10.1949, quoted in *Jawahrlal Nehru's Speeches 1949–1953*, p. 128.

[9] Nehru, in interview with R. K. Karanjia. See his *Mind of Mr. Nehru*, p. 91.

[10] For a description of the influence of the concept of *himsa* in Indian political thought, see, for example, an article by R., "India and the Cold War," in *Middle East Journal,* Vol. 9, No. 3, Summer 1955, p. 261 ff.

[11] Brecher, *The New States of Asia,* p. 116.

[12] *Asian Relations Report*, p. 23.

[13] Poplai (ed.): *Select Documents on Asian Affairs: India, 1947–1950, Vol. II: External Affairs*, Introduction, p. XVII.

[14] Poplai, *ibid.,* Introduction, p. XX.

[15] Speech in the Constituent Assembly (Legislative), 8.3.1949, quoted in Nehru, *India's Foreign Policy* (present author's italics).

[16] 22.3.1949.

[17] Nehru in speech in Canadian Parliament, 24.10.1949, quoted in *Jawaharlal Nehru's Speeches . . .* , p. 128 (present author's italics).

[18] See, for example, Nehru's reply to a debate in the Lok Sabha on 20.8.1958 (quoted in *India's Foreign Policy*) in which he was most scathing in his criticism of the idea of a "third force."

[19] There exists a considerable volume of literature on the semantics of terms such as neutralism, neutrality, positive neutralism, non-alignment, etc. India has been variously described as following a doctrinaire or dogmatic neutralism (Sayegh, *Dynamics of Neutralism in the Arab World*), neutralist as opposed to non-aligned (Brecher, *New States of Asia . . .*), messianic neutralist (Leo Hamon, *Non-Engagement et Neutralism, op. cit.*), while Nehru himself stated that he did not like the label "neutral" (statement at the UN Correspondents' Association in New York on 4.10.1960, quoted in *India's Foreign Policy,* p. 85), nor did he approve of the term "positive neutrality" (Lok Sabha, 22.11.1960, quoted in *India's Foreign Policy*). It is not proposed to join this discussion on semantics here.

[20] *Hindu,* 28.4.1960, quoted also in Char, *Profile of Nehru,* p. 77.

[21] S. C. Jha, former ambassador of India in Paris, in an interview with the author.

[22] See, for example, his attack on the Manila treaty in his speech at the Lok Sabha on 29.9.1954, quoted in *India's Foreign Policy*, p. 89.

[23] *The Times,* London, 8.7.1954.

[24] From July 17, 1954, there were already border incidents in the Wu-je area, a fact kept quiet by the Indians until the White Paper on relations with China was published in 1959—see Rowland *History of Sino-Indian Relations,* p. 89.

[25] See, for example, M.R. Masani's "India: Do's and Dont's for Americans," in *Foreign Affairs*, Vol. 30, No. 3, April 1952, p. 45.

[26] Chou En-lai at Geneva conference on 28.4.1954—see *Indian Views of Sino-Indian Relations No. 1* (Indian Press Digest Monograph Series), 1956, p. 47; See also Rowland, *op. cit.*, p. 92.

[27] *Ibid.* At a press conference in New Delhi after signing the Tibet agreement, Chou En-lai replied in answer to a question that he thought it was desirable for the appropriate responsible persons of the principal Asian countries to consult with each other—*The Times*, London, 28.6.1954.

[28] For the different attitudes of China and the Soviet Union to India, see John Gittings (ed.), *Sino-Soviet Dispute, 1956–1965—Extracts from Recent Documents*, Royal Institute of International Affairs, London, 1964, p. 33. For details on the switch in Chinese foreign policy after Bandung, see Zagoria, *Sino-Soviet Conflict, 1956–1965*; Zagoria put the date of the change at the end of 1957. Thus, "by November 1957, it was apparent that the Chinese Communists were considering abandoning the cautious, consolidating, Bandung-spirit, Right strategy, in effect since 1954, and that they were laying the groundwork for a forward surge" (p. 66).

[29] Quoted by Tyson, *Nehru*, pp. 69–70.

12 THE CASE OF INDONESIA

A diagram of the power structure of Indonesia, which was adopted by the Indonesian Parliament on June 9, 1966, gives the fount of all power in Indonesia as "the *esprit* and the basic conception of the nation known as *Pantja Sila*." From this fount emanate not only the Constitution of 1945, but also all the power institutions in the country—Congress of the People, Parliament, President, Supreme Court, etc.

Thus the *Pantja Sila,* or "Five Principles"—not to be confused with the Indian *Panch Sheel*—formed, in the words of General T. N. J. Suharto, president of Indonesia from 1968, "the philosophical base of our state,"[1] or, according to Muhammad IIatta, "the state ideology."[2] These principles, according to Suharto, "constitute the principal points of view of our nation, from generation to generation and going back many centuries. They thus contain the characteristics of our personality; the *Pantja Sila* is at one and the same time the aim and the accomplishment of our ideas."[3] The first of these principles is belief in Divine Omnipotence and characterizes the strong Muslim feelings of the majority of the population. The second is Humanism,[4] belief in the need to ameliorate the value and the conditions of Man. Suharto adds the following explanation to this principle: it is belief in the right of liberty of each nation, and consequently, a belief that every form of colonialism in the world must be obliterated. The third principle is nationalism, or the unity of Indonesia; in view of the geographical complex of thousands of islands which together compose the Republic of Indonesia, this principle is self-evident. The fourth calls for democracy, and the fifth for social justice—the raising of the standard of living of the entire nation.

The five principles, first propounded by Ahmad Sukarno on June 1, 1945, in the first session of the Commission preparing for independence, formed the basis of Sukarno's political thought, and became a major part of the Preamble to the country's Constitution. The Preamble to the 1945 Constitution was specific regarding the principles guiding the foreign policy of Indonesia. It stated implicitly that liberty was the right of each nation in the world and that colonialism must be abolished, for it stood in contradiction to humanism and justice. Indonesia, according to the Preamble, should participate in the establishment of a world order based on independence, peace and social justice.

These were the planks on which Indonesia's foreign policy has rested, and they have been confirmed by the regime which gradually eased President Sukarno out of power. In its first decree in 1966,[5] later to be confirmed and strengthened in 1968,[6] the Congress of the People passed a series of recommendations to serve as principles of Indonesia's foreign policy. They included:

> Indonesia should renounce its membership of any bloc or military pact;
> Asian problems should be solved by the Asians themselves, including the question of Vietnam;
> the UN resolution on decolonization has not been fully applied. Indonesia must always support every struggle for independence, whichever it may be;
> the strengthening of Afro-Asian solidarity should be the *principal part* of the independent and active foreign policy of Indonesia, a policy which is anti-imperialist and anti-colonialist;
> Afro-Asian organizations such as the Afro-Asian Islamic Organization or the Afro-Asian Journalists' Organization should be strengthened. This is in conformity with the firm policy of Indonesia in respecting and applying the ten principles of *Bandung*.[7]

These precepts have to be examined more closely for they form the basis of Indonesia's initiative on behalf of Afro-Asia. Thus, anti-colonialism has had a central place in the thinking of Indonesia, and, closely combined with it, a deep-rooted antagonism to the West. Anti-Westernism had been imprinted on the minds of the people, particularly the youth, during the Japanese occupation in World War II. After the war came the long-drawn-out struggle for independence against the Dutch. That struggle, and the support given Holland by the US and other Western countries, left its mark in a decidedly anti-Western orientation; it also led to Indonesia taking a particularly extremist line against colonialism in general. One of the first statements of the Indonesian representative at the UN was that "Indonesia will provide its help to all the peoples still colonized in their struggle for independence."[8]

By the time Indonesia became independent, the cold war between the Western and the Communist blocs had become the dominant feature in the political behaviour of the world. Yet anti-Western feelings in Indonesia did not in themselves bring her nearer to the Communist bloc. There existed a large Communist Party in Indonesia, but there were equally parties—the Muslim ones—which were fiercely opposed to Communism. Thus the internal political structure of Indonesia reflected the foreign policy stand which she took from the the very beginning of independence of seeking to balance between the two blocs. Indonesia, like India, sought to create an "area" which adhered neither to the West nor to the Communists. But whereas for India this was to be an "area of peace," for Indonesia the question of anti-colonialism and of deciding "ourselves what our new world is to be"[9] took precedence over the need for world peace. And, whereas for India Afro-Asian solidarity was to be a means of enlarging the "area of peace," for Sukarno the "best weapon in the struggle against domination lies in preserving Afro-Asian solidarity."[10]

However, if anti-colonialism and an active non-alignment were inherent in the general attitudes of all the political parties (except of the Communists in the case of non-alignment) there were marked differences of interpretation by the various parties. Thus, the Socialists, under the leadership of Sjoetan Sjahrir, advocated a "positive neutralism" and the formation of a "third force" which would lessen the dangers of polarization in the world and reduce tension in Asia. On the other hand, the Masjumi[11] Party, which in the first years after independence was easily the largest party in Indonesia and came to power in 1950, was more intent on setting up some form of pan-Islamic cooperation and took concrete steps in that direction (see Chapter 3, p. 42, and note 35). This trend, however, was not to last long. In April 1951, a new coalition government came to power headed by the National Party (PNI).[12] The National Party, like the Socialists, believed in a militant neutralism and the need of a third force. The ideas of pan-Islamism were dropped, and in their place two immediate foreign policy objectives were advocated: support of liberation movements, in this case specifically those of Morocco and Tunisia, and the establishment of an organizational framework for countries with neutralist and anti-colonialist tendencies similar to those of Indonesia in order to activate the idea of a "third force." The Indonesians soon set about putting these ideas into practice.

We thus come to the series of moves, described in Chapter 3, which led to the Indonesian proposal at the Colombo conference to hold an Asian-African conference, and eventually to Bandung itself. The Indonesians had no clear-cut plans in taking this initiative. They had no definite views on how this Asian-African togetherness was to operate. Their views changed several times in the course of the years. Thus, for example, on May 29, 1954, less than a month after the Colombo talks, the Indonesian ambassador in Cairo handed to the Egyptian premier an invitation to the forthcoming Asian-African conference. Its aim, according to the invitation, was "to discuss the problems of every participating country [sic!] to coordinate their efforts and to lay down a permanent and unified policy towards international events."[13] This was tantamount to setting up a political bloc. Several days later the ambassador issued another statement, giving some intimation of the proposed ideological trend of the forthcoming conference: it was to be neutralist, opposing treaties with the US, and upholding the rights of people oppressed by imperialism."[14] This extremist approach was speedily modified after the talks which Indonesian Premier Dr. Sastroamidjojo had with Nehru in New Delhi in the autumn of 1954. When Sastroamidjojo was interviewed by the Far East editor of *International News Service* shortly after his trip to New Delhi, he defined the major objective of the conference as "to view the position of Asia and Africa and their peoples in the world of today and the contribution they can make to the promotion of world peace and cooperation." Asked what common denominator could be expected to unify the invited nations, he replied: "Some of the common denominators might be the social, economic and cultural problems and relations of the countries represented in the conference, since most of the invitees are today facing more or less the same economic situation in their respective countries. Another issue of common interest might be the question of colonialism."[15] This toning down of Indonesian expectations from the conference was undoubtedly a result of the talks with Indian leaders. Later, in hindsight, Indonesians were to dilute their demands even more. Thus, in 1958, Muhammad Hatta wrote that Indonesia had no desire to "set up a third bloc in partnership with the states of Asia and Africa. She wishes to see a meeting from time to time among the Asian and African states, like that of 1955, as a '*moral union*' which can influence in the interest of peace, those states which are banded into blocs."[16]

These and other declarations give the impression that the Indonesians had no clear ideological aims regarding the conference other than a general desire to create a body which could combat colonialism more effectively and assert the rights of the newly independent, ex-colonized countries. There were, however, more pragmatic reasons for Indonesia's eagerness to sponsor an Afro-Asian conference: Dr. Sastroamidjojo was in a minority in Parliament. His National Party was becoming increasingly dissatisfied because of the chaotic economic situation in the country. The opposition of the Socialists, the Masjumi, the Christian parties and the Communists was becoming stronger. There was growing criticism of corruption in high places, of patronage, of the government's ineffectiveness in dealing with administrative and economic problems. In the outlying islands, in particular, there was wide conviction that Java was benefiting disproportionately from the country's foreign exchange.[17] With general elections due in May 1955, the idea of a large-scale international conference held in Indonesia was a heaven-sent opportunity to rally support to the government: it would silence Communist opposition by the hand stretched out to Peking; it would gain nationalist favour by the strong support Indonesia would give to Muslim causes in the Afro-Asian world.

Detractors of Indonesia's leaders consider that these internal reasons were the principal motives for their determination to initiate an Asian-African conference.[18]   It is, today, impossible to judge the relative weight of internal problems against more altruistic foreign policy objectives in the decision to be active in the Afro-Asian sphere. However, it is clear from the behaviour of Indonesia's political leaders, and in particular of President Sukarno himself, that their interest in Afro-Asia far transcended pragmatic gains on the internal political front. Sukarno has considered himself as having a special mission both to consolidate and maintain the solidarity of the Afro-Asian camp and to act as a champion of all peoples still under colonial rule.

The anti-colonialist fervour, which in India gradually declined as an increasing number of countries became independent, was kept aflame in Indonesia throughout the 1950s by its claim to West Irian (Netherlands New Guinea), an issue in which the Western countries were again considered to have taken a stand hostile to Indonesia. The tension over West Irian increased even more when Western countries —in particular the US operating from Taiwan and the Philippines and the British from Malaya and Singapore—were accused of giving help to the rebels of Sumatra and Celebes in the general uprising in 1958. On the other hand the Soviet Union and China gave their unflinching support to Indonesia over West Irian, and, when the 1958 rebellion broke out, rushed arms to the Indonesian armed forces which the West had previously refused to supply. These developments, combined with the facts that from 1957 parliamentary democracy had been replaced by guided democracy and that the powerful Indonesian Communist Party had been incorporated into the government, caused Indonesia to veer to an increasingly hostile posture with regard to the West, a posture which she attempted to impose on the Afro-Asian Movement as a whole. The pro-Chinese line taken by the Indonesian delegates in the Afro-Asian Peoples' Solidarity Organization enjoyed the blessing of the government till the Suharto takeover in late 1965. Sukarno himself addressed several of these meetings, while in the official conferences of Afro-Asian or non-aligned states the president insisted time and again that the struggle against colonialism and imperialism took precedence over peaceful coexistence and world peace. "There will be peaceful coexistence between the developing countries and the imperialist states only when we can face them with equal strength. And that equal strength we can obtain only through solidarity among us . . . we cannot develop economically, nor socially, nor culturally until we have removed these forces of domination," he once declared.[19] In these sentences can be found the underlying causes for Sukarno's profound belief in Afro-Asian solidarity.

Sukarno, then, continued to advocate a "second Bandung," and throughout the late 1950s and early 1960s he sought tirelessly to gain support for another Afro-Asian conference. But even on Indonesia, the most articulate of all countries in favour of Afro-Asian solidarity, the Sino-Indian conflict had its effects. Thus, a leading newspaper in Surabaya wrote: "Chinese aggression has nullified the effects of the Bandung conference ... if the Afro-Asian countries remain quiet at seeing Peking's invasion, then let us consider that the Bandung conference has been dissolved."[20] A Jakarta newspaper commented that "the gay atmosphere prevailing in the Afro-Asian conference in Bandung in April 1955 is still fresh in our memory. Now four years have elapsed and what was acclaimed in the Bandung conference has vanished. There is not one of the results of the Bandung conference that we can be proud of."[21]

Disillusionment had set in in Indonesia, as well as in other countries of Asia and Africa. Yet Sukarno persisted in his pressure for a "second Bandung." and, once again, internal considerations played their part in this persistence. The steps taken by Indonesia which led to the abortive conference at Algiers in 1965 have been described in Chapter 5; they need not be repeated here. The failure of that conference was followed shortly afterwards by the abortive Communist coup in Indonesia, by General Suharto's rise to power, and by the gradual disappearance of Sukarno from the political scene. These developments put an end to Indonesia's *active* role in the Afro-Asian domain. Henceforward she was only to pay lip service to these principles which had been so dear to the previous regime. Instead, the new regime attempted to consolidate its position by an appeal for large-scale economic aid from all quarters, and by the establishment of regional cooperation with Thailand, Malaysia, the Philippines and Singapore, in place of the more nebulous Afro-Asian solidarity.

Indonesia, the greatest champion of Afro-Asian solidarity of all, thus gradually ceased to be active, and, as had occurred with regard to India, the decline of Indonesia's interest coincided with the decline of the movement as a whole, and contributed to it. The causes of that decline will be examined more closely in Chapter 14.

NOTES

[1] Speech by Suharto at the Foreign Correspondents Club in Tokyo, 30.3. 1968. The speech is printed in full in *Grandes Lignes de la Politique Exterieure et Interieure de l'Indonesie,* Ambassade de la République d'Indonesie, Alger 1968; see p. 6 for quotation in text.

[2] Hatta, "Indonesia between the Power Blocs," in *Foreign Affairs,* April 1958, p. 481.

[3] Suharto, quoted in *Grandes Lignes . . ., op. cit.,* p. 6.

[4] Instead of using the word humanism, in regard to the second of the five principles, Sukarno used the term "internationalism." See Conte, *Bandoung,* pp. 24–25.

[5] Congress of the People, Note No. 1/MPRS/1966.

[6] Congress of the People, Note No. 4/MPRS/1968.

[7] See *Grandes Lignes . . ., op. cit.,* p. 28. (Present author's italics.)

[8] Quoted by Queuille, *Histoire de l'Afro-Asiatisme,* p. 71.

[9] Sukarno in speech at opening session of the Jakarta Preparatory Conference for a "second Bandung," 11.4.1964—see *Times of India,* 12.4.1964.

[10] Jakarta Preparatory Conference—*Times of India,* 12.4.1964.

[11] The Madjelis Sjuro Muslimin Indonesia was led by a group of religious Socialists, who followed the modernist schools of thought in Islam. Largely for this reason the more conservative wing broke away in 1952 and formed its own party, the Nahadul Ulama, a step which seriously weakened the Masjumi. For a good description of Indonesian political parties, see G. Kahin (ed.), *Major Governments of Asia,* New York, 1963, p. 61 ff.

[12] Partai Nasionalis Indonesia. In the words of Kahin, *ibid.,* p. 614, this was the party of the bureaucratic middle class and of the territorial civil service.

[13] Radio Damascus, 30.5.1954.

[14] *Al-Ahrām,* Cairo, 6.6.1954.

[15] *Asian-African Conference Bulletin,* Foreign Ministry, Jakarta, No. 1, March 1955.

[16] Hatta, "Indonesia between the Power Blocs," *op. cit.,* p. 481. (Present author's italics.)

[17] The Achinese of northern Sumatra came out in armed revolt shortly after Dr. Sastroamidjojo took office.

[18] See, for example, *Economist,* London, 25.12.1954, which asserted that Indonesia was preoccupied with external affairs principally as a sop to the people to divert them from the constantly deteriorating internal situation.

[19] At the "second Belgrade" conference of non-aligned states, held at Cairo in October 1964. For full text of speech see BBC Monitoring Report ME/1677/E/1-7 (Cairo Radio in English, 0700 GMT, 7.10.1964).

[20] *Suara Rakjat,* Surabaya, 2.9.1959, brought in *National Press Digest,* Jakarta, 9.9.1959.

[21] *Abadi,* Jakarta, 9.9.1959, brought in *National Press Digest,* Jakarta, 12.9. 1959.

13 AFRICA (SOUTH OF THE SAHARA) AND THE AFRO-ASIAN MOVEMENT—WITH SPECIAL REFERENCE TO TANZANIA

The birth of the Afro-Asian Movement was, as we have seen, largely an Asian affair. Africa was drawn in only gradually, and played a junior role throughout the formative years. At the Bandung conference in 1955 there was only minimal African representation.[1] Similarly, the Afro-Asian group at the United Nations was, in its first years, strictly speaking an Arabo-Asian group, and even after Ethiopia and Liberia had joined it, their representatives attended the meetings irregularly. As for the Afro-Asian Peoples' Solidarity Organization, it was, from the outset, dominated by the Russians, the Chinese and the Egyptians, and repeated efforts on the part of African delegations to make a greater impact on the Organization failed.[2]

There were a number of reasons for this state of affairs, the first and most important being, naturally enough, that the majority of African states gained their independence only during and after 1960. This fact, which explains why only three African states south of the Sahara participated at Bandung (there being no other independent "Black" states at the time), does not, however, justify the muted role of the Africans in expressing their solidarity with the Afro-Asian Movement nor does it explain their minor impact on the non-governmental AAPSO. We have, therefore, to seek further causes for this unequal relationship between Africa and Asia within the Afro-Asian Movement.

The first political and national stirrings in Africa were almost exclusively pan-African, and not, as in Asia, particular to any territory or people within the continent. Whereas in Asia particularistic nationalisms—Indian, Chinese, Japanese, etc.—gave birth to more universalist notions of Asianism and Afro-Asianism, in Africa it was the other way around. The Pan-African congress long preceded any

238

particularistic nationalist movements on African soil; the political education of African leaders such as Nkrumah, Azikiwe, Johnson and Kenyatta was, from the first, steeped in pan-Africanist concepts.

This is not the place to recount the history of the Pan-African Movement. But these pan-African overtones to the African national movements had a profound effect both on African political thinking in general and on the attitude of Africans to the Afro-Asian Movement in particular. For from the beginning there existed a strong sense of *African* identity, over and above Afro-Asian solidarity, which had no equal in Asia. The political connotations of pan-Africanism which occupied the minds of the leaders of the British territories of Africa found their match in the ideas of *Négritude* and of an "African personality" propagated in the French territories. This intellectual and political activity created a feeling of African separatism, which later marked the foreign policy attitudes of all African states and affected their approach to the Afro-Asian Movement.

There existed, in fact, a certain rivalry between the pan-African aims centred on Accra and the Afro-Asian policies of Cairo and other centres. The Cairo conference of AAPSO in December 1957 was followed by the first conference of independent African states in Accra in April 1958. The first Afro-Asian Economic Conference, which was held in Cairo in December 1958, was matched by the first All-African Peoples' Congress which opened on the same day in Accra. The second AAPSO plenary assembly which took place in Conakry in April 1960 was forestalled by less than a week by an African "Positive Action" conference convened by Nkrumah in Accra.[3] Commenting on the conference of independent African states in Accra, *The Times* of London declared: "Dr. Nkrumah will have to concern himself whether the relative emphasis is to be placed on the extension of the Afro-Asian Movement or on the independent development of what is well described as the 'African personality.'"[4] In fact, there was no such choice, before either Nkrumah or any of the other African leaders. To them it was self-evident that Africa came first, and their allegiance to Afro-Asian ideals was motivated at least partly because they were convinced that the larger body could be of help in solving African problems. Oscar Kambona, a former foreign minister of Tanzania (then Tanganyika), put it this way: "We began to feel that Afro-Asia—apart from its role of narrowing cold-

war conflicts—could help with material and moral aid in the liberation of southern Africa."[5] Thus, at the conference of independent
African states at Accra in 1958, all the speakers with the exception
of Muhammad Fawzī, foreign minister of the United Arab Republic,
made African unity the major theme of their speeches. Nkrumah, and,
indeed, most African nationalists, chose an African path, and this
was particularly expressed at the first conference of the All-African
Peoples' Congress in Accra that December. The AAPC was interested
exclusively in African problems. According to a leaflet distributed
before the Accra conference, the purpose of the meeting was:

> To formulate concrete plans and work out the Gandhi tactics
> and strategy of the African non-violent revolution regarding
> colonialism and imperialism, racialism and discrimination,
> tribalism and religious separatism, and the position of chief-
> tancy under colonial rule and under a free democratic society.[6]

Similarly, the objectives of the Permanent Secretariat of the AAPC
in Accra were to promote understanding and unity among the peoples
of Africa, to accelerate the liberation of Africa from imperialism
and colonialism, to develop the feeling of being one community
among the peoples of Africa, with the object of the emergence of a
United States of Africa.[7] This was a far cry from Afro-Asianism.

As more African states became independent, the All-African
Peoples' Congress lost its importance. A more responsible voice for
Africa, through its governments, was required. Its place was taken by
the OAI. Though less extremist and flamboyant than its non-official
predecessor, the OAU was, by its nature and definition, an inward-
looking body. The militant pan-African slogans were dropped, the
dreams of a United States of Africa were laid aside, but the interests
of all states in Africa, moderate and militant alike, remained bound
by the periphery of their own continent far more so than those in
other continents.

Obviously, however, the African states could not shut themselves
off from the problems of the world. They could not be isolationist,
if only because of their urgent need of foreign aid and because they
canvassed for support for the non-independent territories in Africa.
They therefore had to develop foreign policy attitudes beyond immediate African questions. Above all, this process was exacerbated

because the cold-war conflicts did not bypass Africa. The Congo crisis, in particular, and the subsequent embroilment of the great powers forced the Africans to take a stand regarding two opposing approaches, which eventually found expression in the rival association of African countries into the militantly anti-colonialist "Casablanca" and more moderate "Monrovia" groups.

This polarization into two opposing units did not, however, mean that each group openly supported one of the two sides in the cold war. Virtually all of the African states, whether of the "Casablanca" or "Monrovia" group, professed to follow a policy of non-alignment vis-à-vis the great-power conflict. There exist scores of statements and declarations by the majority of African leaders on the virtues of non-alignment.[8] Yet this much-abused term covers a multitude of foreign policy postures. A number of African countries such as Senegal, the Ivory Coast, Chad, Kenya and Nigeria, to mention only some, had foreign troops on their soil or their armies were commanded by officers of their former colonizers. The regimes of others—Kenya, Uganda, Tanganyika (Tanzania) and Gabon—were propped up with the help of troops from Great Britain or France when mutiny and rebellion threatened to overthrow them, and yet professed to be non-aligned. Still others followed a policy consistently hostile to one of the two world blocs.

Despite these anomalies, however, the majority of African leaders followed, by self-definition, a non-aligned policy in that they had no wish to become involved in issues which they did not consider to be their own; non-alignment became a means to enable Africa not to be drawn "into areas of conflict which so far have not spread south of the Sahara" and in regard to which "we cannot affect the outcome," to use Nkrumah's words in 1958.[9]

There were a number of reasons for taking this stand, not least among them the strong desire for self assertion, or even self-significance, which has been described in Chapter 2 as one of the common denominators creating a community of interests among both African and Asian newly independent countries. Another reason, also mentioned in that chapter, was the right of full political independence springing from Africa's position as the world's underdog.[10]

Over and above the basic desire of most Africans to be non-committed in cold-war conflicts, three factors more than any others influenced their foreign policy. These were (1) the degree to which an African regime was willing to accept some form of presence of the former colonial power in exchange for hastening on the process of raising its country's standard of living. The regime of President Houphoüet-Boigny of the Ivory Coast which accepted French presence at the cost of slowing down the process of Africanization formed an extreme in one direction, that of former President Nkrumah of Ghana provided an extreme example in the opposite; (2) the degree to which foreign aid received by an African regime was conditional to its following certain foreign policy lines; (3) the stand taken by non-African regimes on colonialism in general and on the liberation of the non-independent African territories in particular.

In most former French territories the first factors have operated to create a situation whereby on most foreign policy questions not directly affecting Africa these countries are, at the very least, strongly influenced by France. In other territories the third factor has operated so strongly as to bring about a rupture in diplomatic relations, as occurred, for example, between several African countries and Great Britain over the Rhodesian issue.

These three factors, then, link up with the basic stand of African states on non-alignment. They affect the degree of non-alignment adopted by each country and provide the weight which tips the balance in favour of one power bloc or the other. Parallel to their approach to non-alignment has been the relationship of the African leaders to the Afro-Asian Movement. All consider themselves part and parcel of it, just as all consider themselves to be basically non-aligned. But some treat the subject with more importance, while others hardly pay it any attention.

No African regime can be described as typical. There is thus no obvious justification for choosing Tanzania for the case study in this chapter, except, perhaps, because it does not easily fall into any of the African pigeonholes. It was not a member of the Casablanca group, nor was it in the Monrovia or Brazzaville groupings. It has been labelled militant and left-leaning, but on certain questions, such as that of Biafra, it sided with such conservative regimes as the Ivory Coast and Gabon. The foreign policy of Tanzania, then, is in many ways specially suitable for study here.

Unlike the situation in India and in many other countries, no clear-cut foreign policy had been adopted before Tanganyika achieved independence in 1961. When the Tanganyika African National Union (TANU) was created in 1954 by the reorganization of the Tanganyika African Association, it received little financial help from abroad, and what little it did receive was closely supervized by the British colonial administration. The party had to look inwards. It had to consolidate its position, especially in the rural areas, in the face of severe restrictions placed in its way by the colonial administration. It had to combat the settlers' organizations, which sought to obtain independence on the basis of government by minority, and it had to overcome the efforts of the opposition, which concentrated on organizing the urban elites. With such problems on its hands, the party "was not in a situation to choose which world bloc to support; there was no such problem. We didn't play any role in world politics, and the cold war did not have any influence on where we could get finance." These words by Oscar Kambona, one of the founders of TANU, and later foreign minister of Tanzania, explain the lack of any foreign policy by the party until independence.[11]

The moves towards independence and the organizing and strengthening of the party were the major interests of the Tanganyikan leaders during the 1950s. This concentration on internal problems continued after independence. In the years 1961–62 the emphasis was put on the process of Africanization; the tendency of the trade union movement to enter into "cold-war politics" was staved off by the general drive to replace expatriates by Africans, especially in the security forces.[12] "In this manner the heat was taken off the trade union pressure, which could have divided Tanganyika along cold war lines," Kambona said.

However, the cold war was thrust on Tanganyika like other countries in Africa. According to Kambona's analysis "The Congo issue divided Africa. We had to make our choice to join one or the other group or to keep out. We tried to get the two groups into one, in order to avoid embarrassment. We had to be moderate enough to win over Monrovia, but militant enough to win over Casablanca."[13] Tanganyika failed in its mission to play broker between the two rival African groupings, but succeeded in sidestepping the cold-war issues involved in the Congo crisis. Instead she developed a foreign policy orientation bound almost exclusively to African issues. "The liberation of Africa was the number one priority. *Everything else fitted in there,"* declared Kambona.[14] When Tanganyikan President Nyerere and Foreign Minister Kambona visited the US in 1963, they refused to discuss financial aid in their talks with President Kennedy, concentrating all their efforts "on the need to liberate southern Africa."[15]

It was largely to bring additional weight to this question of southern Africa that Nyerere and Kambona decided to play a more active role in the Afro-Asian Peoples' Solidarity Organization, and to be host to its assembly in 1963 (see Chapter 8, p. 162ff.) held at Moshi. However, despite the militant and one-sided nature of AAPSO, the Tanganyikans did not depart from their position of keeping a distance from cold-war conflicts. At Moshi, as has been shown, Nyerere powerfully emphasized Tanganyika's approach to the two superpower blocs in his opening speech. But the mere fact that Tanganyika's leaders were so consistent in their opposition to drawing nearer to either bloc made them espouse the Afro-Asian cause. This was the one association of states (apart from the UN itself) outside the confines of Africa to which membership was reconcilable with the strict laws of non-alignment which Tanganyika had set itself. Moreover, in East Africa, according to Kambona, Nehru and Gandhi had had tremendous influence. Their works had been widely read there. East Africans looked largely to India for leadership. India had put Tanganyika's case for independence before the UN trusteeship council. Thus, India's pull towards Afro-Asianism had a great effect in Tanganyika. When Oscar Kambona took over the office of foreign minister in 1963, he adopted as his guiding principles the Bandung Declaration which, in his own words, "almost formed the basis of Tanganyika's foreign policy."[16] Above all, the Afro-Asian Movement, both in its official guise at the UN and in its unofficial form as AAPSO, was willing to provide that support for the decolonization of non-independent territories in Africa which Tanganyika sought.

However, Tanganyika's enthusiasm over AAPSO was short-lived, precisely because that organization was not, according to Tanganyikan standards, strictly non-aligned. By becoming so completely part of the cold war, not only between East and West but even more so between the Soviet and Chinese brands of Communism, AAPSO involved its African members in issues which they felt were not their own. Similarly, as the question of holding a "second Bandung" became increasingly involved in great-power questions, the less enthusiastic the Tanganyikans (or Tanzanians, as they were by now called) became. In the UN they became one of the leading African delegations to organize the separate, African group within the wider Afro-Asian context.[17]

President Nyerere persistently followed this early formula of non-engagement. His relations with the great powers were largely influenced by their relations with Tanganyika. Thus British aid to quell the army brought an amelioration of relations with Great Britain which continued until the Rhodesian crisis. The Zanzibar question, and the suspicions aroused by it among the Western powers, brought about a worsening of relations, especially with the US and the Federal Republic of Germany, but also with the Soviet Union. According to Kambona, the Russians opposed the union of Tanganyika and Zanzibar, on the ground that Zanzibar was an area of Russian influence.[18] The Chinese, on the other hand, supported the idea, and were the main gainers by it. The scope of their activities in the early 1970s makes impressive reading; by 1972 there were more than 16,000 Chinese engaged in different activities in Tanzania (some 16,000 constructing the Tanzanian-Zambian railway and some 600 experts in other fields). This does not, however, mean that Tanzania had forgone its old policy of non-alignment and adopted a pro-Chinese orientation. A careful policy of checks and balances had been applied regarding Chinese aid: thus, the first agreement to let the Chinese train the Tanzanian army was followed by a decision to call in the Canadians to train the army; Chinese instructors in the police force were offset by instructors from Israel; the patrol boats given by China were matched by patrol boats given by Western Germany; the textile mill built by Chinese at a value of £2,500,000 was overtaken by a mill at a value of £3 million that the French were building at Mwanza.

If the Chinese were held in check politically, ideologically they made a great impact in Tanzania, as elsewhere in Africa. Their approach was deceptively simple. For the past millennium there existed a hegemony of the white peoples, they said.[19] This hegemony is being wielded today by the US and the Soviet Union. But for the first time people who are not white are becoming a force to be reckoned with. Their solidarity can bring down white hegemony.

This argumentation is translated into questions of African

significance by African nationalists. The two major problems for them are the decolonization of non-independent Africa, and the question of white man versus black. In their eyes the white part of the world has not done enough, either to support the struggle for independence of those parts of Africa, particularly in the south, which are under "white" domination, or to narrow the gap in the standard of living between the white and the black, or the developed and the underdeveloped parts of the world. This lack of sympathy by the whites is widely construed as emanating from a tacit understanding between the two superpowers. Peaceful coexistence, or a *démarche* in the cold war, is thus seen by many African nationalists as working for their detriment. Thus the Chinese reasoning against peaceful coexistence, and against Soviet attempts to defreeze the cold war, fell on fertile ground. Chinese insistence on the need for self-reliance, her mobilization of the rural masses, and her emphasis on the peasant as the vanguard of the revolution all fitted African considerations. Thus, the central point in President Nyerere's famous "Arusha Declaration" was the need for self-reliance, which he defined as raising the productivity of the whole working population, developing local resources by the nation's own efforts, and raising the standard of living of the rural masses thereby creating a domestic consumer's market which would in turn encourage local industries and eventually lead to the growth of exports.

Chinese influence, which at first worked in favour of solidarity in Afro-Asia, eventually had the opposite effect. Kambona described the Sino-Indian conflict as "a tremendous shock." Tanzania, he claimed, accepted the Chinese explanation; he and others were willing to agree that India's leadership of Asia was decadent, while China was an emergent force. But the result was not that Tanzania entered the fray whole-heartedly on the side of China. The Sino-Indian conflict and the Sino-Soviet rift led Tanzania and other African states to retract from Afro-Asian obligations and withdraw into their African shell. "Both the Russians and the Chinese wanted us to take sides," Kambona recalled. "But as champions of the African liberation movements we refused, as this would have split the movements into pro-Russian and pro-Chinese factions." Once more, the problem was translated into *African* terms, and first and foremost, into the question of the decolonization of non-independent Africa.[20]

Thus the more the Afro-Asian Movement became involved in the conflicts of the great powers, China included, the less were the African members willing to play an active role. From the start of the preparations for a "second Bandung" a group of African states—the Ivory Coast, Dahomey, Upper Volta, Niger and the Republic of Malagasy—decided not to attend, while many other African states wavered in their intentions. President Nkrumah continued with his preparations for the conference of the Organization of African Unity, which was held in Accra on October 21, 1965, despite the pleas of the Algerian hosts of the "second Bandung" to postpone the OAU conference to a date after the "second Bandung" meeting. African hesitations increased when the Moscow-Peking conflict over Russian participation in the "second Bandung" burst in all its fury, and crystallized into open opposition when Algerian President Ahmad Ben Bella was overthrown just before the conference should have been held. These doubts were openly expressed by President Nyerere at a press conference given by him on October 29, 1965. He declared that he had no intention of participating at the forthcoming conference for two reasons, one of which he did not wish to elaborate (presumably the overthrow of Ben Bella). Concerning the other reason, the aim of the conference was to demonstrate the unity of the Afro-Asian third force. Part of the Afro-Asian group had already decided not to come, and there was thus no show of unity. But even if all had decided to take part, he would still object to Tanzania's participation, for the conference would become a stage for quarrel and dissent instead of demonstrating unity and cooperation. It would not solve a single burning problem; it would, instead, only fan the flames of discord. The conference, therefore, should be postponed until true cooperation really existed among all its participants.[21]

Thus Nyerere and most African leaders, in effect, bowed out of Afro-Asianism. The Organization of African Unity answered their needs much more fully. The common denominators which still bound them to the countries of Asia were not, in themselves, strong enough to overcome their African separatism and their refusal to be drawn into conflicts which did not directly affect the African continent.

NOTES

[1] Ethiopia was represented by her foreign minister, Hapte Walde Aklilou; Liberia by Secretary of State Momolu Dukuly, and the Gold Coast, not yet independent, by Kojo Botsio.

[2] For a detailed account of these efforts see: D.Kimche, "Black Africa and the Afro-Asian Peoples' Solidarity Movement," *Asian and African Studies,* Jerusalem, Vol. 4, 1968, p. 107 ff.

[3] Colin Legum, for one, is convinced that this parallelism was not accidental. For his explanation of it, see his "Pan-Africanism and Communism," in Hamrell (ed.), *The Soviet Bloc, China and Africa,* p. 22.

[4] *The Times,* London, 10.4.1958.

[5] Oscar Kambona, in conversation with writer, on 15.9.1968.

[6] Quoted in *The Times,* London, 24.11.1958.

[7] *The Times,* London, 15.12.1958. See also Nkrumah's speech at the opening session, *The Times,* London, 9.12.1958.

[8] Many of these are quoted by Legum in his "Pan-Africanism . . . " pp. 112–7. See also, and in particular, Kwame Nkrumah, "African Prospects," *Foreign Affairs,* Vol. 37, No. 1, October 1958, p. 46ff. For a non-conformist view see President Houphouët-Boigny's statement on positive neutralism, made on 23.1.1965, and quoted by Pierre Chauleur in his "Le role de l'armée en Afrique noir," *Revue Militaire Générale,* Paris, April 1965, p. 518.

[9] Nkrumah, "African Prospects," *ibid.,* p. 48. For an examination of non-alignment and "neo-alignment" in Africa, see Ali Mazrui, *Towards a Pax Africana: A Study of Ideology and Ambition,* London, 1967, p. 147ff.

[10] See Colin Legum's excellent paper, "From Illusions to Reality," given in Addis Ababa in September 1966 in the conference on "Africa and the World" organized by the Haile Selassi I Prize Trust, p. 4.

[11] Much of this examination of Tanzania's foreign policy orientations is based on a series of interviews which the author held with Oscar Kambona.

[12] Significantly enough, one of the last government branches which was "africanized" was the foreign service, which remained largely in expatriate hands till Oscar Kambona became foreign minister in 1963.

[13]   Kambona to author; see Note 11, above.

[14]   *Ibid.* (emphasis of present author).

[15]   According to Kambona, *ibid.*

[16]   A good method of measuring Tanganyika's policy requirements is to see according to what principles her embassies were set up abroad. Tanganyika's representation abroad was decided upon after Kambona became foreign minister. He told this author that his considerations were the following: equal representation in the Communist and Western capitals; a mission in countries which might be persuaded to give large-scale technical aid (the choice was Sweden); one in India, because of the large number of Indians in Tanganyika; it had also been intended to open one in Jakarta, not because of Afro-Asian considerations, but "because of the Indonesian interest in cloves."

[17]   According to an Israeli diplomat at the UN who was particularly close to the African delegations.

[18]   Kambona, in his conversations with the author, recalled a discussion he had with Nikita Khrushchev while both were visiting the Aswan High Dam in Upper Egypt. Khrushchev told him that the Tanganyikans were progressive conservatives while the Zanzibarians were militant. The two should not be mixed together. To which Kambona retorted that, according to Mao Tse-tung, the Russians were also no more than progressive conservatives.

[19]   The writer has heard this from Oscar Kambona and from others. See also Kudryavtsev in *Mezhdunarodnya Zhizn,* No. 5, 1963, pp. 51–6 (the article appeared in English in *International Affairs,* Moscow, May 1963).

[20]   This subject, indeed, forms the major theme of most Tanzanian speeches and statements on foreign policy objectives. See, for example, the speech of Rashid Kawawa who became prime minister in 1962, at the conference of non-aligned nations held in Cairo in October 1964, and quoted in the BBC Monitoring ME/1680/E/9-11 (from Cairo Radio in English, 0700 GMT, 9.10.1964).

[21]   *Tanganyikan Standard,* Dar-es-Salaam, 30.10.1965.

14 THE DECLINE OF THE AFRO-ASIAN MOVEMENT

The star which had risen so high in the political firmament of the Afro-Asian countries at Bandung did not shine brightly for long. By 1965, after the ill-fated attempt to convene the "second Bandung" conference at Algiers had failed, it gave barely a flicker. True, the Afro-Asian group at the United Nations continued to function, but there was neither a sense of unity nor a feeling of solidarity in its ranks. The Afro-Asian Peoples' Solidarity Organization continued to exist, but after the Havana conference of the peoples of Asia, Africa and Latin America it lost what little unity of action it had mustered before. After the AAPSO Council meeting in Nicosia in 1967, the split between the followers of China and those of the Soviet Union became virtually irrevocable. The Chinese and their supporters walked out of the Nicosia conference after the majority voted to rescind a previous decision to hold the following AAPSO plenary assembly in Peking.

The Afro-Asian Movement thus declined as a factor of importance on the international political scene as rapidly as it had risen to that position ten years earlier. This chapter examines the causes of that decline.

There were numerous contributory factors. Some emanated from local developments within the Afro-Asian countries themselves; others had a more universalistic international setting. They can be divided into three major headings:

tensions within the Afro-Asian Movement;
internal developments within the Afro-Asian countries;
the interrelationships between the countries of Afro-Asia and the major world powers.

Among the tensions within the Afro-Asian Movement the Sino-

Indian dispute was a foremost source of division. Chapter 11 discussed this dispute and the disastrous effect it had on Afro-Asian solidarity; some of those who were most active in the movement regarded this conflict as one of the main reasons for the decline of Afro-Asianism.[1]

Connected with this dispute was the change in the foreign policy orientations of China, with the termination of its "good neighbour" policy in 1957.[2] The change affected most strongly her relations with India, but it had an impact on other countries as well, notably on Burma and the countries of South-East Asia.

The change in Chinese policy had a particularly marked effect on the war in Vietnam. This war, and Chinese, and later American, involvement in it, led to a sharpening ideological polarization within Afro-Asia, with correspondingly heightened tensions. This was, of course, especially felt in Asia. Thus, for example, Thailand's willingness to aid the US war effort in Vietnam inevitably led to a deterioration in relations between Thailand and her neighbours—in particular Cambodia and Burma.

The growing activism on the part of China created a reaction of fear among the smaller states of Asia, especially in Burma, Laos and Nepal.

Fear of the Chinese "giant" had, to a certain extent, an earlier counterpart in a fear of India. Some of India's neighbours—Ceylon, Nepal, Burma, to say nothing of Pakistan—had watched with apprehension the early initiative taken by Nehru within the framework of the Afro-Asian Movement. They had no wish to fall under Indian hegemony, so that they reacted to questions of Afro-Asian solidarity with a certain caution.[3]

The Sino-Indian conflict, although the most spectacular, was by no means the only dispute existing within Afro-Asia; hardly less important was the dispute between India and Pakistan over Kashmir. There were, in addition, the "confrontation" between Indonesia and Malaysia, the tensions between Thailand and Cambodia and between Malaysia and Singapore, and the numerous inter-Arab and inter-African disputes, notably between Egypt and Saudi Arabia, Algeria and Morocco, Somalia and Ethiopia, Somalia and Kenya, Ethiopia and the Sudan, Ghana (of the days of Nkrumah) and Togo, and above all, the tensions caused first by the Congo crisis and later by the war in Nigeria over Biafra. All contributed to impede unity and solidarity in Afro-Asia.

In a category by itself is the Sino-Soviet conflict and its effects on Afro-Asia. Afro-Asia became one of the major cockpits for Sino-Soviet strife, with both China and the Soviet Union putting constant pressure on the countries of Asia and Africa to take sides. The conflict made a mockery of the Solidarity Movement and its numerous daughter-organizations, while the tactics of both the Communist powers on the eve of the "second Bandung" led most participants to take a stand of "a plague on both your houses" and withdraw from the entire Afro-Asian Movement. The Sino-Soviet conflict, moreover, upset the balance of checks and benefits which the countries of Asia and Africa had gained from the cold war. Previously, before the Sino-Soviet complication, the cold war had provided them with two un-written and unspoken guarantees: it provided a second side to turn to in case one of the sides in the cold war sought to gain too predominant a position in one of the Afro-Asian countries or in case that country was subjected to real or imaginary threats; and it assured a steady flow of economic aid, with each side in the cold war competing with the other to gain political support on the strength of that aid. The Sino-Soviet conflict complicated matters in that, while the Chinese could provide neither of these services, yet, ideologically many of the Afro-Asian leaders took a stand which was much closer to that of China than to that of either the Soviet Union or the West. Politically the Chinese were the losers, with only a small minority of Afro-Asian governments supporting China, but on the intellectual level the Sino-Soviet conflict had a tremendously disruptive effect in that political *beliefs,* though close to those held by China, were often sacrificed for political *benefits* such as Soviet aid and the benefits derived from the "traditional" cold-war situation. This internal contradiction increased tensions already existing in the Afro-Asian Movement because of the Sino-Soviet conflict.

In themselves, these various tensions were major causes of the decline of the Afro-Asian Movement. To them must be added internal developments within the Afro-Asian countries. In general, the newly independent countries of Asia and Africa underwent developments typical of nationalist movements as a whole. The first, naturally enough, is the pre-independent stage. The national consensus lies solidly behind the leaders of the nationalist movements, and the people identify themselves entirely with the demands of these leaders for independence and with their struggle against the colonial regimes. The second stage begins with the acquiring of independence, and with it problems immediately begin to arise. The gaining of independence is usually construed by the masses as a tangible act which brings in its wake concrete and material benefits.[4] Not only has this not occured, but frequently the social and economic conditions of the inhabitants have deteriorated after independence, with the departure of the Europeans. The consensus behind the national leaders begins to fall apart; the objective—independence—having been gained there is no more need to identify support of the national leaders with patriotism and opposition to them as treason. Opposition mounts as the absence of economic ameliorations after independence becomes apparent.

This opposition is silenced and overcome in a number of ways. The legitimation to stifling the opposition is sought in continuing the struggle for national goals on the part of the leaders who had led their countries to independence. These goals, however, are unattainable in internal affairs, where there are no short-cuts out of the social and economic difficulties. It is, then, in foreign policy questions that this legitimation is obtained—by continuing the anti-colonialist struggle the leaders identify themselves with the same goals for which they had fought in the pre-independence period.

In this manner, consensus behind the national leaders is maintained, opposition to them is continued to be construed as treason, and difficulties on the "home front" are made the responsibility of outside enemies—"imperialists," "colonialists," "neo-colonialists," etc.—against whom the national leaders wage unceasing battle. These outside enemies are sometimes identified: for Indonesia they were the Dutch in West Irian and the British in Malaysia; for Egypt and the Arab countries they were preeminently Israel and world Zionism; for Nkrumah they were the "plotters" in Togo. In many cases these enemies have been vaguely defined as "neo-colonialists" or "imperialists" against whom the people are called upon to fight. Whether real or imagined, these outside enemies helped the leaders to overcome the difficulties of the immediate post-independence period: consolidating the nation, silencing opposition, explaining away economic shortcomings, etc.

This largely artificial continuation of the pre-independence stage could, at best, be only a limited affair, however. The ending of this second period has been hastened by two factors: the rapid decolonization of the remaining non-independent territories, and the increasing social and economic difficulties in which many of the newly independent countries found themselves. The anti-colonialist struggle lost much of its force and meaning, while the internal crises could no longer be offset by crying "wolf." And as the years have passed the magic glitter of independence has rubbed off and below its surface loom the problems, numerous, ugly, and seemingly unsolvable. The old "national" leaders were evidently not the ones to tackle them, for the problems only increased with time. The stage was thus set for their removal, and the commencement of the third stage in development—of introversion, of greater attention to internal problems at the expense of an active foreign policy, of pragmatism in place of the "grand ideals" which had motivated the "heroic" leaders who had gained independence. The move from the second to the third stage is gradual, and has not occurred in all countries, but the tendency is plain to see. Only a few are left of those who were in the forefront of the anti-colonialist crusade, and who in many ways led the Afro-Asian Movement.

Generals Suharto, Boumedienne and Joseph Ankrah of Ghana have typified the third stage in place of the more flamboyant Sukarno, Ben Bella and Nkrumah. Their type of regime differed vastly from that of their predecessors, and so, for different reasons, have the regimes of Shastri and Indira Gandhi been of a completely different nature to that of Nehru and that of Anwār as-Sadāt's to the rule of Nasser. On a lesser level an entire layer of leaders who brought their countries to independence has been removed—Patrice Lumumba, Sylvano Olympio of Togo, the Congolese Fulbert Youlou, Maurice Yaméogo of Upper Volta, Abubakr Balewa of Nigeria, David Dacko of the Central African Republic, Modeibo Keita of Mali, to mention only some.

The new leaders, with certain exceptions, have not maintained the same interest in Afro-Asianism which some of their predecessors had. They have placed more importance on mobilizing large-scale foreign aid than on maintaining the strict rules of non-alignment; their association with other states has often been limited by the practical benefits they can gain from them. Above all, having largely given up the extrovert policy of fighting the outside enemy practised by their predecessors, they have no more need for such platforms as the conclaves of the Afro-Asian countries.

Thus this internal development in many Afro-Asian countries has become a major cause of the decline of the Afro-Asian Movement. Instead there has been a new emphasis on practical, regional associations, brought together for economic, political or security reasons. Regional organizations have been formed in South-East Asia and in Africa, while the Arabs have maintained their separate entity through the Arab League and the summit conferences of Arab heads of state. In this manner the Afro-Asian body has become increasingly fragmented into separate entities, each following its own course.

There are, however, further causes of the decline of Afro-Asianism, and these must be sought in the interrelationships between the countries of Afro-Asia and the major world powers. These interrelationships have constantly changed inasmuch as both sides have been dynamic and not static. The pattern is thus perpetually shifting. Yet, obviously, there exist certain basic factors which remain constant. The Afro-Asian countries have remained the poor "proletariat" of the world; the basic common denominators binding them together, described in Chapter 2, have remained valid. These common denominators formed the base on which Afro-Asian solidarity was founded. But this solidarity came into being not only because of those common factors *per se,* but because they served to single out the countries of Asia and Africa and differentiate them from the wealthy, white, European and North American sector of the world. Thus, from the very beginning, Afro-Asianism as a coherent, political movement was only one side of the coin; its obverse was colonialism, the role of the great powers, the cold war, etc. The dominant political creed of the Afro-Asian countries—non-alignment—was strictly geared to the East-West conflict; it was, in fact, part of it. So was the striving for the "area of peace" motivating Nehru in his quest for Afro-Asian solidarity. Nehru, U Nu, Sukarno, Nkrumah and other Afro-Asian leaders believed that by common political action on the part of the Afro-Asian nations they could affect the course of the cold war. They believed that solidarity meant power—power to stand up to the great powers, to pursue an independent course in the world, to change the pattern of world events. Yet this belief, so basic to the Afro-Asian Movement, proved to be a fallacy. There exists not a single instance in the history of the cold war in which either of the great powers was pressured by the Afro-Asian or non-aligned countries into acting against what it considered to be its national interests. On the contrary, the history of the cold war teems with examples of a cynical disregard which the great powers displayed to the wishes and feelings of the Afro-Asian non-aligned countries.[5]

It was not by the creation of an "area of peace" that a détente was obtained in the cold war, nor did the deliberations of the Afro-Asian leaders reduce tension at Berlin, in Vietnam, or elsewhere. There is no instance in the history of the United Nations in which a united Afro-Asian vote forced the great powers to pursue a policy which they had previously opposed. Indeed, not even a two-thirds majority at the UN can force the two super-powers to act against their will. This impotence was increasingly realized by the Afro-Asian leaders themselves. Thus, in an article in the *Times of India,* the editor, Prem Bhatio, wrote that Nehru seemed to have become "increasingly doubtful about the capacity of outside powers to influence the thoughts and actions of the two major contestants in the current cold war." Nehru was, according to Bhatio, mainly doutful over the Berlin problem, and felt that the non-aligned had nothing to offer.

Thus one of the underlying aims of Afro-Asian leaders—to create a power which could reduce tensions and influence world events—was not fulfilled. And the policy on which that aim had been based, that of non-alignment, was, with the passage of time, itself increasingly questioned. Both the Americans and the Russians had blown hot and cold on this policy, at times praising it and at others condemning it. The Chinese, at the height of their "good neighbour" policy at Bandung, had demonstrated a sympathy for non-alignment which did not, however, last long. By 1958 the Chinese saw the world in the throes of a sharpening struggle in which there was no place for non-alignment—hence, also, their strong attacks on Yugoslavia. As Lowenthal wrote on the Chinese attitude, "a neutral state is either a state that can be involved in conflict with the West or can be turned into a Chinese buffer—or it's no good."[6] This attitude considerably strengthened when the Sino-Soviet conflict burst upon the world.

For in this conflict *there were no neutrals among the non-aligned.* Both the Chinese and the Russians demanded allegiance, and it was this demand, voiced so strongly in AAPSO meetings, at Havana, and, above all, on the eve of the abortive Algiers "second Bandung" conference, which did irreparable damage to Afro-Asian solidarity.

The Sino-Soviet conflict destroyed the old concept of non-alignment to an even greater extent than the Chinese invasion of India succeeded in doing. At the same time, it became increasingly apparent that there could exist such a thing as a capacity for non-alignment, or, to put it in another way, capacity to resist the pressure of great powers for allegiance, whether that pressure was Chinese, Russian or American. This capacity is affected by the following factors:

The geographical proximity of a country to a great power, or the strategical significance of its geographical placing. The greater the strategical importance, the stronger the pressure for allegiance will be. This can be seen, for example, in the relationship between the US and the central American states, or between the Soviet Union and Mongolia.

The degree to which a country can maintain self-defence in the face of an outside threat or a major internal crisis affecting the security of the regime. The greater a country's capacity for coping with a military threat on its own, the greater its capacity will be to pursue a policy of non-alignment.

Closely connected with the above is the degree to which a country is prone to such threats. Obviously, a country considering itself under constant threat is more liable to bend to pressure from a great power than one which feels it has no need for protection or large-scale military aid.

The degree to which a country accepts large-scale military aid from one of the powers.

Thus, as examples of the last three categories, the non-alignment of both Ethiopia and Somalia was affected by the fact that each felt it needed outside help to cope with the threat posed by the other. The Ethiopians turned to the Americans, the Somalis to the Russians.

President Jomo Kenyatta, of Kenya.

Similarly, the governments of Kenya, Uganda and Tanganiyka were unable to overcome the danger to their existence created by the army mutinies in 1964 and called in British troops. Gabon did the same later, and its regime was saved with the help of French para-troopers. By no stretch of the imagination can the Gabonese regime today be considered non-aligned vis-à-vis French demands. Turkey considered itself threatened by the Soviet Union, and sought the protection of NATO and CENTO. Egypt and Syria, after accepting large-scale military aid from one source—the Soviet Union—could no longer follow a truly non-aligned policy.

The question of capacity for non-alignment became especially important as the approach of the great powers themselves to the Afro-Asian countries changed. The original polarization of the cold-war conflict into two blocs, each competing for the support of the non-aligned countries, was altered by the Sino-Soviet conflict, and, to a much lesser extent, by the Gaullist reorientation of French foreign policy. The Sino-Soviet conflict was one of the major factors leading to a détente in Soviet-American relations in the mid-1960s, which, in turn, led to a lessening in competition for the support of the non-aligned countries. Both the Soviet Union and the United States increasingly tended to provide aid only to countries which were willing, in one way or another, to align or commit themselves. Development in the methods of modern warfare no longer demanded the presence of vast military bases of the Singapore-type as a sign of alignment or commitment; it was not even necessary to enter into formal military pacts. Rather, the form of relationship existing between Egypt and the Soviet Union after the Six-Day War of June 1967 or between Indonesia or Ghana and the United States in 1968, became the prototype of this new form of alignment between a great power and an Afro-Asian country.

Does this mean that non-alignment no longer exists? "The essence of non-alignment," wrote Fayez A. Sayegh,[7] "is the attainment of a state of freedom *from all alien determinants* of foreign policy. It is the achievement of the ability to judge every issue (including issues of the cold war) on its own merits and in the light of one's national interest and principles, and not on the basis of commitments made in advance to other parties nor in the light of such extraneous considerations as alignment with power blocs." To put it in another way, non-alignment becomes "an assertion of the universal right to self-determination in the particular context of the cold war."[8]

An increasing number of Afro-Asian countries find this self-determination in the context of the cold war to be limited by "alien determinants" which, however, are not necessarily against their own national interests. Here lies the weakness of the stand of the non-aligned: they had assumed that alignment was, *per se,* detrimental to their national interests. This may have been so in the "classic" period of the cold war, but it no longer applied to the changing world situation of the 1960s, with the advent of the Sino-Soviet conflict, and with the changing attitude of the great powers to the non-aligned countries of Asia and Africa. Moreover, the policy of playing one bloc against the other and gaining aid from both, no longer applied to the international realities of the late 1960s and early 1970s. The result is that an increasing number of countries in Africa and Asia have taken a stand vis-à-vis the great powers which *does* limit their freedom of choice of foreign policy orientations regarding world issues and therefore curtails their non-alignment. Non-alignment, however, continues to be a badge adorning most members of the Afro-Asian "club," but a badge which has lost its previous meaning. It is worn by those having military agreements with former colonial powers (Kenya, Singapore, Malaysia, Ivory Coast, etc.), and by those closely bound to one of the great powers or openly antagonistic to one of them (Egypt or Syria—Soviet Union; Iran or Indonesia—United States; or India—openly antagonistic to China).

This change in character of non-alignment in the decade since Bandung had an effect on the Afro-Asian Movement as a whole, and has been an additional cause of its decline.

There were thus numerous reasons for the eclipse of Afro-Asianism in the 1960s, arising from factors operating within Afro-Asia itself, and from those affecting its relationship with the other side of the coin, the wealthy, white European–North American sector. All, however, would not have been sufficient to have brought about its demise if Afro-Asianism had been a movement based on ideological foundations strong enough to withstand the trials and tribulations to which it was subjected.

This, however, has patently not been so. Afro-Asianism rested on a number of common denominators and on a belief that by an association of Afro-Asian states various advantages would be gained and power to influence world events. These advantages were differently construed by different members of the Afro-Asian community. For some, the mere fact of being associated with other states on an equal footing strengthened their images, at home and abroad, as independent, sovereign, national entities. For others the Afro-Asian association implied an alternative to the cold-war conflict, and for yet others a form of escapism from the cold war. There were those who saw the material advantages to be gained from adhering to the Afro-Asian group and playing off one bloc against the other, and there were others who saw in the Afro-Asian association a means of creating an "area of peace" between the two cold-war contenders, and thus contributing to the maintenance of world peace.

All these were legitimate interests. But these interests could, and did, change with changing circumstances, for they were in no way anchored in a solid ideology. The common denominators which brought the countries together in the first place cannot be described as ideology. As S.C. Jha told the author: "there is no Afro-Asian ideology. But there do exist certain common purposes of Afro-Asian countries as most of them were under colonial domination."[9] These common purposes provide the possibility of working together to achieve common ends: amelioration of the standard of living, removal of foreign domination, independence from the economies of the great powers, industrialization, and, above all, narrowing the gap that separates them from the wealthy countries of Europe and North America.

Oscar Kambona put it in an even more extreme manner. The Afro-Asian Movement did not succeed, he claimed, because it continued to bandy empty slogans instead of concentrating on such practical issues as marketing ("the prices of manufactured goods are rising and those of raw materials are going down—this is the biggest problem of Africa and Asia today").[10] There is thus a basis for the continuing of Afro-Asian cooperation on practical issues in such bodies as SUNFED, or, to quote J. D. B. Miller, in the "practical enunciation of common demands which diplomats, civil servants and other experts have worked out on the basis of their own practical experience and that of the other states."[11] Afro-Asianism, however, to all intents and purposes, has ceased to function as a coherent political movement.

NOTES

[1] Thus, for example, S. C. Jha of India told the author (14.11.68) that "the importance of the movement was greatly reduced. The whole of the Afro-Asian Movement was retarded and irretrievably damaged by the aggression."

[2] See Zagoria, *ibid.,* p. 66.

[3] Thus according to Brecher, *New States of Asia,* p. 100, the failure to create permanent machinery as a follow-up to conferences such as Bandung was largely due to (a) rivalry between China and India, neither of which was willing to concede Asian leadership to the other, and (b) fear among the smaller states that one of the two or both would dominate the system.

[4] The author came across an extreme example of this belief in Guinea, where villagers demanded that a road be built to the local cemetery shortly before independence was acquired; they believed that with independence the dead would rise from their graves!

[5] The most blatant was, perhaps, the resumption of nuclear bomb tests by the Soviet Union on the eve of the opening of the conference of non-aligned nations at Belgrade in September 1961.

[6] Richard Lowenthal, "Sino-Soviet Split and its Repercussions in Africa," in Hamrell (ed.), *The Soviet Bloc, China and Africa,* p. 134. See also article by Adie, "China, Russia and the Third World," *China Quarterly,* July-September 1962, p. 200 ff., for discussion on Chinese and Russian attitudes to the Afro-Asian countries.

[7] Sayegh, *Dynamics of Neutralism in the Arab World,* p. 39 (present author's italics).

[8] Sayegh, *ibid.,* p. 40.

[9] Interview with S.C. Jha, Paris, 14.11.1968.

[10] Interview with Oscar Kambona, London, 15.9.1968.

[11] Miller, *op. cit.* p. 42.

CONCLUSIONS

The history of the Afro-Asian Movement, as recounted in these pages, lasted barely twenty-five years—a brief span, indeed, in the long and chequered history of Asia and Africa. These twenty-five years, however, cover a period of paramount importance for the two continents. It witnessed the disintegration of colonial rule and heralded the dawn of a new era, of the independent, sovereign nation-states of Asia and Africa.

This has been a period of transition in the political history of Afro-Asia. The process of decolonization has been a gradual one, with the phenomena characterizing a colonial society often continuing long after political independence was attained. It has also been a period of political adaptation: the world has had to learn to live with the new states of Africa and Asia, and, at the same time these states have had to learn to adjust themselves to the political realities of the world surrounding them.

These political realities, in the first formative years of the majority of the Afro-Asian nation-states, were dominated by the cold war between the two super-powers, the United States and the Soviet Union. The attitudes of both these powers to the new states of Asia and Africa were governed by the exigencies of the cold war—the mixture of wooing, bullying, flattery, threats and "presents" in the form of aid which characterized the policies of these powers towards Afro-Asia during much of this period amply bear this out. On the other hand, the foreign policy orientations of the states of Africa and Asia were overshadowed by the need to come to terms with this cold war which, despite themselves, engulfed them.

It is in this context that the Afro-Asian Movement must be examined. To a great extent, it was the product of this period of transition and mutual adjustment between the states of Afro-Asia and the rest of the world.[1] It was not a movement blossoming out of any deep ideological motivations. Rather, it was the child of political expediency, whose parentage was the urge to hasten the process of decolonization on the one side and the need to react to the great-power conflict on the other. The rise and decline of the Afro-Asian Movement were largely dependent on these two factors. They formed the backdrop to the urge for Afro-Asian solidarity in the late 1940s and 1950s. They also provided the causes for the decline of the movement in the 1960s. The reasons for this decline, as set out in the previous chapter, can all be set within the framework bound by these two issues.

The internal rivalries within Afro-Asia, foremost among them the Sino-Indian conflict, were a direct result of the process of decolonization. The post-colonial era brought to the surface religious differences, tribal frictions and national rivalries which had been held in check under colonial rule, and these proved stronger than the common denominators which had formed the basis for Afro-Asian solidarity. Moreover, the speeding up of the process of decolonization, and the concomitant lessening in importance of the anti-colonialist struggle, served to weaken one of the most powerful common links in Afro-Asian solidarity, namely, the struggle for freedom from colonial rule.

At the same time, the character of the movement changed in accordance with developments in the great-power conflict. The gradually unfolding Sino-Soviet clash, the emergence of policentrism in place of the former rigid global division into two opposing blocs, the change in tactics of both the Soviet Union in the Khrushchevian post-Stalin period and of the United States in Kennedy's post-Dulles rule, the gradual détente which followed in the wake of nuclear stalemate—all these developments had their immediate effect on the character and objectives of the Afro-Asian Movement.

Additionally, as seen in previous pages, there existed marked divergences in the attitude of the members of the Afro-Asian Movement to the cold war. This was as evident at Bandung as it was within the Afro-Asian group at the United Nations, or in the Afro-Asian Peoples' Solidarity Organization. It was particularly true regarding the movement's leaders. Thus, Nehru, U Nu and others considered the conflict to be one step from disaster: the cold war had to be defused, and this was to be the supreme task of the Afro-Asians. Abdel Nasser, Sékou Touré, Oscar Kambona and others viewed the cold war in a completely different light. It opened up possibilities for political manoeuvre by the weaker nations which would not be feasible in a situation of détente between the powers. The cold war raised the importance of the nations of Afro-Asia, for each power was interested in obtaining their support and preventing the other side from gaining a foothold. A détente, on the other hand, opened vistas of a division of Afro-Asia into zones of influence or, at best, of lack of interests on the part of the great powers and a subsequent lessening of importance of the countries involved. The cold war, therefore, was in the eyes of Abdel Nasser and those who thought like him a favourable state of affairs which should be perpetuated and could be advantageously exploited. This was a far cry, indeed, from the views of Nehru.

There were also the policy considerations of the Chinese and their followers, which, again, were different from those of many other Afro-Asian countries. For them there was no place for true non-alignment, advocated by so many members of the Afro-Asian Movement. The Chinese attitude to the movement went through a number of stages: the first, propounded at Bandung, was of reconcilement. China was then in the throes of her "good neighbour" policy; she wanted to be recognized and accepted, and was even willing to pay lip-service to non-alignment and peaceful coexistence to achieve this aim. The second stage was marked by a growing hostility to the tenets of non-alignment. For the Chinese the Afro-Asian Movement now had a twin aim: as an instrument to prevent a détente between the United States and the Soviet Union, and as a vehicle to further revolution against the "white citadel": primarily the capitalist West, but eventually the Soviet Union as well. The third stage fell under the shadow of the Sino-Soviet split. Chinese efforts were now supremely directed against Soviet "revisionism."[2] What could be clearer than the following statement, made by one of the pro-Chinese delegates, at the eighth council meeting of AAPSO, in Nicosia in February 1967: "For the struggling and fighting people of Africa, Asia and Latin America things like peaceful coexistence, peaceful transition, disarmament and the like are only disguised forms of collaboration with imperialism, old and new colonialism."[3] These "things" not only formed part of the most basic policy orientations of the Soviet

Union, but were also fundamental precepts of a number of Afro-Asian countries, India included. With such a divergence of views, there was not much chance for Afro-Asian solidarity!

Thus Afro-Asianism meant different things to its principal members, ranging from the "area of peace" of Nehru to the militant anti-colonialism of Sukarno and Nkrumah and the instrument for revolution of the Chinese. It is, however, open to question whether the existence of the Afro-Asian Movement *per se* contributed to the hastening of the process of decolonization or influenced in any manner the major decisions of the great powers. The fact is that the Afro-Asian Movement was neither able to affect the issues of the cold war in any way, nor, in the long run, to act as an alternative to the power blocs for its members. As Nehru himself pointed out at Bandung the stage had, not yet been reached where Afro-Asians could help each other.

Afro-Asianism did not prove to be an effective alternative politically, militarily or economically to links with the developed world. India was a case in point, being vitally in need of vast economic aid on a scale which only the great powers could supply. Moreover, when the Sino-Indian war broke out, she received help not from the countries of Afro-Asia, which, much to her chagrin, refused to be drawn into taking sides, but from the great powers. A close observer of the Indian political scene has, indeed, claimed that her excessive dependence on the great powers has been the reason that "in Afro-Asian politics India has been reduced to the position of a second-rate power with no influence even on nations with close geographic proximity.[4] Indian dependence on one of the great powers was greatly increased during and immediately after the Indo-Pakistani war in December 1971. The Soviet Union actively helped the Indians by air-lifting vital arms and supplies to India via Egypt. As a result of this aid, the ties between India and the Soviet Union were considerably strengthened after the war.

India has been no exceptional case. In the latter years of the 1960s most countries of Asia and Africa sought to strengthen their links with the great powers on the one hand, and to place renewed emphasis on regional cooperation on the other. The associations formed were far more pragmatic, based not on militant slogans or lofty ideals which had characterized the Afro-Asianism of Sukarno or Nehru, but on the national needs of the countries concerned, whether in the economic, political or military domains.[5] Thus, neither Shastri nor Indira Gandhi displayed any great interest in foreign affairs as Nehru had shown. Their interests lay almost exclusively in the overwhelming difficult internal problems pressing on India, and in external factors directly affecting India's security, such as the Kashmir issue, the situation in East Bengal (later to become Bangla-Desh), or China. In all these issues the Soviet Union was of greater consequence than the United States, and it is therefore hardly surprising to see India's foreign policy orientation shifting away from the strict non-alignment which had so characterized it in the past.[6] Indeed, in the view of one of the foremost students of Indian current affairs, the repeated use of the expression "non-alignment" by Indira Gandhi had become a convenient means for covering up her lack of interest in world affairs, apart from those directly affecting India, and in these her views coincided with those of the Soviet Union.[7] Similarly, Egypt, because of her desire to obtain large-scale military aid from Russia, moved ever closer to the Soviet orbit; here, too, non-alignment had largely lost its meaning. The national interests of Egypt prescribed close relations with the Soviet bloc, and this took precedence over more general Afro-Asian solidarity. It was, indeed, this virtually total dependence of Egypt on the Soviet Union which brought about the crisis between the two nations that led to the forced withdrawal of Soviet forces from Egypt in July 1972.

Yet, despite this dramatic turn of events, the Egyptians still remained largely dependent on the Soviet Union and by no stretch of the imagination could they be considered to be reverting to a true non-aligned stance in their foreign policy orientation. Neither the Soviets nor the Egyptians deemed it necessary to abrogate the treaty of friendship which had been signed a year earlier by the Presidents of Egypt and the Soviet Union. At the other end of the scale post-Sukarno Indonesia was becoming increasingly dependent on massive Western aid, resulting in a concomitant departure from the militant anti-Western orientation which had dominated Indonesia's foreign policy in the days of Sukarno.

Thus in place of the old Afro-Asian brotherhood there has been increasing emphasis on bilateral and regional associations, based on *practical* national interests. This is in conformity with the normal procedure for determining foreign policy orientations, and use of this procedure has demonstrated that the period of transition, mentioned earlier, has been drawing to an end.

The twenty-five years of transition marked a tremendous upheaval, a major turning-point in the political history of Afro-Asia. But there was no concomitant change in the social or economic field. The peoples of Asia or Africa may have become politically independent, but change in political status has had little effect on their standard of living, nor has it done away with the poverty, ignorance and disease which, no less than the colonial masters, had been the enemies of the people for so long.

The Afro-Asian Movement, so active in the political field, spared little time for economic and social problems. Yet it is precisely here that common Afro-Asian policies are most needed. It has been said by one of the most active advocates of Afro-Asian solidarity that "the nations of Africa and Asia have to meet the challenge of science"[8] and that Afro-Asia should be used as a moral force to attack "the anomalous discrepancy in the distribution of wealth in our times."[9] These are, indeed, the greatest challenges facing the countries of Africa and Asia today. Poverty, illiteracy, unemployment, disease, inadequate housing, unbalanced diets, maladministration are still the hallmarks of large sections of Afro-Asia. Most of the countries do not have the resources to tackle these evils on their own. They need outside help from more developed countries and from the international agencies of the United Nations. Yet economic aid in itself is no magic palliative, as the experience of the past twenty-five years has shown. Economic aid only too often serves to increase the gap between the rich and the poor of the recipient countries without offering any basic remedy to the fundamental maladies affecting their societies.

The challenge of science, the need to adjust institutionally to the technical and scientific aspects of Western civilization of the late twentieth century, is the one common problem, overshadowing all others, which faces all Afro-Asian countries. The extent that this problem is solved affects the degree of effectiveness of outside economic aid. One without the other is useless.

Can Afro-Asianism take up this challenge? Can the struggle for economic development play the role that anti-colonialism did for the last half century? Can the movement be regalvanized by this new unifying theme?

The Afro-Asian Movement was, as we have pointed out, the product of a period dominated by the twin phenomena of decolonization and the cold war. Within the bounds of these two issues the movement had a role to play. Within this context peoples of many different languages, religions, races, and often conflicting political creeds were able to come together in a single political movement. Without the twin issues of the struggle against colonialism and the cold war such a cumbersome and variegated grouping was unable to hold together for any length of time, let alone be effective.

Efforts to continue the old forms—whether in the guise of AAPSO, ALAAPSO or as a grouping of non-aligned countries—have largely failed to succeed. After the Chinese and their allies walked out of the 1967 Nicosia gathering of AAPSO, the Solidarity Movement lost what little credence it had left, even among the militants of Asia and Africa. Similarly, the third summit conference of the heads of state of non-aligned countries held at Lusaka, Zambia, in September 1970, made but scant impression on world public opinion; the new foreign policy orientations of countries such as India, Indonesia and Egypt, described earlier in this chapter, made a mockery of the term 'non-aligned.'

Instead, the challenge is being taken up in the domain of regional cooperation, within both Africa and Asia. In the words of Singapore's foreign minister "the alternative to regional cooperation in Asia is endemic violence, further pauperization and further degradation for Asians."[10] In his views "what is immediatly needed is a total commitment to economic development by Asian countries. . . . Now that anti-colonialism is a dead doctrine, regionalism could fruitfully fill the vacum that now exists."[11] The same can be said for Africa, where the Organization of African Unity has already largely replaced the Afro-Asian Movement as the major political instrument enabling full cooperation of all the countries of the continent.

The move to regional cooperation is growing steadily. It already exists in the form of African regional bodies and in the Association of South-East Asian Nations. It is reflected in the demands for an Asian common market,[12] and in the growing attention paid by the countries of the Third World to the manifold challenges posed to them by the highly technological world of the 1970s.[1,3]

It is in this form of practical, regional cooperation that the spirit of Afro-Asianism may yet live on. For this is the path that the countries of Asia and Africa—and indeed, of Latin America—will have to follow in order to take their rightful place in the world of the twenty-first century.

NOTES

[1] Soviet political commentators also considered the Afro-Asian Movement to have emerged in the period of transition, though from a slightly different viewpoint. Thus, Etinger and Melikyan, in *Policy of Non-Alignment,* p.6: "The neutralist trend in the newly-liberated countries springs from the laws governing our epoch of transition from capitalism to socialism."

[2] For a clear and concise summary of Chinese policy vis-à-vis the Afro-Asian Movement, see Neuhauser, "Third World Politics: China and AAPSO, 1957–1967," *Harvard East Asian Monographs,* 27, 1968. See also Zagoria, *op. cit.*

[3] *Statement by Charles Kauraisa, head of the South West Africa Delegation to the 8th Session of the Council of the Organization of Afro-Asian Solidarity, February 13–17, 1967, Nicosia, Cyprus.* Document issued by Conference Secretariat, Nicosia, n.d., p. 2.

[4] Pohekar, *India's Relations with Asia and Africa,* p. 3.

[5] S. Rajaratnam, the foreign minister of Singapore, bluntly voiced this view in an interview: "Our foreign policy is an extension of our national interests. Unlike some countries we will not sacrifice national interests for world objectives." See *Sunday Times,* Kuala Lumpur and Singapore, 28.9.69, p. 10. Indonesia's new links with the Western powers which she developed in the latter half of the 1960s, and her adherence to the Association of South-East Asian Nations, together with her erstwhile enemy Malaysia, was another example of this new tendency.

[6] The closer relations between the Soviet Union and India were a direct result of the Indo-Chinese conflict. They also reflected in the steadily growing economic aid given by the Soviet Union to India. See, for example, the joint communiqué issued in Moscow on September 17, 1969, at the termination of a visit there by the Indian external affairs minister, Dinesh Singh. The two sides expressed inter alia satisfaction that cooperation between them was "reaching considerable development in the political, economic, cultural, scientific and other fields," and stated that there existed "a coincidence or proximity of positions on (urgent international

271

problems) by the Soviet Union and India"—see *Times of India,* New Delhi, 18.9.69, p. 1. Soviet aid to India rose to new heights on the eve of the Indian-Pakistan war in December 1971, and the Communist countries of East Europe were among the first to recognize the new Republic of Bangla-Desh which was established as a result of that war.

[7] A view expressed by the secretary-general of the Indian Council for World Affairs, Professor Poplai, in an interview with the author.

[8] C. P. Romulo, "Asia, Africa and the World," in *Emerging World—Jawahrlal Nehru Memorial Volume,* New York, 1964, p. 193.

[9] *Ibid.,* p. 194.

[10] S. Rajaratnam, "Regionalism: A Dream?" in *Asia Magazine,* Hong Kong, 28.9.1969, p. 25.

[11] *Ibid.,* p. 27.

[12] See, for example, the declaration of the Philippines ambassador to Jakarta that the Philippines and Indonesia should take the initiative in forming the Asian common market—*Djakarta Times,* Jakarta, 29.9.69. pp. 1–2.

[13] Thus, for example, the conference of foreign ministers of non-aligned countries, which convened in Georgetown, Guyana, in August 1972, discussed, inter alia, the following issues:

a) evaluation of the outcome of the UNCTAD conference held at Lima, Peru, earlier that year;

b) the effect of the world monetary crisis of 1972 on the non-aligned countries;

c) review of the results of the world conference on human environment at Stockholm in June 1972—with specific reference to development and environment;

d) review of the international development strategy.

APPENDIX 1

Some of the more important conferences and meetings of the Afro-Asian Peoples' Solidarity Organization and its affiliate organizations

26.12.1957– 1. 1.1958   Founding Assembly, AAPSO, Cairo.

7–13.10.1958   First Afro-Asian Writers' Conference, Tashkent.

8–11.12.1958   First Afro-Asian Economic Conference (AFRASEC), Cairo.

2– 8. 2.1959   First Conference of Afro-Asian Youth, Cairo.

11–13. 2.1959   First Council Meeting, AAPSO, Cairo.

11–15. 4.1960   Second Plenary Assembly, AAPSO, Conakry.

9–12. 1.1960   Executive Committee, AFRASEC, Aswan.

9–13.11.1960   Executive Committee, AAPSO, Beirut.

14–23. 1.1961   First Afro-Asian Women's Conference, Cairo.

21. 1.1961   Emergency Council on Congo, AAPSO, Cairo.

21–22. 2.1961   Solidarity Fund, AAPSO, Conakry.

27.2– 2. 3.1961   Preparatory Committee for Second Conference of Afro-Asian Writers, Cairo.

10–14. 4.1961   Council Meeting, AAPSO, Bandung.

28–29. 7.1961   Solidarity Fund, AAPSO, Conakry.

7– 9.12.1961   Executive Committee, AAPSO, Gaza.

11–17.12.1961   Assembly Meeting, AFRASEC, New Delhi.

12–   2.1962   Second Conference of Afro-Asian Writers, Cairo.

19–31. 3.1962   Afro-Asian Conference for Development of Rural Areas, Cairo.

25. 5.1962   Executive Committee, Cairo.

25–28. 5.1962   Preparatory Committee for Conference of Afro-Asian Lawyers, Conakry.

10.10.1962   Afro-Asian Conference on Railways, Cairo.

273

15–20.10.1962	Second Conference of Afro-Asian Lawyers, Conakry.
4–10. 2.1963	Third Plenary Assembly, AAPSO, Moshi, Tanganyika.
10–15. 2.1963	Preparatory Committee for Afro-Asian Journalists' Conference, Jakarta.
17–18. 4.1963	Afro-Asian Conference for Rural Development, New Delhi.
26–30. 4.1963	Afro-Asian Journalists' Conference, Jakarta.
9–12. 9.1963	Executive Committee, AAPSO, Nicosia.
22–23.11.1963	Executive Committee of Afro-Asian Lawyers, Conakry.
5– 9.12.1963	Conference of AFRASEC, Karachi.
7.12.1963	Afro-Asian Housing Conference, Cairo.
12.2– 2. 3.1964	Afro-Asian Conference on Rural Reconstruction,[1] Kuala Lumpur.
24. 2.1964	Afro-Asian Legal Consultative Committee, Cairo.
22–27. 3.1964	Council Meeting, AAPSO, Algiers.
16–23. 6.1964	Afro-Asian Economic Seminar,[2] Pyongyang.
3. 9.1964	Afro-Asian Conference on Insurance, Cairo.
24.10.1964	Afro-Asian Medical Conference, Cairo.
22–27. 2.1965	Afro-Asian Economic Seminar, AAPSO, Algiers.
6–13. 3.1965	Afro-Asian Islamic Conference, Bandung.
10–16. 5.1965	Fourth Plenary Assembly, AAPSO, Winneba, Ghana.
3–14. 1.1966	First Conference of Asian, African and Latin American Peoples' Solidarity Organization, Havana.
12–16. 2.1967	Council Meeting, AAPSO, Nicosia.
26–30. 3.1967	Afro-Asian Writers' Conference, Beirut.

[1] This conference was attended by official delegates of the Afro-Asian countries.
[2] Organized by China.

APPENDIX 2

Delegates attending the AAPSO Council meeting, held at Nicosia in February 1967

The following is a copy of document No. (5)c, issued by the Permanent Secretariat of AAPSO, giving a list of delegates attending the conference. (The original document also gave the room numbers of the delegates. Spelling of the names is taken from the document.)

Doc. No. (5)c

LIST OF ARRIVALS 13/2/1967

1. ALGERIA
   1. Mr. Nohamed Meghraoui
   2. Mr. Ahmed Zemirline

2. ANGOLA
   3. Mr. Francisco Barros
   4. Mr. Jorgo Paul

3. BAHREIN
   5. Mr. Ahmed Ibrahim El Zwadi
   6. Mr. Kassem Khaled
   7. Mr. Seif Ben Ali

4. BOTSWANA
   8. Mr. P. Matante
   9. Mr. Peter Dick Maruping
   10. Mr. Bobby Mack
   11. Mr. Nusi Theo

5. BURUNDI
   12. Mr. Bigirimana

6. CONGO (BRAZZAVILLE)
   13. Mr. Elenga

7. CONGO (LEOPOLDVILLE)
   14. Mr. Gaston Sumialot
   15. Mr. Casimir M'Bagiara
   16. Mr. Eduard Marcel Sumbu

8. CYPRUS
   16. Dr. Vassos Lyssarides
       (Head of Delegation and
       Chairman of Session)

9. GAMBIA
   17. Mr. Ibrahima Garba Juhumba

10. "PORTUGUESE" GUINEA
    18. Mr. Amilcar Cabral
    19. Mr. Saude Maria Victor

11. INDIA
    20. Dr. Anup Singh
    21. Mr. Romesh Chandra
    22. Mr. M. Kalimullah
    23. Mr. Baren Ray
    24. Mr. C. N. Malviya

12. IRAN
  25. Mr. Amir Debadi
    Torkestani Abdoilhossein
    Etebar

13. IRAQ
  26. Mr. Abdel Wahab
    El Salloum

14. JORDAN
  27. Mr. Karim Said

15. KENYA
  28. Mr. John Ndisi

16. KOREA
  29. Mr. Zen Byeng Chul
  30. Mr. Ryu Hai Yeng
  31. Mr. Rim Mi Hong

17. LEBANON
  32. Mr. Farid Gebrane
  33. Mr. Ma'arouf Saad
  34. Mr. Farouk Massarani

18. LESOTHO
  35. Mr. M. W. L. Mapefane

19. MADAGASCAR
  36. Miss Gizele Rabesahala

20. MALI
  37. Toure Youssef

21. MAURITIUS
  38. Mr. Sibsurun Teekaram

22. MONGOLIA
  39. Mr. Ch. Lodoidamba
  40. Mr. G. Dugre
  41. Mr. D. Damba
  42. Mrs. L. Ider

23. MOROCCO
  43. Mr. Abdel Rahman
    El Yousoufi

44. Mr. Hamid Barrada
45. Osman Benani

24. MOZAMBIQUE
  46. Mr. Marclino Dos Santos

25. OMAN
  47. Mr. Mohamed Amin Abdallah

26. PALESTINE
  48. Mr. Khairi Hammad
  49. Mr. Abdel Kerim El Karmy

27. RWANDA
  50. Mr. Francois Rukeba
  51. Mr. Papias Gatwa

28. SOMAL REPUBLIC
  52. Hon. Hassan Haji Omar Omoi

29. SOMALILAND "FRENCH"
  53. Mr. Mobarak Ahmed
    Mobarak

30. SOUTH AFRICA
  54. Mr. Robert Resha
  55. Mr. M. Piliso
  56. Mr. Alfred Nzo
  57. Mr. Johnny Makatini
  58. Mr. Tennyson Makiwane
  59. Mrs. R. V. Nzo
  60. Mr. M. A. Makiwane

31. SOUTH WEST AFRICA
  61. Mr. Charles Kauraisa
  62. Mr. Katjimuina Veii
  63. Mr. Moses K. Katjuongua

32. OCCUPIED SOUTH YEMEN
  64. Mr. Nasser Ahmed El Oragi

33. SUDAN
  65. Sheikh Ali Abdel Rahman

34. SWAZILAND
  66. Mr. Herbert F. Nkosi

35. TANZANIA
    67. Mr. D. A. Hassan

36. UAR
    68. Mr. Khaled Mohie Eddin
    69. Mr. Ahmad Bahaa Eddin
    70. Dr. Fawzi El Sayed
    71. Dr. Rifaat El Mahgoub
    72. Mr. Ahmad Mokhtar Kotb
    73. Madam Amina El Said
    74. Miss Bahia Karam
    75. Mr. Ahmad El Sayed Wahsh
    76. Mr. Farouk Abdel
        Salah Hassan
    77. Mr. Mohammed Abdel
        Rahman Diab
    78. Mr. Wageeh Diaa
        Eddin Mohammad

37. USSR
    79. Mr. Piotr Pimenov
    80. Mr. Rostislav Ulyanovsky
    81. Mr. Chinguiz Aitmatov
    82. Mr. Vladmir Yarovoi
    83. Mr. Dmitry Dolidze
    84. Mr. Mirza Makhmutov
    85. Mr. Georgy Kim

38. NORTH VIETNAM
    86. Mr. Houang Bac
    87. Mr. La Cong Ngyen

39. SOUTH VIETNAM
    88. Mr. Le Phong
    89. Mr. Le Anh Keit
    90. Mr. Nguyen Thanh Cong

40. YEMEN
    91. Mr. Abdallah El Alawi

41. ZAMBIA
    92. Mr. Simbule Zambias
    93. Mr. P. W. Lumbi

42. ZIMBABWE
    94. Mr. George B. Nyandoro
    95. Mr. J. Z. Moyo
    96. Mr. M. M. Noko
    97. Mr. Stephen Nkomo

43. ARAB PENINSULA
    98. Mr. Mohammed Nidal

OBSERVERS
Tri-Continental Executive
Secretariat:
    99. Mr. Osmany Cienfuegos
    100. Mr. Domingo
         Amuchastecui
    101. Mr. Gabriel Molina
    102. Mr. Silvio Rivera

[The following names appear at the end of the document and refer apparently to late-comers to the conference]

JAPAN
1. Minoru Ito
2. Mitsuhizo Kaneko
3. Hiroshi Ide

MALTA
1. Joe Camilleri
2. Salu Sant

SYRIA
1. Amin
2. Ismail
3. Aadad
4. Sundi

BIBLIOGRAPHY AND SOURCES

The following list of books, articles and other sources is by no means all-inclusive: it does *not* include the numerous books of more general subject-matter which contain relevant material on the subject, such as the Royal Institute of International Relations' Surveys of International Affairs, or Andre Fontaine's *Histoire de la Guerre Froide,* to mention two examples. The sections below on "Africa—General" and "Asia—General" are selective only, as is the list of articles. Lastly, this list of source material, naturally enough, cannot do justice to the extremely valuable material which the writer obtained orally, in interviews, discussions and conversations with participants in the making of the Afro-Asian Movement.

AFRICA—GENERAL
(Books with relevant material on the Afro-Asian Movement, or on foreign policy orientations of African states.)

AUSTIN, D., and H. N. WEILER (eds.), *Inter-State Relations in Africa,* Part I, Freiburg, 1965.

BREZINSKI, Z., *Africa and the Communist World,* Stanford, 1963.

COOLEY, J. K., *East Wind over Africa,* New York, 1965.

DIA MAMADOU, *African Nations and World Solidarity,* London, 1962.

DIALLO, D., *L'Afrique en Question,* Paris, 1968.

DUMOGA, J., *Africa between East and West,* London, 1969.

EMERSON, R., and M. KILSON (eds.), *Political Awakening of Africa,* New Jersey, 1965.

LEGUM, C., *Pan-Africanism: A Short Political Guide,* New York, 1965.

LESSING, P., *Africa's Red Harvest,* London, 1962.

MAZRUI, ALI A., *Towards a Pax Africana,* London, 1967.

McKAY, V., *Africa in World Politics,* New York, 1963.

NKRUMAH, K., *Africa Must Unite,* London, 1963.

PADELFORD, N. J., and R. EMERSON (eds.), *Africa and World Order,* New York, 1963.

PADMORE, G., *Pan-Africanism or Communism—the Coming Struggle for Africa*, London, 1946.
POTEKHIN, I., *Africa Looks Ahead*, London, 1963.
ROTBERG, R., *A Political History of Tropical Africa*, New York, 1965.
SHALTEN, FRITZ, *Communism in Africa*, New York, 1966.
SITHOLE, N., *African Nationalism*, London, 1954.
THIAM, DOUDOU, *Foreign Policy of African States*, New York, 1965.
TOURÉ, SÉKOU, *L'Expérience Guieenne et l'Unité Africaine*, Paris, 1959.
WODDIS, J., *Africa—The Way Ahead*, London, 1963.
———, *Africa—The Roots of Revolt*, London, 1960.
ZARTMAN, I. W., *International Relations in the New Africa*, New York, 1966.

ASIA—GENERAL

(Books with relevant material on the Afro-Asian Movement
or on foreign policy orientations of Asian states.)

BRECHER, M., *New States of Asia: A Political Analysis*, London, 1963.
EDWARDES, M., *Asia in the Balance*, London, 1962.
CARPARE D'ENCAUSSE, H., *Le Marxisme et l'Asie*, Paris, 1959.
JOHNSTONE, W. C., *Burma's Foreign Policy—A Study in Neutralism*, Cambridge, Mass., 1963.
KAHIN, G. M., *Nationalism and Revolution in Indonesia*, New York, 1952.
KENNEDY, J., *Asian Nationalism in the Twentieth Century*, London, 1968.
KOTELAWALA, Sir J., *An Asian Prime Minister's Story*, London, 1956.
LEV, D. S., *Transition to Guided Democracy: Indonesian Politics, 1957–1959*, New York, 1966.
MODELSKI, G. (ed.), *New Emerging Forces: Documents on the Ideology of Indonesian Foreign Policy*, Data Paper 2, Canberra, 1963.
MYRDAL, G., *Asian Drama: An Enquiry into the Poverty of Nations*, 3 vols., London, 1968.
PANIKKAR, K. M., *Asia and Western Dominance*, London, 1953.
SMITH, R. M., *Cambodia's Foreign Policy*, New York, 1965.
VLEKKE, B. H. M., *Indonesia in 1956 : Political and Economic Aspects*, The Hague, 1957.
WINT, G., *Spotlight on Asia*, London, 1955.
——— (ed.), *Asia: A Handbook*, New York, 1966.

AFRO-ASIA AND THE THIRD WORLD

ALLAIS, M., *Le Tiers Monde en Carrefour*, Paris, 1962.

BENNABI, M., *L'Afro-Asiatisme,* Cairo, 1956.
CALVOCORESSI, P., *World Order and New States,* London, 1962.
CROZIER, B., *Morning After: A Study of Independence,* London, 1963.
EMERSON, R., *From Empire to Nation: the Rise to Self-Assertion of Asian and African Peoples,* Cambridge, Mass., 1960.
ETINGER, Y., and O. MELIKYAN, *Policy of Non-Alignment,* Moscow, n.d.
FANON, F., *Wretched of the Earth,* London, 1965.
FARAJALLAH, S. B., *Le Groupe afro-asiatique dans le cadre de Nations Unis.* Geneva, 1963.
HOVET, T., JR., *Bloc Politics in the United Nations,* New York, 1962.
———, *Africa in the United Nations,* Evanston, Ill., 1963.
JANSEN, G. H., *Afro-Asia and Non-Alignment,* London, 1966.
JHABVALA, D. S., *Afro-Asian Solidarity,* Calcutta, 1957.
LACOUTRE, J., and BAUMIER J., *Le Poids du Tiers Monde,* Paris, 1962.
LOHIA, R., *Third Camp in World Affairs,* Bombay, 1951.
LONDON, K. (ed.), *New Nations in a Divided World: The International Relations of the Afro-Asian States,* New York, 1963.
MARTIN, L. W. (ed.), *Neutralism and Non-Alignment,* New York, 1962.
MILLER, J. D. B., *Politics of the Third World,* London, 1966.
POPLAI, S. L. (ed.), *Asia and Africa in the Modern World,* Bombay, 1955.
QUEUILLE, P., *Histoire de l'Afro-Asiatisme jusqu'à Bandoung: la Naissance du Tiers-Monde,* Paris, 1965.
RADOVANOVIÉ, L., *Policy of Non-Aligned Countries,* Belgrade, 1964.
ROSSI, M., *Third World,* New York, 1963.
SIGMUND, PAUL E., *Ideologies of the Developing Nations,* New York, 1967.
CENTRE D'ETUDE DES RÉLATIONS INTERNATIONALES, *Les Pays nouvellement indépendants dans les relations internationales,* colloquium, 26–27 November 1960, Paris.
———, *The Emerging World—Jawahrlal Nehru Memorial Volume,* New York, 1964.
———, *President Tito's Meetings with Statesmen of Asian and African Countries,* Belgrade, 1961.

AFRO-ASIAN CONFERENCES

ABDULGANI, R., *Bandung Spirit, Moving on the Tide of History,* Djakarta, 1964.
BAUMIER, J., *La Route de Bandoung,* Paris, 1956.
CONTE, A., *Bandoung, tournant de l'histoire,* Paris, 1965.
GUITARD, O., *Bandoung,* Paris, 1961.

HASSOUNA, A. K., *First Asian-African Conference Held at Bandung*, League of Arab States, Cairo, 1955.

HEYKE, H. E., *Die Asiatisch—Afrikanische Konferenz von Bandung (bis 24 April 1955). Zur Deutung der politischen Leitmotive und Kräfte*, Heidelberg, 1963.

KAHIN, G. M., *The Afro-Asian Conference, Bandung, Indonesia, April* , New York, 1956.

LEGUM, C., *Bandung, Cairo and Accra*, London, 1958.

ROMULO, C. P., *Meaning of Bandung*, North Carolina, 1956.

WRIGHT, R., *Colour Curtain*, London, 1956.

——, *Selected Documents of the Bandung Conference*, New York, 1955.

——, *Afro-Asia Speaks from Bandung*, Ministry of Foreign Affairs. Djakarta, 1955.

——, *Asian Relations, Report of Proceedings—Documentation of the First Asian Relations Conference*, New Delhi, 1948.

——, *Conference of Heads of State or Government of Non-Aligned Coun- Belgrade, September 1–6, 1961*, Belgrade, 1961.

AFRO-ASIAN PEOPLES' SOLIDARITY ORGANIZATION

JACK, H. HOMER, *Cairo: The Afro-Asian Peoples' Solidarity Organization— A Critical Analysis*, Chicago, 1958.

LENTIN, A. P., *La Lutte Tricontinentale*, Paris, 1966.

SMETS, P. F., *De Bandoung à Moshi; contribution à l'étude des conférences afro-asiatiques (1955–1963)*, Brussels, 1964.

——, *Second A.A.P.S. Conference, Conakry 11–15 April 1960*, Permanent Secretariat for AAPS, Cairo, 1960.

——, *A.A.P.S. Conference: Cairo, December 26, 1957–January 1, 1958*, Moscow, 1958.

——, *Afro-Asian Solidarity Committee: A Documentary Study*, Saigon, 1958.

——, *What Happened at Moshi*, Indian Association for Afro-Asian Solidarity, New Delhi, n.d.

CHINA AND THE SOVIET UNION

CRANKSHAW, E., *New Cold War: Moscow v. Peking*, London, 1963.

DUTT, V. P., *China's Foreign Policy, 1958–62*, Delhi, 1964.

FEJTÖ, F., *China-URSS: La Fin d'une Hégémonie*, Paris, 1964.

HAMRELL, S. (ed.), *Soviet Bloc, China and Africa,* London, 1964.
HINTON, H. C., *Communist China in World Politics,* London, 1966.
LONDQUIST, S., *China in Crisis,* London, 1963.
NEUHAUSER, C., *Third World Politics: China and A.A.P.S.O.1957–1967,* Harvard East Asian Monographs, 27, Cambridge, Mass., 1968.
RAO, G. N., *Indo-Chinese Border—A Reappraisal,* Bombay, 1968.
ROWLAND, J., *A History of Sino-Indian Relations,* Princeton, 1967.
ZAGORIA, D. S., *Sino-Soviet Conflict: 1956–1965,* Princeton, 1962.
———, *China and the Asian-African Conference—Documents,* Peking, 1955.

EGYPT AND THE ARAB WORLD

ABU JABER, KAMEL S., *Arab Ba'th Socialist Party,* New York, 1966.
'ABD EL-NASSER, GAMAL, *Speeches and Press Interviews,* Cairo, 1958–62.
———, *Egypt's Liberation: The Philosophy of the Revolution,* Washington, 1955.
———, *Where I Stand and Why,* Washington, 1959.
BINDER, L., *Ideological Revolution in the Middle East,* New York, 1964.
CREMEANS, C., *Arabs and the World,* New York, 1963.
DIB, G. M., *Arab Bloc in the U. N.,* Amsterdam, 1956.
SAYEGH, F. A., *Dynamics of Neutralism in the Arab World,* San Francisco, 1964.
CARNEGIE ENDOWMENT FOR INTERNATIONAL PEACE, *Egypt and the U.N.,* New York, 1955.

INDIA

BALABUSHEVICH, V. V., and B. PRASED (eds.), *India and the Soviet Union— A Symposium,* New Delhi, 1969.
BHARGAVA, G. S., *India—UAR Relations—An Assessment,* New Delhi, 1966.
BRECHER, M., *Nehru: A Political Biography,* London, 1959.
———, *India and World Politics—Krishna Menon's View of the World,* London, 1968.
———, *India's Foreign Policy—An Interpretation,* New York, 1957.
BRIGHT, J. S., *Before and After Independence,* New Delhi, 1950.
CHAR, K. T., *Profile of Nehru,* Bombay, 1965.
KARANJIA, R. K., *Mind of Mr. Nehru,* London, 1960.
KARUNAKARAN, K. P., *India in World Affairs, 1947–1950,* London, 1952.
KUNDRA, J. C., *India's Foreign Policy 1947–54,* Groningen, 1955.

MENDE, T., *Conversations with Nehru*, London, 1956.

MURTI, B. S. N., *Nehru's Foreign Policy*, New Delhi, 1953.

———, *India's Stand on Korea*, New Delhi, 1953.

MURTI, K. S., *Indian Foreign Policy*, Calcutta, 1964.

NEHRU, J., *A Bunch of Old Letters*, Bombay, 1958.

———, *India and the World*, London, 1936.

———, *Nehru: India's Foreign Policy—Selected Speeches by J. Nehru, 1946–61,*Publications Division, Ministry of Information, New Delhi, 1961.

———, *Jawaharlal Nehru's Speeches: 1949–1953*, New Delhi, 1957.

———, *Jawaharlal Nehru's Speeches, 1957–63*, Vol. 4, New Delhi, 1964.

———, *Prime Minister Jawaharlal Nehru in China*, Embassy of the People's Republic of China, New Delhi, 1957.

NORMAN, D. (ed.), *Nehru, The First Sixty Years*, 2 vols., London, 1965.

PATEL, S. R., *Foreign Policy of India—An Inquiry and Criticism*, Bombay, 1960.

POHEKAR, S., *India's Relations with Asia and Africa*, Laski Memorial Lecture, Ahmadabad, 1964.

POPLAI, S. L., *Selected Documents on Asian Affairs: India,1947–1950,*London, 1959.

POWER, P. F. (ed.), *India's Non-Alignment Policy—Strength and Weaknesses*, Boston, 1967.

PRASAD, B., *Origins of Indian Foreign Policy—the Indian National Congress and World Affairs*, Calcutta, 1962.

RAJAN, M. S., *India in World Affairs 1954–56,*New Delhi, 1964.

SINGH, IQBAL, *India's Foreign Policy*, Bombay, 1946.

TYSON, G., *Nehru, The Years of Power*, London, 1966.

LOK SABHA SECRETARIAT, *Panchsheel*, New Delhi, 1957.

———, *Foreign Policy of India, 1947–58,*New Delhi, 1958.

———, *Foreign Policy of India, 1947–59,*New Delhi, 1966.

SELECTED LIST OF ARTICLES

ADIE, W. A. C., "China, Russia and the Third World," *China Quarterly*, London, No. 11, July–Sept. 1962, pp. 200ff.

ARDANT, P., "Le Neo-Colonialisme, Thème, Mythe, et Réalité," *Revue Française de Science Politique*, Vol. XV, No. 5, Oct. 1965.

BENNINGSEN, A., "Sultan Galiev: l'U.R.S.S. et la revolution coloniale," *Journal a Plusiers Voix*, 20.12.1956.

BETHEL, P. D., "Havana Conference," New York, 24.3.1966, pp. 25–129.

CARRIERE D'ENCAUSSE, H., "La Politique sovietique en Moyen Orient," *Cahiers de la Republic*, Dec. 1956.

GUYOT, COMMANDANT, "L'Inde, son influence dans le Tiers Monde," *Centre de Hautes Etudes Administratives sur l'Afrique et l'Asie Modernes (C.H.E.A.M.)*, Paris, 1963.

HATTA, MUHAMMAD, "Indonesia's Foreign Policy," *Foreign Affairs*, New York, April 1953, pp. 441–53.

———, "Indonesia Between the Power Blocs," *Foreign Affairs*, New York, April 1958, Vol. 36, No. 3, p. 480ff.

HOWARD, H. H., "The Arab-Asian States in the U.N.," *Middle East Journal*, Washington, Vol. 7, No. 3 (Summer 1958), pp. 279–92.

JACKSON, D. B., "Whose Men in Havana," *Problems of Communism*, April–May 1966, pp. 1–10.

JHA, C. S., "The Algiers Conference," *India Quarterly*, New Delhi, Vol. XXI, No. 4, Oct.–Dec. 1965, p. 37 ff.

KRIPALANI, J. B., "For Principled Neutrality," *Foreign Affairs*, New York, Oct. 1959, pp. 46–60.

KUDRYAVTSEV, V., "Reflections at the Foot of Mt. Kilimanjaro," *International Affairs*, Moscow, May 1963.

MAKSOUD, C., "Reflections on Afro-Asianism," *Conspectus I*, No. 3 (1965), pp. 11–19.

NKRUMAH, K., "African Prospect," *Foreign Affairs*, New York, Oct. 1958, pp. 45–54.

PAUKER, G., "Rise and Fall of Afro-Asian Solidarity," *Asian Survey*, Berkeley, Sept. 1965, pp. 425–32.

POWER, P. F., "Peoples' Solidarity Movement: Evolution and Continuity," *Mizan*, London, Vol. 9, No. 1, Jan. 1967.

SAKRIKAR, D., "Bandung to Algiers: A Critical Survey," *United Asia*, Bombay, No. 17, May–June 1965.

SERGEYEVA, N., "Meaning of Bandung," *New Times*, Moscow, No. 17, 26.4.65.

SIHANOUK, N., "Cambodia Neutral: the Dictate of Necessity," *Foreign Affairs*, July 1958, pp. 582–7.

STACKELBERG, G. A. VON, "Afro-Asian Solidarity and the Sino-Soviet Dispute," *Bulletin of the Institute for Study of the USSR*, Munich, Vol. XI, August 1964, No. 8.

STEVENS, G., "Arab Neutralism and Bandung," *Middle East Journal*, Washington, Vol. 11, No. 2, Spring 1957.

STOCKWIN, H., "Afro-Asian Attitudes," *Far Eastern Economic Review*, Hongkong, No. 49, 30.9.65, pp. 633–5.

THOMSON, J. S., "Burmese Neutralism," *Political Science Quarterly*, June 1957, pp. 261–84.

VANDERWEGHE, L., "Le Neutralisme afro-asiatique," *Chronique de Politique Entrangére,* Paris, March 1960, pp. 179–222.
R., "India and the Cold War," *Middle East Journal,* Summer 1965.

PERIODICALS

Bulletin of the Institute for the Study of the USSR (Munich); *Mizan Newsletter* (London); *Peking Review* (Peking); *India Quarterly* (New Delhi); *China Quarterly* (London); *Intelligence Digest* (London); *Jeune Afrique* (Tunis); *International Affairs* (Moscow); *New Times* (Moscow); *Tricontinental* (Havana); *World Marxist Review* (Prague); *New Age* (New Delhi).

PRESS

The Times, London; *Le Monde,* Paris; *New York Times,* New York; *Current Digest of the Soviet Press; Neue Zürcher Zeitung;* Press of India, Japan, Burma, Indonesia, Ghana, Nigeria, Tanzania, Egypt and Israel.

OTHER SOURCES

Conference documents (including unpublished protocols of the Asian-African conference held at Bandung, unpublished protocols of the preparatory conference held at Jakarta in 1964, and conference documents of AAPSO and of the tricontinental conference); publications of the Permanent Secretariat of AAPSO in Cairo; publications of embassies of Afro-Asian countries; United Nations publications; B.B.C. monitoring .

INDEX

Abdel Nasser, Jamāl, 63, 70, 72, 74, 81, 82, 83, 84, 85, 89, 90, 91, 94, 95, 96, 97, 100, 105, 137, 138, 146, 166, 206, 218, 222, 225, 254, 265

Abdul Raḥmān, Tunku, 193

Abidjan, 2

Abrahams, Peter, 10

Accra, 2, 89, 90, 92, 120, 121, 192, 239, 240, 247

Aden, 73, 74

Afghanistan, 30, 33, 34, 36, 73, 85 92

Afro-Asian Chambers of Commerce, 146, 149

Afro-Asian Conference for Economic Cooperation, 145, 146

Afro-Asian Economic Conference, 239

Afro-Asian Economic Seminar, 184, 188, 190

Afro-Asian Islamic Organization, 191, 230

Afro-Asianism, 17, 21, 22, 31, 33, 74, 104, 114, 117–18, 123, 224, 238, 240, 247, 251, 254–255, 260–261, 266, 268, 270

Afro-Asian Journalists' Association, 184, 188, 230

Afro-Asian-Latin American Peoples' Solidarity Organization (ALAAPSO), 160, 161, 209

Afro-Asian Lawyers' Association, 184, 188

Afro-Asian Organization for Economic Cooperation (AFRASEC), 149

Afro-Asian Peoples' Solidarity Organization (AAPSO), 18, 87, 123, 126, 135–138, 144–147, 149–151, 153–154, 156–158, 160–162, 164–167, 174–193, 198, 200, 204–211, 224, 234, 238–239, 244, 250, 252, 257, 264–265

AAPSO Council, 135, 144, 156, 185, 186, 188, 250

AAPSO Executive Committee, 154, 158, 160, 180

AAPSO General Assembly, 151

Afro-Asian Solidarity Conference, 130

Afro-Asian Trade Unions Conference, 184

Afro-Asian Women's Conference, 188

Afro-Asian Youth Movement, 144

Afro-Malagasy Union (UAM), 118

Akintola, Chief Samuel L., 10

Albania, 69

Algeria, 38, 72, 91, 93, 102, 119, 120, 121, 122, 135, 136, 145, 157, 188, 189, 190, 210, 247, 251

Algiers, 1, 100, 114, 118–122, 144, 145, 185, 188, 189, 190, 235, 250, 257

287

'Alī Muḥammad, 45, 51, 67, 69, 70
All-African Peoples' Congress (AAPC), 239, 240
All-India Muslim League, 1
Angola, 191
Ankrah, Joseph, 254
Anti-Fascists Peoples' Freedom League, 11
Appiah, Joe, 10
Arab Chambers of Commerce, 146
Arab Congress (1913), 1
Arab League, 29, 38, 39, 43, 61, 73, 101, 255
Arabian Gulf, The, 135
Argentina, 101, 160
Armistice Supervisory Commission for Indochina, 47
Aruna Asag Ali (Mrs.), 183
Arusha Declaration, 246
Arzoumanian, Arzumania A., 132, 133
Asian Conference for the Relaxation of International Tension (ACRIT), 126
Asian Pacific Peace Liaison Committee, 127
Asian Relations Conference, 29, 32
Asian Relations Organization, 32, 33
Asian Solidarity Committee, 127
Atlantic Charter, The, 8
Attlee, Clement Richard, 31
Aung San, 29, 32
Australia, 33, 34
Austria, 101
Ayūb Khan, Muḥammad, 105
Azikiwe, Dr. Nnamdi, 7, 239

Baguio, 50
Baku, 3
Balewa, Sir Abubakr Tafawa, 254
Bali, 184

Bandaranaike, Sirimavo (Mrs.), 100, 105, 115
Bandaranaike, Solomon W.R.D., 32, 98
Bandung, 1, 5, 18, 25, 37, 39, 45, 46, 53, 59–61, 63–79, 80–87, 89–91, 94–95, 98–100, 103, 105, 117, 121, 122, 126–129, 133, 135, 137, 145, 147, 156–158, 160, 162, 164, 177, 184–185, 191, 198, 219–222, 230, 232, 235, 238, 250, 256, 260, 264–266
Bandung, Declaration of, 80, 244
Bandung Manifesto, 80
Bandung, Second (1965), 1, 96, 98, 102, 104, 106, 118, 225, 234, 244, 247, 250, 252, 257
Barahoti, 49
Basutoland, 204
Bay of Pigs, 95
Bechuanaland, 192
Beirut, 146, 154, 156
Belgium, 8
Belgrade, 23, 84–86, 90–91, 95–97, 99–101, 105–106, 114, 117, 224
Ben Barka, Mehdi, 200
Ben Bella, Aḥmad, 91, 115, 119, 190, 210, 247, 254
Berlin, 5, 256
Berlin Wall, 95
Bevin, Ernest, 31
Bhatio, Prem, 256
Bhilai Steel Works, 86
Biafra, 242, 251
Bierville, 4
Binder, Leonard (Prof.), 83
Black Dragon Secret Society, 7
Boateng, Kwaku, 192
Bogor, 51, 52, 61
Bois, William du, 7, 18
Bolivia, 101

Bose, Subhas Chandra, 7
Boumedienne, Houari, 119, 120, 254
Bouteflika, 'Abd al-'Azīz, 121, 122
Brazil, 101, 160
Brazzaville, 8, 242
Brecher, M. (Prof.), 5, 215, 216
Brijoni Island, 84, 100
British Commonwealth, 43, 67, 95, 119
Brussels, 4, 5, 6, 214
Brutents, K., 178
Bulganin, N.A., 83, 84, 86, 137
Bulgaria, 69
Burma, 11, 12, 22, 29, 31, 32, 36, 42, 43, 45, 46, 47, 51, 52, 60, 61, 65, 67, 70, 73, 85, 86, 88, 92, 101, 102, 120, 138, 251
Burundi, 116

Cairo, 29, 38, 39, 42, 43, 61, 63, 74, 82, 88, 91, 95, 96, 98, 100, 102, 105, 106, 114–118, 127–131, 133, 135–138, 144–147, 149–151, 153, 154, 161, 162, 166, 184–185, 188–189, 193, 200, 205–209, 232, 239
Cambodia, 23, 67, 93, 251
Cameroons, The, 135–136, 157
Canada, 245
Casablanca, 89–90, 96, 121, 241–243
Castro, Fidel, 94, 201, 207, 209, 210
Celebes, 234
Central African Republic, 52, 254
Central Treaty Organization (CENTO) 25, 150, 151, 259
Césaire, Aimé, 3
Ceylon, 12, 29, 32–33, 43, 45–46, 65–66, 68, 70, 88, 98–100, 103, 105, 138, 160, 166, 184, 188, 251
Chad, 24, 135, 241
Chandra, Romesh, 131
Chiang Kai-shek, 33, 51

Chile, 101, 204
China, 6, 7, 8, 11, 12, 13, 18, 24, 25, 29, 32–34, 36, 40–41, 44–50, 51, 53, 59–61, 63–68, 70–71, 73–75, 86–87, 93, 96, 100, 103, 105, 114, 116–122, 126–127, 130, 135–136, 147, 151, 153–154, 157–158, 161–162, 164–165, 174–193, 198, 200, 201, 202, 204, 205, 208, 209, 210, 219, 220, 221, 224, 225, 234, 238, 244–247, 250–252, 256–257, 259, 260, 264–267
Chou En-lai, 48–49, 60, 65–69, 71, 74, 82, 105, 121, 158, 164, 185, 219
Churchill, Winston, 8
Cienfuegos, Osmany, 203, 206
Colombia, 160, 201
Colombo, 45–48, 50, 98–102, 145, 183–184, 232
Colombo Bureau of Afro-Asian Writers, 161
"Colombo Powers," 47, 50–52, 67, 73, 98, 164
Columbia University, 221
Communism, Communist, 3, 4, 7, 10, 11, 13, 17, 18, 23, 24, 26, 33, 36, 45, 47, 59, 60, 63–71, 74, 84–85, 174–175, 177–180, 187, 193, 201, 208, 210, 211, 231, 233, 244, 252
Communist Party (India), 86, 178, 179
Communist Party (Indonesia), 231, 233, 234
Communist Party (USSR), 3, 85
Conakry, 144–145, 149, 150, 153–154, 156, 162, 184, 239
Congo (Brazzaville), 116, 117, 158, 193
Congo (later changed to Zair), 23, 114–115, 145, 150, 154, 157, 192, 201, 224, 240, 243, 251, 254

Cremeans, Charles, 97
Cuba, 94–96, 154, 160, 200–210
Cuban Institute for Friendship between Peoples, 156
Cuellar, Diego Montana, 210
Cyprus, 39, 91, 100, 135, 180, 183, 184, 201, 204
Czechoslovakia, 23, 69

Dacko, David, 254
Dahomey, 24, 120, 247
Damascus, 130, 144
Dar-u-Islam, 156
Dia, Mamadou, 17, 20
Diallo, Abdoulai, 204, 205
Dienbienphu, 44, 47, 60
Dulles, John Foster, 44, 59, 60, 64, 88, 264

Eastern Peoples, Congress of (1922), 3
Ecuador, 101, 160
Eden, Anthony, Lord Avon, 46, 64
Egypt, 4, 6, 22–23, 26, 33–34, 36, 43, 61, 63, 70, 74, 82–83, 85, 88–89, 91–92, 95–96, 98–101, 104–105, 115, 119–120, 127, 129–130, 132, 136–138, 144–147, 149–151, 153–154, 156–158, 161, 165–166, 185, 188, 191–193, 204–208, 211, 224, 232, 238, 240, 251, 253, 259, 260
Einstein, Albert, 6
Eisenhower, Dwight, 88, 131
Esthonia, 38, 42, 69, 73
Ethiopia, 33–34, 36–38, 42, 64, 72–73, 85, 92, 97, 100, 238, 251, 257
European Common Market, 147, 149
Export Developing Council (India), 149

Fanon, Franz, 19

Fawzi, Muḥammad, 89, 240
Federal Republic of Germany, 245
Finland, 101
Formosa Straits, 59, 66, 126
France, 4, 8–11, 18–20, 37–39, 43–44, 64, 69, 88, 94, 114, 131, 154, 220, 225, 239, 241–242, 245, 259
Fulani, 20

Gabon, 241–242, 259
Gafurov, Bobodjan, 86, 187
Galāl, Fuad, 158
Galiev, Sultan, 3
Gandhi, Indira, 225, 254, 266–267
Gandhi, Mahatma, 6, 7, 216, 218, 219, 240, 244
Garvey, Marcus, 7
Gaulle, Charles de, 8
Gaza, 158, 160, 161
Geneva, 44–46, 49, 98
Germany, 8, 9, 96, 117
Ghana, 19, 91, 97, 99, 102, 115, 116, 130, 136, 150, 182, 192, 242, 251, 254, 259
Goa, 135, 225
Gold Coast, 2, 72, 73
Great Britain, 6, 8–12, 18–20, 25, 30–32, 44, 46, 64, 88, 94, 131, 147, 150, 154, 185, 220, 234, 239, 241–243, 245, 253, 259
Greater Asia, Association (1924), 7
Greece, 32
Guatemala, 158, 201
Guinea, 26, 89, 91, 101, 103, 118, 114–115, 149–151, 154, 161, 164, 166, 204

Haile Sellasie, Emperor, 97
Hamon, Leo, 25
Harisi, Muḥammad al-, 130
Hassuna, 'Abd al-Khāliq, 39, 61

Hatta, Muḥammad, 4, 8, 229, 233
Hausa, 20
Havana, 158, 190–193, 198, 200–211, 250, 257
Haykal, Muḥammad Ḥasanayn, 104, 105, 122
Hindu Congress, 32
Hitler, Adolf, 9
Ho Chi Minh, 3, 4
Holland, 8, 11, 33, 41, 73, 230, 253
Houphouët-Boigny, Dr. Felix, 3, 118, 242
Hungary, 69, 88

India, 3, 5, 6, 7, 8, 12, 19, 22, 24, 29–33, 36, 39–43, 45, 47–52, 60–61, 63, 65–68, 70–71, 81, 83, 88, 92, 95–96, 99, 100–101, 103, 105, 115–122, 127, 131, 136, 138, 149–150, 154, 157–158, 161–162, 164, 166–167, 183–184, 188, 191, 193, 204, 210, 214–225, 234–235, 238, 242, 244, 246, 251, 257, 260, 264, 266–267
Indian Congress Party, 49
Indian Council of World Affairs, 217, 218
Indian Muslim Congress, 32
Indian National Congress, 1, 5–8, 29–30, 164, 214, 219
Indian Ocean, 216
Indochina, 4, 11, 33, 43–46, 59, 126
Indonesia, 1, 5, 8, 11–12, 29, 33–36, 38, 41–43, 45–47, 51, 53, 60, 65, 67, 73–74, 88, 92, 98, 99, 101–103, 105, 116, 118–121, 127, 130, 135–136, 147, 154, 156–158, 166, 184–185, 190–192, 204, 210, 229, 232, 234–235, 253, 259–260, 264
Inter-Asian Relations Conference, 31, 34

International African Service Bureau, 10
International Association of Domestic Lawyers, 156
International Conference for World Peace (1926), 4
Iran, 24, 30, 33, 36, 42, 65, 67–68, 70, 73, 92, 151, 191, 210, 260
Iraq, 33, 36, 39, 63–65, 67, 70–71, 73, 98, 136
Irish Republic, 101
Irwin, Lord, 7
Isip, 147
Israel, 17, 24, 36–37, 52, 61, 63, 67, 73, 166, 184, 253
Ivory Coast, 2, 118, 241, 242, 247, 260

Jakarta, 51, 65, 102–104, 118, 136, 144, 162, 184, 191, 235
Jamaica, 101
Jamāli, Dr. Faḍhil, 64, 67, 71
Japan, 1, 7, 8, 10–12, 17, 41, 47, 65, 70, 73, 99, 102, 127, 136, 157, 161, 192, 204, 210, 238
Java, 4, 53, 73, 233
Jha, C. S., 19, 99, 120–121, 219, 261
Johnson, Wallace, 7, 10, 239
Jones, F. C. 47
Jordan, 73, 102, 130, 158
Junblāt, Kamāl, 154

Kahin, G. (Prof.), 71
Kale, John, 153
Kalimullah, M., 157
Kambona, Oscar, 116, 165–166, 239, 243–246, 261, 265
Karl Marx University, 157
Kashmir, 45, 93, 191, 219, 222, 225, 251, 267
Kazakhstan, 66

Keita, Modeibo, 95, 115, 254
Kennedy, J. F., 95, 97, 114, 244, 264
Kenya, 82, 115, 130, 135, 165, 185
    241, 251, 259, 260
Kenyatta, Jomo, 3, 7, 10, 31, 165, 239
Khrushchev, Nikita, 83, 84, 96, 94–
    95, 97, 146, 161, 186–187, 264
Koinage, Peter, 165
Korea (General), 36, 39, 40, 42, 44,
    59, 135
Kotelawala, Sir John, 44–45, 47,
    51–52, 66. 68–69
Kudryavtsev, V., 176, 177
Kuo Chien (Mrs.), 186
Kuo Mo-jo, 87, 127
Kuomintang, 4
Kuznetsov, A. E., 65, 119
Kwadri, Gidi, 130

Lansbury, George, 6
Laos, 37, 73, 93, 95, 101–102, 251
Laski, Harold, 3
Latin America, 38, 97, 105, 154,
    160–161, 166, 176–177, 182, 184,
    190, 198, 200–201, 203–221, 250,
    265
Latvia, 69, 73
Lebanon, 33, 36, 38, 63, 65, 70, 73,
    92, 100, 102, 154
Legum, Colin, 21, 161
Leipzig, 157
Lenin, Leninism, 2, 17, 176, 185, 202
Liberia, 24, 34, 36–38, 64, 70, 72–73,
    92, 238
Libya, 63, 65, 70, 73, 102
Lima, Luis Turcios, 201
Lithuania, 69
Liu Ning-yi, 164
Lok Sabha, 39, 44, 50, 59, 81
London, 3, 12, 18, 44, 47, 63, 68, 71,
    95, 119, 189, 214, 239

London School of Economics, 3
Lowenthal, Richard, 256
Lumumba, Patrice, 23, 95, 156, 187,
    254
Lyssarides, Dr. Vassos, 183

MacMillan, Harold, 94
Mahendra, King, 115
Malagasy, Republic of (Madagas-
    car), 135, 247
Malaviya, H. D., 130, 150
Malaya, 11, 12, 29, 32, 33, 91, 92, 99,
    119, 166, 204, 210, 234
Malaysia, 103, 121, 191, 193, 235,
    251, 253, 260
Maldives, The, 191
Malenkov, G. M., 86
Mali, 95, 101, 116, 150, 192, 254
Mamedy, Camara, 164, 166
Manchester, 7, 10, 29
Manchuria, 8
Manila, 35, 47
Manila Treaty, 50, 219
Mao Tse-tung, 12, 33
Marx, Marxism, 3, 17, 176, 177,
    185
Massamba-Debat, Alphonse, 117
Mauritania, 92
Mauritius, 204
Menderes, Adnan, 63
Mendes-France, Pierre, 38
Menon, Krishna, 3, 48–50
Mexico, 4, 101
Miller, J.D.B., 261
Mirskii, G., 176–178
Moluccas, 8
Mongolia, 24, 91–92, 130, 135, 147,
    186, 204, 206, 257
Monrovia, 90, 241–243
Morocco, 43, 72, 82, 93, 135, 184,
    193, 232, 251

Moscow, 4, 5, 13, 65, 83, 85, 86, 101, 114–116, 188–189, 192, 247
Moscow Nuclear Test Ban Treaty, 182, 186
Moshi, 162, 164 167, 180, 182, 192, 244
Mozambique, 191
Muḥyī ad-Dīn, Khaled, 131
Murumbi, Joseph, 115
Muslim Masjumi Party (Indonesia), 42, 231, 233
Mwanza, 245
Myrdal, Gunnar (Prof.), 8, 12

Nagasaki, 7, 11
Nairobi, 167
National Party (Indonesia), 42, 231, 233
Nazir, Muḥammad, 42
Nehru, Jawaharlal, 3, 4, 5, 6, 7, 8, 21, 24, 29–33, 36, 39–41, 44–45, 47, 50–52, 59–61, 63–67, 69–71, 73–75, 81–86, 90–91, 94–99, 114–115, 126, 138, 149, 214–221, 224–225, 232, 244, 254–256. 264–266
Nehru, Rameshwari (Mrs.), 130, 152
Nepal, 73, 115, 138, 204, 210, 251
New Delhi, 29. 31–36, 38–40, 43, 49–50, 65, 88, 98, 126–127, 144–145, 149, 218, 232
New Guinea, 8, 73
New York, 7, 94
Nicosia, 166, 180, 182–184, 250, 265
Niger, 20, 24, 193, 247
Nigeria, 20, 130, 167, 191, 241, 252ff.
Nkrumah, Dr. Kwane, 3, 10, 31, 91, 94, 97, 115, 120, 182–183, 192, 239–242, 247, 251, 253–255, 260, 266
North Africa, 37–39, 43, 63, 74
North Atlantic Treaty Organization (NATO), 64, 259

North East Frontier Agency, 49
North Kalimantan, 191, 192, 204, 210
North Korea, 24, 52, 130, 145, 147, 185, 192
North Rhodesia, 165
North Vietnam, 12, 24, 60, 65, 68, 102, 121, 130, 147, 192
Nyerere, Julius, 120, 165, 244–247

Obote, Sir Milton, 115
Okāsha, Sarwat, 161
Okinawa, 135
Olympio, Sylvano, 254
Oman, 130, 191, 205
Oppressed Nationalities, Association of (Anti-Imperialist League), 4–7
Oppressed Peoples, Association of (1927), 214
Organization of African Unity (OAU), 90, 101, 104, 120, 240, 247, 269

Pakistan, 12, 24, 25, 33, 36, 39, 40, 43, 45, 46, 51, 52, 63, 64, 67, 68, 69, 70, 72, 73, 92, 96, 99, 100, 103, 105, 118, 119, 210, 224, 225, 251
Palestine, 4, 31, 32, 37, 46, 63, 67, 68, 74, 82, 135, 149, 156
Pan-African Congress, 1, 7, 10, 18
Pan-Africanism, 1, 7, 239
Pan-African Movement, 7. 29, 239
Pan-African Movement for East and Central Africa (PAFMECA), 165
Pan-Asian Front (China), 7
Pan-Asianism, 1, 7, 32, 40, 46, 238
Paris, 3, 44, 160
Parti Démocratique de Guinée, 149, 150
Peking, 13, 52, 192–193, 200, 220–221, 233, 235, 247

Perana Qila, 29
Peru, 160
Philippines, The, 12, 24, 33–34, 36, 50, 63–64, 67–68, 70–71, 73, 92, 94, 96, 147, 234, 235
Pinay, Antoine, 64
Pnompenh, 19
Poland, 69
Poplai, S. L. (Prof.), 217
Portugal, 150, 222
Pyongyang, 145, 184

Qudsi, Nazim al-, 34

Rabat, 185
Radek, Karl, 3
Rangoon, 43, 52, 128
Rashidat, Shafik, 130
Rashidov, Sharaf, 129, 132, 133, 202
Red Fort, 29
Rhodesia, 151, 242, 245
Rif'at, Muḥammad, 149
Rolland, Romain, 6
Romulo, Carlos, 34, 35, 64–66
Roosevelt, F. D., 8
Royal Institute of International Affairs, 47
Rumania, 69

Sādāt, Anwar, as-, 82, 129, 131, 132, 254
Sahara, 72, 73, 150, 238, 241
Sastroamidjojo, Dr. 'Ali, 42, 45–46, 50–55, 67, 126, 232–233
Saudi Arabia, 33, 36, 67, 73, 92, 102, 191, 251
Sayegh, Faiz A., 23, 24, 82, 259
Sékou Touré, 89, 91, 115, 117, 120, 150, 265
Senegal, 17, 118, 241
Senghor, Dr. Leopold, 4

Shastri, Lal Bahadur, 115, 225, 254, 266
Sibā'ī, Yusuf, as-, 136, 138, 151, 153, 157, 158, 160, 189
Sihanouk, Prince, 23
Silva, Pedro Medina, 201
Singapore, 25, 121, 234–235, 251, 259, 260, 265
Singh, Anup, 127, 130
Sithole, Rev. Ndabaningi, 9
Sjahrir, Soetan, 8, 11, 42, 231
Socialist Party, The (Indonesia), 42, 231, 233
Soebehan, Muḥammad, 147
Sofronov, Anatoly, 127
Solidarity Fund, 145
Somalia, (Somaliland), 135, 251, 257
South Africa, 36, 52, 138, 166
South Arabia, 191
South Arabian Protectorates, 73
South China Sea, 44
South East Asia Collective Organization, 50
South East Asian Nations Association, 269
South East Asia Treaty Organization (SEATO), 25, 50, 64, 127, 150, 151
South Korea, 24, 52
South Rhodesia, 165
South Vietnam, 24, 65, 70, 102, 192, 193
Soviet Afro-Asian Solidarity Committee, 181
Soviet Union, The, 3, 4, 5, 13, 18, 23, 24, 26, 30, 40, 44, 46–47, 52, 60, 65–70, 72, 74, 80, 83–88, 92, 95, 100–101, 103, 114, 122, 126–127, 129–130, 132–133, 136–137, 145–147, 150–151, 154, 156–158, 160–162, 164–167, 174–193, 198, 200–202, 204–210, 215, 234, 238, 244–

Soviet Union, The (contd.), 247, 250, 252, 256–257, 259–260, 263–267
Stalin, Joseph, 26, 95, 264
Stepanov, Lev, 17, 179
Stockholm, 126, 160, 161
Subandrio, Dr., 102
Subarjo, Dr., 42
Sudan, 64–65, 70, 73, 102, 130, 136, 251
Suez, 88–89, 98, 138, 224
Suharto, T. N. J., 229, 234–235, 254
Sukarno, Aḥmad, 5, 8, 23, 41, 51, 61, 67, 82, 91, 94–98, 102, 104, 116, 156, 191, 224–225, 229–231, 233–235, 254–255, 266–267
Sumatra, 234
Sun Yat-sen, 7
Sun Yat-sen, Madame, 4, 6
SUNFED, 93, 99, 261
Surabaya, 235
Suslov, M.A., 178
Sweden, 101
Syria, 4, 33–34, 36, 69–70, 91–92, 130, 136, 259–260

Taiwan, 24, 51–52, 66, 71, 127, 150, 153, 234
Tanganyika African Association, 243
Tanganyika African National Union (TANU), 243
Tanzania (Tanganyika), 26, 116, 120, 162, 165–166, 183, 192, 238–239, 241–247, 259
Tashkent, 144–145
Thailand, 17, 24, 37, 42, 63–64, 67, 73, 92, 96, 102, 192–193, 204, 235, 251
Tibet, 48–49, 74
Tibetan Treaty, 48

Tibet Pact, 219
Tikhonov, Nikolai, 127
Tito, Josip Broz, 84–85, 88, 94–97, 100, 115
Tobago, 101
Togo, 135, 215, 253, 254
Tokyo, 11
Tonkin, Gulf of, 36
Torrado, Oswaldo Dorticos, 201
Tri-Continental Solidarity Organization 191–193, 208, 209
Trinidad, 101
Tshombe, Moise, 115
Tunisia, 37, 72, 82, 93, 154, 232
Turkey, 6, 17, 24, 63–64, 67, 70–72, 96, 99, 102, 158, 191, 259
Turkmenistan, 66
Tursu-Zade, Mircos, 181

U Nu, 33, 44–45, 52, 61, 65, 70, 82, 86, 255, 264
U Thant, 121
Uganda, 115, 121, 135, 153, 157, 165, 241, 259
United Nations Organization (U.N.), 21, 31, 34–37, 39–42, 46, 51, 68, 80, 91–95, 97, 99, 121, 127, 135, 144, 154, 157, 190, 193, 224, 230–231, 238, 244–245, 250, 256, 264, 268
U.N. Charter, 35, 64, 68, 71–72, 80, 89, 133
U.N. General Assembly, 2, 36–38, 89, 92–95
U.N. Security Council, 38
United States of America, 2, 7, 8, 10, 12, 13, 23, 25, 31, 33–34, 37, 43–44, 46, 50, 59–60, 64, 66, 71, 80, 84, 87–88, 92, 95, 114–117, 126, 131, 147, 150, 154, 157, 160, 184–185, 188, 190, 193, 201–204, 208, 210, 219–220, 231–232, 234, 244–245,

U.S.A. (contd.), 251, 256–257, 259, 260, 263–265, 267
Upper Volta, 24, 120, 247, 254
Uruguay, 101, 204
Uzbekistan, 66

Venezuela, 101, 193, 201
Vienna, 95
Vietminh (League for the Independence of Vietnam), 11, 36, 37, 43, 44, 60
Vietnam (General), 60, 95, 114, 135 203, 205, 230, 251, 256
Vivekanada, Swami, 218
Voroshilov, Marshal, 66

Waris, Ḥassan, 130
Warsaw Pact, 86
Washington, 65
Welbeck, Nathaniel, 182–183
Wen Yuan-ning, 32
West Germany, 204, 245
West Indies, 7

West Irian (Netherlands New Guinea), 73, 234, 253
Wilson, Woodrow, 2
Winneba, 191, 192, 193, 200
World Federation of Trade Unions (WFTU), 129
World Peace Council (WPC), 137, 156, 160–161, 166, 176
World Peace Organization (WPO), 126, 129, 198
Wu Hsueh-tsien, 201

Yameogo, Maurice, 254
Yazīd, Muḥammad, 188, 189
Yemen, 33–34, 36, 73, 92, 102, 135
Youlu, Fulbert, 254
Yugoslavia, 84, 85, 94, 96, 101, 104–105, 115–117, 256

Zanzibar, 245
Zimbabwe, 9
Zimerline, Aḥmed, 157
Zorlu, 70